Scholastic Success With
3rd GRADE
WORKBOOK

SCHOLASTIC
Teaching
Resources

NEW YORK • TORONTO • LONDON • AUCKLAND • SYDNEY
MEXICO CITY • NEW DELHI • HONG KONG • BUENOS AIRES

Acknowledgments

Maps workbook copyright © 2002 by Linda Ward Beech

Scholastic Inc. grants teachers permission to photocopy the reproducible pages from this book for classroom use. No other part of this publication may be reproduced in whole or in part, or stored in a retrieval system, or transmitted in any form or by any means, electronic, mechanical, photocopying, recording, or other wise without written permission of the publisher. For information regarding permission, write to Scholastic Inc., 557 Broadway, New York, NY 10012.

Cover art by Anne Kennedy
Cover design by Anna Christian
Interior illustrations by Jon Buller, Micheal Denman, Reggie Holladay,
Susan Hendron, Anne Kennedy, Kathy Marlin, Bob Masheris, and Mark Mason
Interior design by Quack & Company

ISBN 0-439-56971-0

10 08 09

READING COMPREHENSION

TESTS: READING

CONTEMPORARY CURSIVE

GRAMMAR

Scholastic Professional Books

WRITING

Scholastic Professional Books

Scholastic Professional Books

Scholastic Professional Books

"Nothing succeeds like success."

Alexandre Dumas the Elder, 1854

Dear Parent,

Congratulations on choosing this excellent educational resource for your child. Scholastic has long been a leader in educational publishing—creating quality educational materials for use in school and at home for nearly a century.

As a partner in your child's academic success, you'll want to get the most out of the learning experience offered in this book. To help your child learn at home, try following these helpful hints:

❖ Provide a comfortable place to work.

❖ Have frequent work sessions, but keep them short.

❖ Praise your child's successes and encourage his or her efforts. Offer positive help when a child makes a mistake.

❖ Display your child's work and share his or her progress with family and friends.

In this workbook you'll find hundreds of practice pages that keep kids challenged and excited as they strengthen their skills across the classroom curriculum.

The workbook is divided into eight sections: Reading Comprehension; Reading Tests; Contemporary Cursive; Grammar; Writing; Maps; Addition & Subtraction; and Math. You and your child should feel free to move through the pages in any way you wish.

The table of contents lists the activities and the skills practiced. And a complete answer key in the back will help you gauge your child's progress.

Take the lead and help your child succeed with the *Scholastic Success With: 3rd Grade Workbook!*

The activities in this workbook reinforce age-appropriate skills and will help your child meet the following standards established as goals by leading educators.

Mathematics

★ Uses a variety of strategies when problem-solving

★ Understands and applies number concepts

★ Uses basic and advanced procedures while performing computation

★ Understands and applies concepts of measurement

★ Understands and applies concepts of geometry

★ Understands and applies properties of functions and algebra

Writing

★ Understands and uses the writing process

★ Uses grammatical and mechanical conventions in written compositions

Reading

★ Understands and uses the general skills and strategies of the reading process

★ Can read and understand a variety of literary texts

★ Can understand and interpret a variety of informational texts

Geography

★ Understands the characteristics and uses of maps and globes

★ Knows the location of places, geographic features, and patterns of the environment

Scholastic Success With

READING COMPREHENSION

SQ3R

Do you know about SQ3R? It is a formula to help you understand what you read. It can be useful for any reading assignment. SQ3R is especially helpful when you are reading a textbook, like your social studies or science book. Each letter of the formula tells you what to do.

S = Survey

Survey means to look over the assignment. Look at the pictures. Look at the title and the headings, if there are any. Read the first sentence or two.

Q = Question

Question means to ask yourself, "What is this assignment about? What is the author trying to tell me?" Once you get an idea of what you are going to read, then you can read with a better understanding.

3R = Read, Recite, Review

1. Read the assignment, looking for the answers to the questions you had. Concentrate. Picture in your mind what the words are saying.

2. Recite in your mind, or write on paper, the main ideas of what you have just read. Write the main ideas in your own words.

3. Review what you have learned. Make notes to help you review.

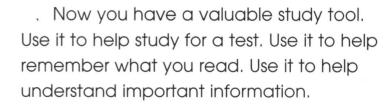

Now you have a valuable study tool. Use it to help study for a test. Use it to help remember what you read. Use it to help understand important information.

Let's practice. Read the assignment on page 13. Use the SQ3R formula step by step.

Scholastic Professional Books

Name _____ 6/9

The Invention of the Telephone

Alexander Graham Bell invented the telephone. He was a teacher of the deaf in Boston. At night, he worked on experiments using a telegraph. Once when the metal in the telegraph stuck, Bell's assistant plucked the metal to loosen it. Bell, who was in another room, heard the sound in his receiver. He understood that the vibrations of the metal had traveled down the electric current to the receiver. He continued to work on this idea.

March 10, 1876, was the first time Alexander Graham Bell successfully spoke words over a telephone line. He was about to test a new transmitter when he spilled some battery acid on his clothes. He cried out to his assistant who was in another room, "Mr. Watson, come here! I want you!" Watson heard every word clearly on the telephone and rushed into the room.

Bell demonstrated his invention to many people. Over time, more and more telephone lines were installed, and people began to use the invention in their homes and businesses.

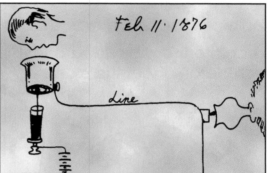

partial page from inventor's notebook

Did SQ3R help you? Let's find out.

1. **Who invented the telephone?** The person who invented the telephone is Alexander Graham Bell

2. **What was his regular job?** He was a techer for the deaf.

3. **What did Mr. Bell say to Mr. Watson during the first telephone conversation?**
   He said! Mr. Watson come here! I want you!

4. **Who was Mr. Watson?** He was Mr. Bells assistint.

5. **How did people first learn about the telephone?** Because Mr. Bell demonstrated it.

On another piece of paper, write a paragraph telling why you are glad the telephone was invented. Read your paragraph to a friend.

The Milky Way

The **main idea** of a story tells what the story is mostly about. **Details** in a story tell more information about the main idea.

What do you think of when you hear the words, "Milky Way"? Do you think of a candy bar? Well, there is another Milky Way, and you live in it! It is our galaxy. A galaxy is a grouping of stars. Scientists have learned that there are many galaxies in outer space. The Milky Way is a spiral-shaped galaxy with swirls of stars spinning out from the center of it. Scientists believe there are about 200 billion stars in the Milky Way. One of those stars is the sun. Nine planets orbit the sun. One of them is Earth. Even from Earth, on a clear night away from city lights, you can see part of the Milky Way. It is called that because so many stars close together look like a milky white stripe across the sky. However, if you looked at it with a telescope, you would see that it is made up of thousands of stars.

Complete the main idea and each detail about the story.

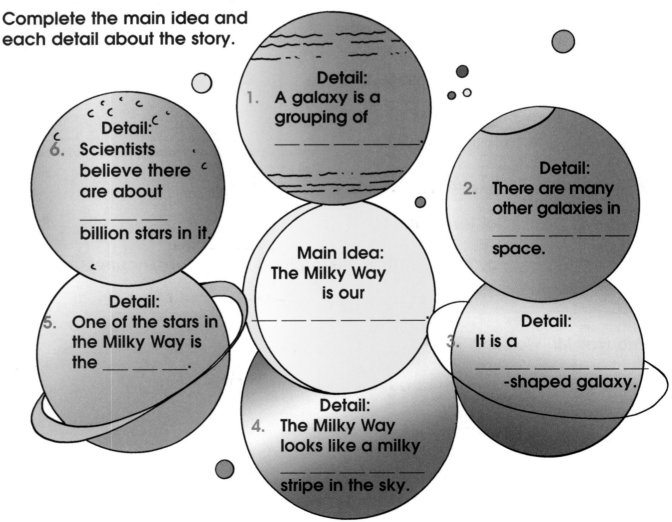

Detail:
1. A galaxy is a grouping of _____

Detail:
6. Scientists believe there are about _____ billion stars in it.

Detail:
2. There are many other galaxies in _____ space.

Main Idea:
The Milky Way is our _____

Detail:
5. One of the stars in the Milky Way is the _____.

Detail:
3. It is a _____ -shaped galaxy.

Detail:
4. The Milky Way looks like a milky _____ stripe in the sky.

Scholastic Professional Books

Wagon Train

Will and Kate thought it would be a great adventure to travel west with the wagon train. In the spring of 1880, their family left their home in Pennsylvania and joined a wagon train headed for California. For months, their only home was the wagon. A large canvas was spread over metal hoops on top of the wagon to make a roof. Will helped his father oil the canvas so that the rain would slide off and keep them dry inside. Each day Kate and Will gathered wood as they walked beside the wagon. In the evening when the wagons stopped, Kate and her mother built a campfire for cooking supper. They hauled supplies with them so that they could cook beans and biscuits. Sometimes the men went hunting and brought back fresh deer meat or a rabbit for stew. When it rained for several days, the roads were so muddy that the wagons got stuck. There was always danger of snakes and bad weather. There were rivers and mountains to cross. There was no doctor to take care of those who got sick or injured. Will and Kate were right. Traveling with a wagon train was a great adventure, but it was a very hard life.

Unscramble the words to make a complete sentence that tells the main idea.

wagon dangerous. on a Life hard and was train _____

_____

Choose a word from the wagon to complete each detail.

1. __ __ __ __ __ __ the canvas

2. __ __ __ __ __ __ __ __ __
   wood

3. __ __ __ __ __ __ __ over a
   campfire

4. __ __ __ __ __ __ __ supplies

5. __ __ __ __ __ __ __ for meat

6. __ __ __ __ __ __ __ __ out
   for snakes

7. __ __ __ __ __ __ __ for
   the rain to stop

8. __ __ __ __ __ __ __ __ rivers
   and mountains

9. __ __ __ __ __ __ __ sick or
   hurt with no doctor to help

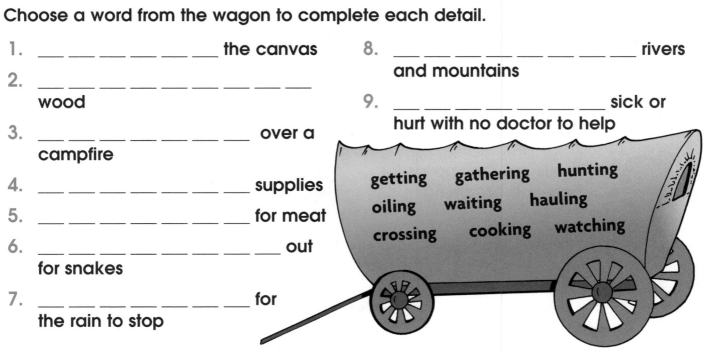

getting   gathering   hunting

oiling   waiting   hauling

crossing   cooking   watching

What a Nose!

An elephant's trunk is probably the most useful nose in the world. Of course, it is used for breathing and smelling, like most noses are. However, elephants also use their trunks like arms and hands to lift food to their mouths. They suck water into their trunks and pour it into their mouths to get a drink. Sometimes they spray the water on their backs to give themselves a cool shower. An adult elephant can hold up to four gallons of water in its trunk. Elephants can use their trunks to carry heavy things, such as logs that weigh up to 600 pounds! The tip of the trunk has a little knob on it that the elephant uses like a thumb. An elephant can use the "thumb" to pick up something as small as a coin. Trunks are also used for communication. Two elephants that meet each other touch their trunks to each other's mouth, kind of like a kiss. Sometimes a mother elephant will calm her baby by stroking it with her trunk. Can your nose do all those things?

Find the statement below that is the main idea of the story. Write _M.I._ in the elephant next to it. Then find the details of the story. Write _D_ in the elephant next to each detail. Be careful! There are two sentences that do not belong in this story.

 Elephants use their trunks to greet each other, like giving a kiss.

 Elephants use their trunks to give themselves a shower.

 Some people like to ride on elephants.

 Elephants can carry heavy things with their trunks.

 Mother elephants calm their babies by stroking them with their trunks.

Elephants use their trunks to eat and drink.

 Elephants use their noses for smelling and breathing.

 Elephants have very useful noses.

 Giraffes are the tallest animals in the world.

💡 **On another piece of paper, finish this story: When I was on safari, I looked up and saw a herd of elephants. Underline the main idea.**

Scholastic Professional Books

The Math Contest

Story elements *are the different parts of a story. The* **characters** *are the people, animals, or animated objects in the story. The* **setting** *is the place and time in which the story takes place. The* **plot** *of the story includes the events and often includes a* **problem** *and a* **solution**.

Every Friday, Mr. Jefferson, the math teacher, held a contest for his students. Sometimes they played math baseball. Sometimes they had math relays with flash cards. Other times, they were handed a sheet of paper with a hundred multiplication problems on it. The student who finished fastest with the most correct answers won the contest. One Friday, there was a math bee. It was similar to a spelling bee, except the students worked math problems in their heads. There was fierce competition, until finally, everyone was out of the game except Riley and Rhonda. Mr. Jefferson challenged them with problem after problem, but both students continued to answer correctly every time. It was almost time for class to end, so Mr. Jefferson gave them the same difficult problem. They had to work it in their heads. Riley thought hard and answered, "20." Rhonda answered, "18." Finally they had a winner!

To find out who won the game, work the problem below in your head. Write the answer on the blank.

$$6 + 4 + 6 - 4 - 4 + 6 + 6 = \_\_\_\_\_$$

Now, to see if you are correct, circle only the 6's and 4's in the box. The answer will appear.

Answer each question below.

7	4	6	5	3	1	2	6	4	8	0
6	9	1	4	3	5	6	2	8	6	7
5	0	8	6	0	4	9	7	3	1	4
3	1	7	4	0	6	5	8	7	2	6
7	0	6	5	8	4	9	3	2	9	6
8	4	9	8	0	6	1	5	7	8	4
6	2	7	3	9	2	4	8	1	6	5
6	4	4	6	1	9	0	6	6	2	3

1. Name the three people in the story. _____, _____, and _____

2. Circle where the story takes place.
   a. in the gym
   b. in the cafeteria
   c. in Mr. Jefferson's classroom

3. Circle the problem in the story.
   a. Mr. Jefferson held the contest on Thursday.
   b. Class was almost over, and the contest was still tied.
   c. Riley and Rhonda both answered incorrectly.

4. Who answered the difficult question correctly? _____

Best Friends

Amy dreaded recess every day. She did not have any friends to play with. All the girls in her class were paired up with a best friend or in groups, and she always felt left out. So, instead of playing with anyone, Amy just walked around by herself. She wanted to seesaw, but that is something you need to do with a friend. She liked to swing, but she could not go very high. She wished someone would push her to get her started.

One day, the teacher, Mrs. Gibbs, walked up and put her arm around Amy. "What's the matter, Amy? Why don't you play with the other children?" she asked kindly.

Amy replied, "Everyone has a friend except me. I don't have anyone." Mrs. Gibbs smiled and said, "Amy, the way to get a friend is to be a friend." Amy asked, "How do I do that?"

Mrs. Gibbs answered, "Look around the playground. There are three classes of third-graders out here during this recess time. Find someone who is alone and needs a friend. Then go to that person and ask them to play." Amy said she would think about it, but she was afraid she would be too embarrassed. She wasn't sure she could do it.

The next day, Amy noticed a dark-haired girl all alone on the playground. She worked up her courage and walked over to the girl. "Hi! My name is Amy. Do you want to play with me?" she asked.

"Okay," the girl said shyly. As they took turns pushing each other on the swings, Amy found out that the girl's name was Ming. She and her family had just moved from Japan. She did not know anyone and could not speak much English yet. She needed a friend.

"Want to seesaw?" Amy asked. Ming looked puzzled. Amy pointed to the seesaw. Ming smiled and nodded. Amy was so happy. She finally had a friend!

Scholastic Professional Books

On each blank, write the letter of the picture that correctly answers the question. One answer is used twice.

1. Where does this story take place? _____

2. Who is the main character in the story? _____

   Who are the other two characters in the story? _____ and _____

3. What is the problem in the story? _____

4. How does Amy solve her problem? _____

5. What is Ming's problem? _____

   How does Ming's problem get solved? _____

A. Mrs. Gibbs

B. playground

C. Ming needed a friend, too.

D. Ming

E. Amy

F. Amy asked Ming to play, and they became friends.

G. Amy needed a friend.

Think about what you did during recess or another part of your day. On another piece of paper, list the characters, setting, problem, and solution. Use this list to write a story. Read the story to a friend.

The Tallest Trees

Redwood trees are the tallest trees in the world. Some grow over 300 feet high, which is taller than a 30-story building. Think of it this way: If a six-foot tall man stood at the base of a redwood tree, the tree would be 50 times taller than the man! These giant trees grow near the **coast** of California and Oregon. The **climate** is foggy and rainy there, which gives the redwoods a **constant** supply of water. Redwoods can grow for hundreds of years; in fact, some have lived for over 2,000 years! The **bark** is very thick, protecting the trees from insects, **disease**, and fires. The bark of redwood trees is a reddish-brown color. Redwood trees are very important to the lumber companies because the trees are so large that each one can be cut into lots of **lumber**. You may have seen lumber like this in redwood fences or redwood patio furniture. However, many of the trees are protected by law in the Redwood National Park. Lumber companies cannot cut trees that grow there. This is so the trees will not become **extinct**.

Put an *X* beside the correct definition of each bolded word in the story.

1. coast ____ land by the sea ____ a desert

2. climate ____ time ____ weather

3. constant ____ happens regularly ____ never happens

4. bark ____ leaves ____ outer covering of trees

5. disease ____ illness ____ high temperatures

6. lumber ____ plastic pipes ____ wood cut into boards

7. extinct ____ no longer existing ____ expensive

Read an article about another type of tree. On another piece of paper, list five new words from the article. Use a dictionary to learn the meaning of each word.

Scholastic Professional Books

Let's Play Soccer!

Soccer is the world's most popular sport. It is played in many countries all over the world. Every four years, an international competition is held. It is called the World Cup.

A **soccer field** is rectangular with a goal on each end. Each **goal** is made of a rectangular, frame-covered net. The game is played with a **soccer ball**. The ball is usually made of leather and is filled with air.

Two teams compete against each other. One point is awarded to a team when it scores a goal. Whichever team scores the most goals wins the game.

There are 11 players on each team. **Forwards** have the most responsibility to score goals. Sometimes forwards are called strikers. They are helped by teammates who play at midfield. These players are sometimes called **halfbacks**. Halfbacks help to score goals and try to keep the other team's ball away from the goal. Other teammates play farther back on the field to defend their goal. They try to keep the other team from getting close enough to score. They are sometimes called **fullbacks**. Each team has one **goalie** whose job is to keep the other team from scoring by blocking the ball or catching it before it goes into the goal. A goalie may catch or throw the ball, but no other players may use their hands. They may use their feet, legs, chest, or head to move the ball. A **referee** will penalize a team if any players other than the goalie use their hands. Soccer is definitely a team sport. All the positions are important in winning the game.

Label the diagram using the bolded words from the story.

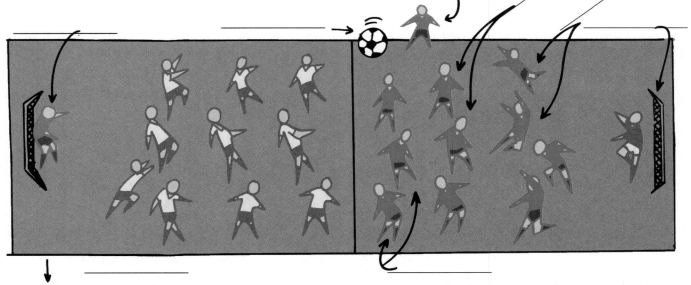

Scrambled Eggs

Sequencing *means putting the events of a story in the order in which they happened.*

The sentences below are scrambled. Number them in the correct sequence.

A. ____ I took a shower.
   ____ I got out of bed.
   ____ I got dressed.

B. ____ She planted the seeds.
   ____ Big pink flowers bloomed.
   ____ Tiny green shoots came up.

C. ____ He ate the sandwich.
   ____ He spread some jelly on them.
   ____ He got out two pieces of bread.

D. ____ He slid down the slide.
   ____ He climbed up the ladder.
   ____ He landed on his feet.

E. ____ We built a snowman.
   ____ Low gray clouds drifted in.
   ____ It began to snow hard.

F. ____ Firefighters put out the fire.
   ____ Lightning struck the barn.
   ____ The barn caught on fire.

G. ____ The pepper spilled out of
         the jar.
   ____ I sneezed.
   ____ My nose began to itch.

H. ____ "My name is Emma."
   ____ "Hi, what is your name?"
   ____ "It's nice to meet you, Emma."

I. ____ I said, "Okay, do a trick first."
   ____ Rover whined for a treat.
   ____ I gave him a dog biscuit.
   ____ He danced on his hind legs.

J. ____ She built a nest.
   ____ Baby birds hatched from
         the eggs.
   ____ I saw a robin gathering straw.
   ____ She laid four blue eggs.

My Crazy Dream

I don't know why, but I went to school in my underwear. Everyone was laughing! I walked up and down the hall looking for my classroom, but I could never find it. Then I went to the Lost and Found box and put on some clothes. I heard my principal say, "Son, are you lost?" However, when I turned around, it was the President of the United States talking to me. He asked me to fly on his jet with him. As we were flying, I looked out the window and saw a pterodactyl flying next to us! How could that be? They are extinct! It smiled and waved good-bye. Then all of a sudden, the airplane turned into a roller coaster. It climbed upward a million miles, then down we went! For hours and hours we just kept going straight down! The roller coaster finally came to a stop, and I was on an island entirely made of chocolate. I ate a whole tree made of fudge! Then a native dressed in green feathers sneaked up behind me and captured me. He put me in a pot of boiling water to make soup out of me. I got hotter and hotter and hotter! Finally, I woke up and realized I had fallen asleep with my electric blanket on high.

Number the pictures in the order that they happened in the dream.

💡 **On another piece of paper, draw a picture of a dream you once had. Then write a sentence about the beginning, middle, and end of the dream on separate strips of paper. Have a friend put the sentences in order.**

Berry Colorful Ink

When sequencing a story, look for key words such as first, then, next, *and* finally *to help you determine the correct sequence.*

In early American schools, students used a quill pen and ink to practice writing letters and numerals. Since these schools did not have many supplies, the students often had to make their own ink at home. There were many different ways to make ink. One of the most common ways was to use berries such as blackberries, blueberries, cherries, elderberries, or strawberries. The type of berry used depended on the color of ink a student wanted. First, the type of berry to be used had to gathered. Then a strainer was filled with the berries and held over a bowl. Next, using the back of a wooden spoon, the berries were crushed. This caused the juice to strain into the bowl. After all the berry juice was strained into the bowl, salt and vinegar were added to the juice and then stirred. Finally, the juice was stored in a small jar with a tight-fitting lid. Not only did the students make colorful inks to use, they also made invisible and glow-in-the dark inks.

Number the phrases below in the order given in the story.

_____ **The mixture was stirred.**

_____ **Using the back of a wooden spoon, the berries were crushed.**

_____ **The ink was stored in a small jar with a tight-fitting lid.**

_____ **Berries were gathered.**

_____ **All the berry juice was strained into the bowl.**

_____ **The strainer was held over a bowl.**

_____ **Salt and vinegar were added to the berry juice.**

_____ **A strainer was filled with berries.**

Look in a cookbook for a recipe you would like to try. Read all the steps. Have someone help you make the recipe. Be sure to follow each step in order.

Simon Says

*When **following directions**, it is important to read the directions carefully and to follow them in the order they are listed.*

When you play Simon Says, you only follow the directions that Simon says. You do not follow any other directions. Play the game following the directions below.

1. Simon says draw a hand in the box below.

2. Simon says draw a ring on the ring finger.

3. Simon says draw fingernails on each finger.

4. Color each fingernail red.

5. Simon says write the names of five school days, one on each finger.

6. Circle your favorite day.

7. Write your teacher's name in the lower left-hand corner of the box.

8. Simon says write an addition problem on the hand, using the numbers 4, 5, and 9.

9. Now write a subtraction problem next to it.

10. Simon says draw a red scratch on the pinky finger.

11. Simon says draw a watch on the wrist.

12. Make the watch show 2:30.

13. Simon says outline the box with a yellow crayon.

14. Simon says write your name in the top right-hand corner of the box.

Sneaky Snakes

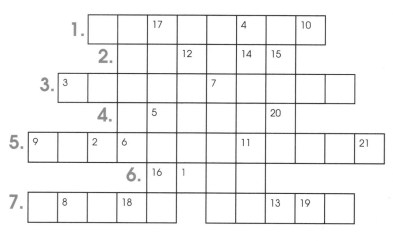

Snakes are very good at hiding. Most snakes can **camouflage** themselves into their environment. That means they have different colors and patterns on their bodies that allow them to blend in with the colors and patterns of things around them. Camouflage helps them hide from their enemies and helps them be **sneaky** when they are trying to capture something to eat. For example, the emerald tree boa lives in the **jungle**. Its green skin makes it nearly invisible among the green leaves of the trees. **Rattlesnakes** live in rocky, dry places. The patterns of black, tan, and brown on their backs help them blend in with their rocky environment. The horned viper lives in the desert. Its skin is the same color as **sand** where it burrows underground. It is hard to see unless it is moving. Also, some snakes that are harmless look very similar to **venomous** snakes. The harmless milk snake is colored orange, with yellow and black stripes, much like the poisonous **coral snake**. The enemies of the milk snake mistake it for a coral snake because they look so much alike.

Find the answers in the story. Write them in the puzzle.

1. **Write the word that starts with a v and means "poisonous."**

2. **Write another word for "tricky."**

3. **Write what helps a snake blend in with its surroundings.**

4. **Write where emerald tree boas live.**

5. **Write what snakes live in rocky places and have black, tan, and brown patterned skin.**

6. **Write what is the same color as the horned viper.**

7. **Write the name of the snake that looks like a milk snake.**

Write the letter from the numbered squares in the puzzle above to fill in each box.

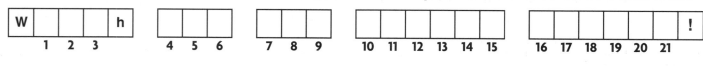

Scholastic Professional Books

Fun With Words

Follow the directions to play each word game.

1. A palindrome is a word that is spelled the same forward or backward. Write each word backward. Circle each word that is a palindrome. Put an X on each word that is not.

   wow _____

   dad _____

   mom _____

   funny _____

   noon _____

   tall _____

   deed _____

2. Some words imitate the noise that they stand for. For example, when you say "pop," it sounds like a popping sound! That is called onomatopoeia. Unscramble each noise word. Write it correctly.

   seechrc _____

   owp _____

   plurs _____

   mobo _____

   lckic _____

   zzisel _____

   chnucr _____

3. Homophones are words that sound alike when you say them but are spelled differently and have different meanings. For example, see and sea are homophones. Draw a line to match each pair of homophones.

   knot   flew

   break   soar

   flu   not

   sore   write

   right   road

   rode   brake

4. Add or subtract letters from each word to change it into another word. Write the new word.

   peach – ch + r = _____

   shirt – irt + oe = _____

   sports – p – rts + ccer = _____

   love – ove + ike = _____

   stove – st + n = _____

   chicken – c – ick = _____

   brother – bro + nei = _____

Some names sound funny when you pronounce them backward. For example, Carol would be pronounced Lorac, and Jason would be pronounced Nosaj! Write your name and each of your classmates' names backward. Then pronounce each name. Are any of the names palidromes?

Where Is Holly?

Drawing conclusions *means to make reasonable conclusions about events in a story using the information given.*

One day, while Mom was washing dishes in the kitchen, she realized that she had not heard a peep out of three-year-old Holly in a long time. The last time she had seen her, she was playing in the living room with some building blocks. "She sure is being good," thought Mom.

Write an X next to the best answer.

1. **Why did Mom think Holly was being good?**

   _____ Holly was washing dishes for her.

   _____ Holly was playing with dolls.

   _____ Holly was being so quiet.

After rinsing the last dish, Mom went to the living room to see what Holly had built. But Holly was not there. "Holly! Where are you?" Mom asked. Mom heard a faraway voice say, "Mommy!" So Mom went outside to see if Holly was there.

2. **Why did Mom go outside to look for Holly?**

   _____ Holly's voice sounded so far away.

   _____ The last time Mom saw Holly, she was riding her tricycle.

   _____ Holly said, "I'm outside, Mommy."

Mom looked down the street, up in the tree, and in the backyard, but Holly was not outside. She called her again but did not hear her voice. So, she went back inside. "Holly! Where are you? Come out right now."

3. **Why did Mom say, "Come out right now."**

   _____ She was mean.

   _____ She heard Holly's voice coming from the closet.

   _____ She thought Holly might be hiding.

Once again, Mom heard a faraway sound. "Help me!" cried Holly. Mom ran to the bathroom, but Holly was not there. She ran to the garage, but Holly was not there either. Finally, she ran to Holly's room and saw Holly's feet sticking out of the toy box, kicking wildly in the air!

4. **What had happened to Holly?**

_____ **She had fallen headfirst into the toy box and could not get out.**

_____ **She was playing with the blocks again.**

_____ **She was playing hide-and-seek with Mom.**

Mom lifted Holly out of the toy box and asked, "Holly, are you all right?" Holly replied, "I think so." Holly then told Mom that she had been looking for her toy piano because she wanted to play a song for her. "Do you want to hear the song now?" Holly asked. "First, let's have a special snack. You can play the piano for me later," Mom suggested. Holly thought that was a great idea!

5. **Where was Holly's toy piano?**

_____ **The piano was under Holly's bed.**

_____ **The piano was at the bottom of the toy box.**

_____ **She was playing hide-and-seek with Mom.**

Mom and Holly walked to the kitchen. Mom made Holly a bowl of ice cream with chocolate sauce and a cherry on top. Holly told Mom that she wanted to go to the the park. Mom really liked that idea.

5. **What will Mom and Holly do next?**

_____ **Mom and Holly will go shopping.**

_____ **Mom and Holly will go for a bike ride.**

_____ **Mom and Holly will play on the swings in the park.**

Read a chapter from a book. On another piece of paper, write a sentence telling what you think will happen next. Read the next chapter. Were you correct?

Who Invented Potato Chips?

A Native American named George Crum invented potato chips in 1853, although that was not his intention! He was a chef at an elegant restaurant in Saratoga Springs, New York, called Moon Lake Lodge. A regular item on the menu was fried potatoes, which was an idea that had started in France. At that time, French fried potatoes were cut into thick slices. One day, a dinner guest at Moon Lake Lodge sent his fried potatoes back to the chef because he did not like them so thick. So, Mr. Crum cut the potatoes a little thinner and fried them. The guest did not like those either. That made Mr. Crum angry, so he thought he would just show that guy. He sliced the potatoes paper-thin and fried them, thinking that would hush the complaining diner. However, his plan backfired on him! The diner loved the crispy, thin potatoes! Other diners tried them and also liked them. So, Mr. Crum's potato chips were added to the menu. They were called Saratoga Chips. Eventually, Mr. Crum opened his own restaurant to sell his famous chips. Now potato chips are packaged and sold in grocery stores worldwide!

Color each chip and its matching bag the same color.

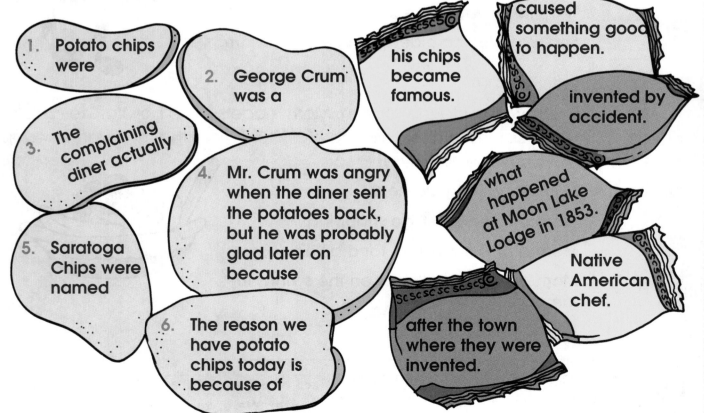

1. Potato chips were

2. George Crum was a

3. The complaining diner actually

4. Mr. Crum was angry when the diner sent the potatoes back, but he was probably glad later on because

5. Saratoga Chips were named

6. The reason we have potato chips today is because of

his chips became famous.

caused something good to happen.

invented by accident.

what happened at Moon Lake Lodge in 1853.

Native American chef.

after the town where they were invented.

The Lake Cabin

As you read the paragraph, imagine the scene that the words are describing. In the picture below, draw everything that has been left out. Color the picture.

My favorite thing to do in the summer is to go to Grandpa's lake cabin. In the evening after a full day of fishing, Grandpa and I sit on the back porch and enjoy the scenery. The sun setting behind the mountain fills the blue sky with streaks of orange and yellow. Colorful sailboats float by us in slow motion. Suddenly a fish jumps out of the water, making tiny waves in rings. A deer quietly walks to the edge of the water to get a drink. Red and yellow wildflowers grow near the big rock. On the shore across the lake, we see a couple of tents. Someone must be camping there. A flock of geese fly over the lake in the shape of a V. Every time we sit and look at the lake, Grandpa says, "This is the best place on earth!"

On another piece of paper, write a paragraph describing the place that you think is "the best place on earth." Read your paragraph to a friend.

Monroe's Mighty Youth Tonic

Way back yonder in 1853, a traveling salesman named "Shifty" Sam Monroe rode into our little town of Dry Gulch. I was there that day when Shifty stood on the steps of his **buckboard** selling Monroe's Mighty Youth Tonic. Shifty announced, "Ladies and gentlemen, **lend me your ears**. I, Sam Monroe, have invented a tonic that will give you back your youth. It will **put a spring in your step**. You'll feel years younger if you take a spoonful of this **heavenly elixir** once a day. It contains a **special blend of secret ingredients**. Why, it once made a 94-year-old cowboy feel so young, he went back to **bustin' broncs** again! An old settler that was over 100 felt so young he let out a **war whoop** that could be heard in Pike County! **It's a steal** at only one dollar a bottle. Step right up and get yours now." Well, I wondered what those secret ingredients were, so I bought a bottle and tasted it. It tasted like nothing but sugar water. So I hid behind Shifty Sam's wagon and waited for the crowd to **mosey** on home. When Shifty went inside to make some more tonic, I **kept my eye on him**. Sure enough, he mixed sugar and water and added a drop of vanilla. We'd been **hornswoggled**! I **hightailed it** right then over to the sheriff's office and had him arrest that no-good varmint. Old Shifty is now spending the rest of his "mighty youth" **behind bars**!

Scholastic Professional Books

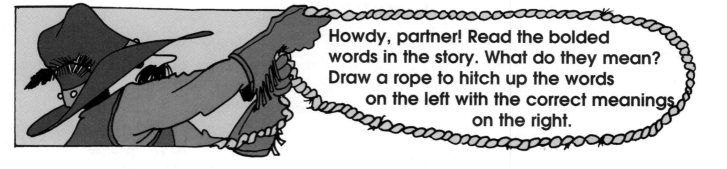

Howdy, partner! Read the bolded words in the story. What do they mean? Draw a rope to hitch up the words on the left with the correct meanings on the right.

1. way back yonder

2. buckboard

3. Lend me your ears.

4. Put a spring in your step.

5. heavenly elixir

6. special blend of secret ingredients

7. bustin' broncs

8. war whoop

9. It's a steal!

10. mosey

11. kept my eye on him

12. hornswoggled

13. hightailed it

14. no-good varmint

15. behind bars

walk slowly

cheated; tricked

watched him closely

making wild horses gentle

ran quickly

evil creature

Listen to me.

in jail

wagon

You are getting it for a low price.

I won't tell what's in it.

makes you feel peppy

many years ago

loud yell

wonderful tonic

Double It Up

*Some words can share the same spelling but have completely different meanings. To figure out the correct meaning of each word, use context clues. Using **context clues** means to look at the meaning of the whole sentence. One meaning for the word will make sense, and the other one will not. Read the following examples:*

The bat flew out of the dark cave. (Would a baseball bat fly out of a cave? No. Then it must be the other kind of bat: a small flying animal.)

He swung the bat so hard that the ball went over the fence. (Would someone swing a small animal in order to hit a ball? Of course not!)

Picture each of the following sentences in your mind to help you decide which meaning is correct for each italicized word. Then fill in the bubble next to the correct meaning.

1. I am sneezing because I have a *cold.*
   ○ opposite of hot
   ○ an illness

2. I rowed up to the *bank* and got out of the boat.
   ○ building where money is kept
   ○ shoreline of a river or creek

3. The garage is 15-*feet* wide.
   ○ a measurement
   ○ body parts used for walking

4. The *mouse* ran under the bushes.
   ○ a small, furry animal
   ○ hand control for a computer

5. I like to put butter on my *roll.*
   ○ hot bread
   ○ to turn over and over

6. Let's give the winner a big *hand*!
   ○ body part with fingers on it
   ○ applause

7. I *can* sing soprano.
   ○ a metal container
   ○ am able to

8. The wolf crept into the sheep *pen.*
   ○ writing instrument that uses ink
   ○ area that is fenced in

 On another piece of paper, write two sentences showing a different meaning for the word "star" in each.

Scholastic Professional Books

Where Am I?

Making inferences *means to use information in a story to make judgments about information not given in the story.*

Read each riddle below. Look for clues to help you answer each question.

1. It is dark in here. I hear bats flying. With my flashlight, I see stalactites hanging above me. I hear water dripping. Where am I?

   _____

2. Let's sit in the front row! Ha ha ha! That's funny . . . a cartoon about a drink cup that is singing to a candy bar. That makes me hungry. I think I'll go get some popcorn before it starts. Where am I?

   _____

3. This thing keeps going faster and faster, up and down, and over and around. It tickles my tummy. The girls behind me are screaming. I hope I don't go flying out of my seat! Where am I?

   _____

4. I can see rivers and highways that look like tiny ribbons. I am glad I got to sit by the window. Wow, we are in a cloud! Yes, ma'am. I would like a drink. Thank you. Where am I?

   _____

5. I am all dressed up, sitting here quietly with my parents. The flowers are pretty. The music is starting. Here she comes down the aisle. I wish they would hurry so I can have some cake! Where am I?

   _____

6. Doctor, can you help my dog? His name is Champ. He was bitten by a snake, and his leg is swollen. I hope he will be all right. Where am I?

   _____

7. How will I ever decide? Look at all the different kinds. There are red hots, chocolates, candy corn, gummy worms, jawbreakers, and lollipops. Boy, this is my favorite place in the mall! Where am I?

   _____

8. This row has carrots growing, and this one has onions. The corn is getting tall. The soil feels dry. I better water the plants today. Don't you think so, Mr. Scarecrow? Where am I?

   _____

On another piece of paper, write two "Where Am I?" riddles of your own. Read your riddles to someone else and have them guess where you are.

On the Border

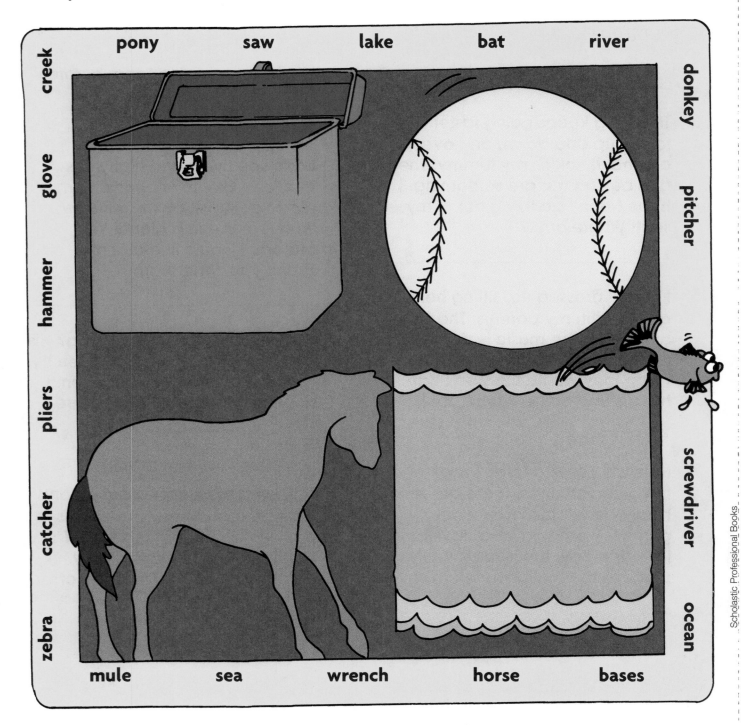

Classifying *means to put things into groups. One way to classify is to look for similarities, ways things are alike.*

Read the words around the border of the picture. Find the words that belong with each picture. Write the words inside the picture. There will be five words in each picture.

pony   saw   lake   bat   river

creek   donkey

glove   pitcher

hammer

pliers

catcher   screwdriver

zebra   ocean

mule   sea   wrench   horse   bases

Moving In

The day we moved to our new house, there was a lot of work to do. Mom gave me the job of organizing the cabinets and closets. I unpacked each box and put things in their proper places. I filled up the medicine chest in the bathroom and the linen closet in the hall. I organized the silverware drawer in the kitchen, as well as the food in the pantry. I lined up Dad's stuff on the garage shelves. Last of all, I filled the bookshelf.

Write each word from the box in the correct category.

Medicine Chest
_____
_____
_____
_____

Linen Closet
_____
_____
_____
_____

Silverware Drawer
_____
_____
_____
_____

Pantry
_____
_____
_____
_____

Garage Shelves
_____
_____
_____
_____

Bookshelf
_____
_____
_____
_____

encyclopedias
eyedrops   teaspoons
car wax   motor oil
quilts   dictionary
cake mix   forks
serving spoons
atlas   aspirin
bandages   blankets
fishing tackle
crackers   novels
pillowcases
cereal   knives
sheets   toolbox
cough syrup
canned soup

THIS END UP

On another piece of paper, make a list of eight things that people might store in an attic.

The Pyramid Game

Every morning before school, Mrs. Cavazos writes five words inside a pyramid on the chalkboard. When class begins, her students are to think of a title for the group of words. The title is to tell how the words are alike. The class then thinks of three words to add to the list.

Write a title for each pyramid of words.

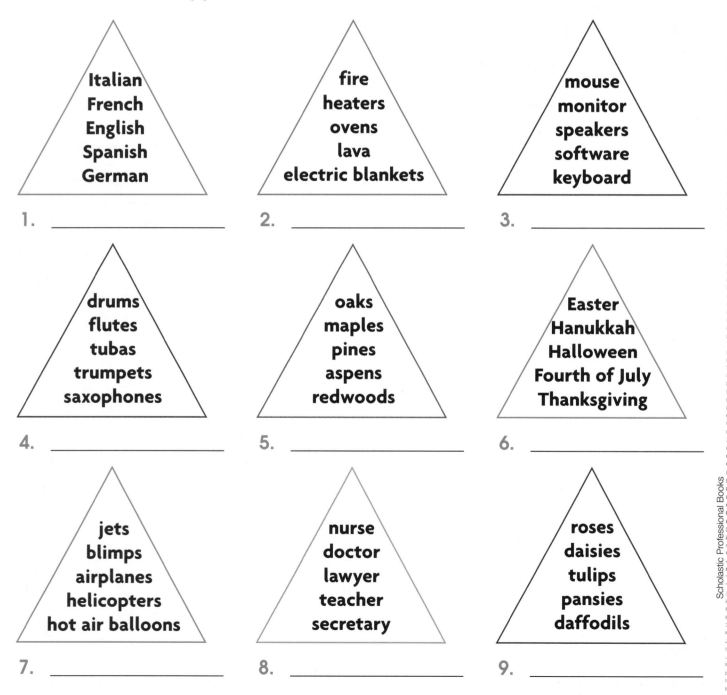

Italian
French
English
Spanish
German

1. _____

fire
heaters
ovens
lava
electric blankets

2. _____

mouse
monitor
speakers
software
keyboard

3. _____

drums
flutes
tubas
trumpets
saxophones

4. _____

oaks
maples
pines
aspens
redwoods

5. _____

Easter
Hanukkah
Halloween
Fourth of July
Thanksgiving

6. _____

jets
blimps
airplanes
helicopters
hot air balloons

7. _____

nurse
doctor
lawyer
teacher
secretary

8. _____

roses
daisies
tulips
pansies
daffodils

9. _____

Scholastic Professional Books

News or Views?

 Facts *are true statement and can be proven.* **Opinions** *are a person's own personal views or beliefs.*

When people talk about things, they often mix news with opinions. Read each cartoon. Write *News* in the box if it is a fact. Write *Views* in the box if it is a person's own personal opinion.

1. **Punky Starr is the best rock singer that ever lived!**

2. **I like our new president. I think he is intelligent and kind.**

3. **Oranges were 3 for $1.00 at the Farmer's Market today.**

4. **Nobody likes me. Everyone thinks I am ugly.**

5. **When it gets dark, we will be able to see the Big Dipper and the North Star.**

6. **The city council will meet on Monday to vote on the new highway.**

7. **Ha ha ha ha! This show is funny.**

8. **The math homework for today is on page 34.**

9. **Your messy room looks like a pigpen!**

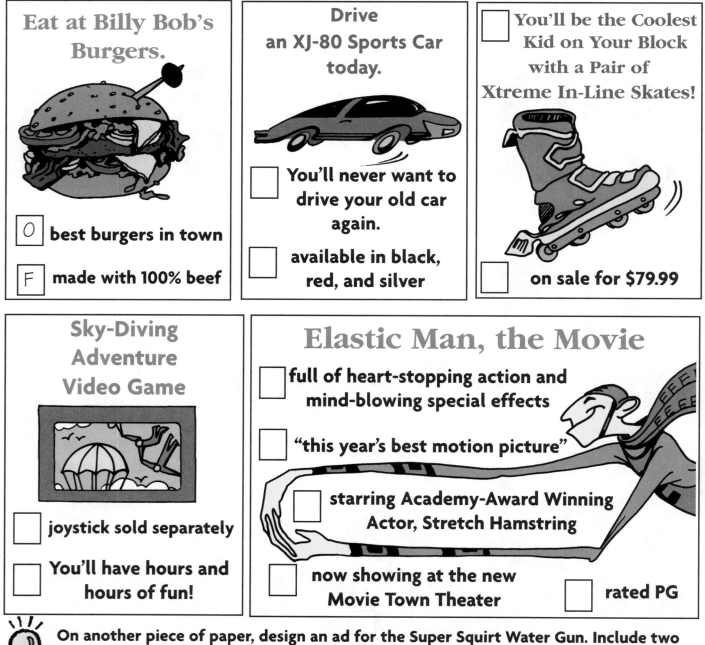

TV Commercials

When you watch TV, you see a lot of commercials advertising different products. The people making the commercial want you to buy their product, so they make it sound as good as possible. Some of the things they say are facts, which can be proven. Other things are just the advertiser's opinion about how good the product is or how it will make you feel. Read each advertisement below. Write an *F* in the box beside each fact and an *O* in the box beside each opinion. The first one is done for you.

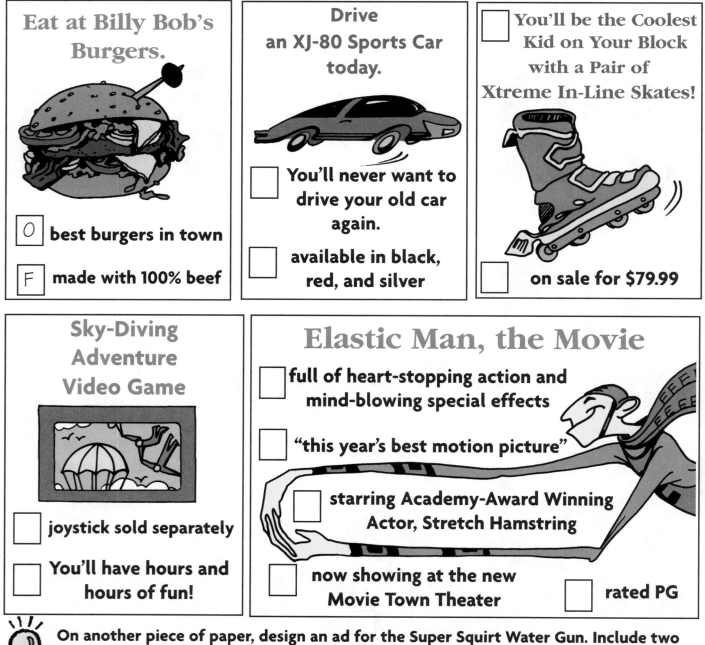

Eat at Billy Bob's Burgers.

[O] best burgers in town

[F] made with 100% beef

Drive an XJ-80 Sports Car today.

[ ] You'll never want to drive your old car again.

[ ] available in black, red, and silver

You'll be the Coolest Kid on Your Block with a Pair of Xtreme In-Line Skates!

[ ] on sale for $79.99

Sky-Diving Adventure Video Game

[ ] joystick sold separately

[ ] You'll have hours and hours of fun!

Elastic Man, the Movie

[ ] full of heart-stopping action and mind-blowing special effects

[ ] "this year's best motion picture"

[ ] starring Academy-Award Winning Actor, Stretch Hamstring

[ ] now showing at the new Movie Town Theater

[ ] rated PG

On another piece of paper, design an ad for the Super Squirt Water Gun. Include two facts and two opinions.

News Report

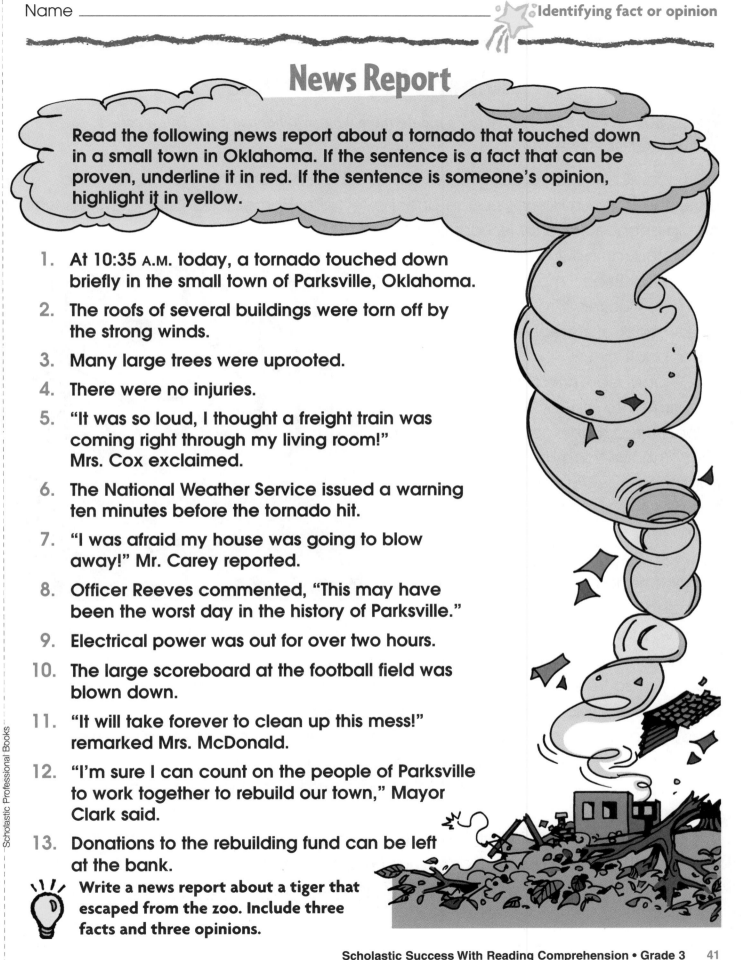

Read the following news report about a tornado that touched down in a small town in Oklahoma. If the sentence is a fact that can be proven, underline it in red. If the sentence is someone's opinion, highlight it in yellow.

1. At 10:35 A.M. today, a tornado touched down briefly in the small town of Parksville, Oklahoma.

2. The roofs of several buildings were torn off by the strong winds.

3. Many large trees were uprooted.

4. There were no injuries.

5. "It was so loud, I thought a freight train was coming right through my living room!" Mrs. Cox exclaimed.

6. The National Weather Service issued a warning ten minutes before the tornado hit.

7. "I was afraid my house was going to blow away!" Mr. Carey reported.

8. Officer Reeves commented, "This may have been the worst day in the history of Parksville."

9. Electrical power was out for over two hours.

10. The large scoreboard at the football field was blown down.

11. "It will take forever to clean up this mess!" remarked Mrs. McDonald.

12. "I'm sure I can count on the people of Parksville to work together to rebuild our town," Mayor Clark said.

13. Donations to the rebuilding fund can be left at the bank.

💡 Write a news report about a tiger that escaped from the zoo. Include three facts and three opinions.

Homer's Big Adventure

Use details from a story to help determine what will happen next. This is called **making predictions**.

Brian was in such a hurry to get to the school bus on time that he forgot to close the door on Homer's cage after he fed him. Homer T. Hamster knew this was his big chance. He crawled out of his cage and ran downstairs, careful to sneak past Brian's mother without being seen. He ducked through a hole in the screen door and stepped out into the great backyard.

"Yippeeee!" cried Homer, throwing his little arms into the air. "I'm free at last!" He zipped through the gate and down the alley. The first thing Homer saw was a huge, snarling German shepherd who thought it was fun to chase anything that could run. "R-r-ruff! R-r-ruff!"

Homer scurried here and there only inches ahead of the dog. He barely escaped by hiding under a flowerpot. "Whew, that was close!" he thought. He waited there awhile, shaking like a leaf.

Then he crept out into the alley again. He looked this way and that. The coast was clear, so he skipped happily along. He looked up just in time to see the big black tires of a pickup truck that was backing out of a driveway. He almost got squooshed! So, he darted quickly into someone's backyard where a boy was mowing the lawn. R-r-r-r-r! Homer had to jump out of the way again.

Back in the alley, he decided to rest somewhere that was safe. He crawled into a garbage dumpster and fell asleep. Later, he heard the sound of a big truck. He felt himself going high up into the air. The dumpster turned upside down, and the lid opened. Homer was falling. "Yikes!" screamed Homer. He had to think fast. He reached out and grabbed the side of the truck, holding on for dear life.

Scholastic Professional Books

The truck rolled down the alley and into the street. As it turned the corner, Homer was flung off the truck and onto the hood of a school bus. He grabbed onto the windshield wipers as the bus drove to the corner and stopped.

The bus driver exclaimed, "Look, kids! There is a hamster riding on our bus!" All the kids rushed forward to see the funny sight. Homer looked through the windshield at all the surprised faces. All of a sudden, Homer saw Brian! Brian ran out of the bus and carefully picked up Homer. "Hey, buddy, how did you get out here? Are you okay?" Brian asked as he petted Homar's fur.

1. **What do you think happened next? Color the picture that seems to be the most likely ending to the story.**

2. **Underline the sentence that tells the main idea of the story.**

   Homer hid under a flowerpot to escape from a German shepherd.

   Homer had many exciting adventures after crawling out of his cage.

   Brian was surprised to see Homer riding the school bus.

3. **Do you think Homer will leave his cage again? Write a sentence to tell why or**

   why not. _____

   _____

On another piece of paper, write a paragraph telling about one more adventure Homer might have had while he was out of his cage. Read your paragraph to a friend.

Mary's Mystery

Monday afternoon, Mom called my sister, Mary, to the door. The florist had just delivered a dozen red roses to her. "For me?" asked Mary. "Who would be sending me flowers?" Mom told her to read the card. It said, "Mary, I'm sorry I hurt your feelings. Can you forgive me?" Mary looked puzzled. She could not think of anyone that had hurt her feelings.

On Wednesday, a delivery boy brought a package to the door. He said, "This is for Mary." It was a box of chocolate candy. Mary liked chocolate very much, but she could not figure out who was sending her gifts, or why.

On Friday, a teenage girl dressed in a sparkly costume rang the doorbell. Mary answered the door. The teenager asked, "Are you Mary?" She nodded her head and said yes, and the teenager told her that she was sent by someone to perform a singing telegram. She sang, "Mary, I want you to be . . . the girl who will marry me . . ." Then she left. Mary looked at Mom. "I am only nine years old! I don't want to get married!" Mom laughed. "There must be some mistake."

That night, a handsome young man came to the door with a ring box in his hand. He rang the doorbell at Mary's apartment. Mary opened the door. When the man saw Mary, he looked surprised. He said, "Oh, I'm sorry. I was looking for Mary's apartment." Mary said, "Well, I am Mary." The man stood there frowning for a moment. Then he started to laugh.

Scholastic Professional Books

"No wonder my girlfriend has not mentioned the gifts I sent her. I bet they have all been coming here." Then he told Mary to step outside and look at the metal numbers over her apartment door. Mary's apartment was #620, but the 6 had come loose and had turned upside down. That made it look like #920. The man said, "I am sorry about the mix-up. My girlfriend, Mary, just moved into apartment #920. I think all the delivery people saw your #920 and stopped here, just like I did. I guess when they found out your name was Mary, they thought they had the right place." Mary laughed. "Now I understand," she said. "Oh, I am sorry, but I already ate the chocolates." The man replied, "That's okay." Then as he turned to walk away he added, "You can also keep the flowers." "Thank you," Mary said grinning, "but I am not going to marry you!"

1. **Underline two sentences below that tell what might happen next. Mark an X on two sentences that tell about something that probably will not happen.**

   The man found the other Mary, his girlfriend, and gave her the ring.

   The man sent Mary a bill because she ate the chocolates.

   Nine-year-old Mary sent the man a dozen roses.

   Mary's mom turned the 9 over to make a 6 again and nailed it tight so their apartment number would be correct.

2. **Circle what the title of the song the singing telegram might have been.**

   "Love Me Always"

   "Crossing the Mississippi"

   "The Champion Cheer"

3. **What did the florist deliver to Mary? _____**

4. **Which gift do you think Mary liked the best? Why? _____**

   _____

5. **On what day did Mary receive the singing telegram? _____**

6. **Where is the setting of this story? _____**

Special Charts

Comparing and **contrasting** means to show the similarities and differences of things. A Venn diagram is a chart made of overlapping circles that can be used to organize the similarities and differences. The overlapping parts of the circles show how things are similar. The other part of the circles show how things are different.

Joe, Kim, and Rob each got a lunch tray, went through the lunch line, and sat together to eat. These students all had the same lunch menu, but each one only ate what he or she liked. Joe ate chicken nuggets, green beans, applesauce, and carrots. Rob ate chicken nuggets, green beans, a roll, and corn. Kim ate chicken nuggets, a roll, applesauce, and salad.

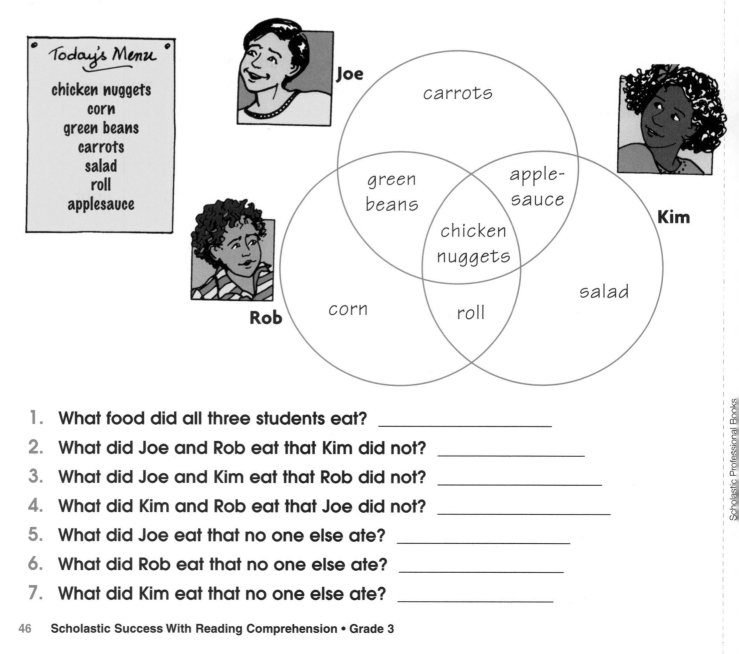

1. What food did all three students eat? _____

2. What did Joe and Rob eat that Kim did not? _____

3. What did Joe and Kim eat that Rob did not? _____

4. What did Kim and Rob eat that Joe did not? _____

5. What did Joe eat that no one else ate? _____

6. What did Rob eat that no one else ate? _____

7. What did Kim eat that no one else ate? _____

Sports Chart

There are three brothers who love to play sports. Each one is good at several different sports. Jeff plays hockey, football, soccer, and baseball. Allen plays hockey, football, tennis, and golf. Seth plays hockey, tennis, soccer, and basketball.

1. **Complete the Venn diagram showing which sports each brother plays. Start with the sport all three brothers have in common. Write it in the shared space of all three circles.**

Jeff

Allen

Seth

1. **What sport do all three boys like to play?** _____

2. **What sport do Jeff and Allen like to play that Seth does not?** _____

3. **What sport do Jeff and Seth like to play that Allen does not?** _____

4. **What sport do Allen and Seth like to play that Jeff does not?** _____

5. **What sport does Jeff like to play that no one else does?** _____

6. **What sport does Allen like to play that no one else does?** _____

7. **What sport does Seth like to play that no one else does?** _____

Sharks

There are over 350 different kinds of sharks. The whale shark is the largest. It is as big as a whale. The pygmy shark is the smallest. It is only about seven inches long.

All sharks live in the ocean, which is salt water, but a few kinds can swim from salt water to fresh water. Bull sharks have been found in the Mississippi River!

Sharks do not have bones. They have skeletons made of cartilage, which is the same thing your ears and nose are made of. A shark's skin is made of spiky, hard scales. The jaws of a shark are the most powerful on earth. When a great white shark bites, it clamps down on its prey and thrashes its head from side to side. It is the deadliest shark.

Sharks eat fish, dolphins, and seals. The tiger shark will eat just about anything. Some fishermen have discovered unopened cans of food, clocks, boat cushions, and even a keg of nails inside tiger sharks. Sometimes sharks even eat other sharks. For example, a tiger shark might eat a bull shark. The bull shark might have eaten a blacktip shark. The blacktip shark might have eaten a dogfish shark. So a tiger shark could be found with three sharks in its stomach!

Some sharks are very strange. The hammerhead shark has a head shaped somewhat like a hammer, with eyes set very far apart. A cookie cutter shark has a circular set of teeth. When it bites a dolphin or whale, it leaves a perfectly round hole in its victim. The sawshark has a snout with sharp teeth on the outside, which makes it look like a saw. The goblin shark has a sharp-pointed spear coming out of its head, and its ragged teeth make it look scary!

The mako shark is the fastest swimmer. Sometimes makos have been known to leap out of the water, right into a boat! These are just a few of the many kinds of fascinating sharks.

Scholastic Professional Books

Complete the chart with the name of the correct shark. If the statement is about all sharks, write *all*.

1. the largest shark	whale shark
2. the smallest shark	
3. the deadliest shark	
4. the fastest swimmer	
5. live in the ocean	
6. have skeletons of cartilage	
7. has a sharp-pointed spear coming out of its head	
8. has a head shaped like a hammer	
9. skin of spiky, hard scales	
10. leaves a round bite mark	
11. looks like a saw	
12. has eaten unopened cans, clocks, and boat cushions	

💡 **Read more about two different kinds of sharks. On another piece of paper, list two similarities and two differences.**

Name _____

Earthquake!

*The **cause** in a story is what made something happen. The **effect** is what happened.*

Earthquakes are one of the most powerful events on the earth. When large sections of underground rock break and move suddenly, an earthquake occurs. This causes the ground to shake back and forth. Small earthquakes do not cause much damage, but large ones do. Some earthquakes have caused buildings and bridges to fall. Others have caused rivers to change their paths. Earthquakes near mountains and cliffs can cause landslides that cover up the houses and roads below. If a large earthquake occurs under the ocean, it can cause giant waves which flood the seashore. When large earthquakes occur in a city, there is danger of fire from broken gas lines and electric lines. Broken telephone lines and damaged roads make it difficult for rescue workers to help people who are in need. Scientists are trying to find ways to predict when an earthquake will happen so that people can be warned ahead of time.

Draw a shaky line under each effect.

Earthquakes can cause . . .
1. landslides
2. tornadoes
3. fires from broken gas and electric lines
4. huge waves that flood the seashore
5. swarms of flies
6. buildings and bridges to fall
7. sunburns
8. rivers to change their paths
9. damaged roads
10. lightning

Read about tornadoes. On another piece of paper, make a list of eight things a tornado might cause.

Scholastic Professional Books

Wacky Water Slides

Have you ever gone to a water park in the summertime? Some of the most popular attractions are the water slides. How do they work? Construction crews put together sections of large plastic and fiberglass tubes to form the slides. They can make the tubes go straight down or around and around. Either way, the tubes must have a starting point that is high off the ground. This is because water slides work by gravity. Gravity is the natural pull of the earth. It is the force that makes things fall to the ground. So, when a swimmer begins to slide from up high, gravity pulls the swimmer down the slide into the pool below. There is another thing that water slides need in order to work. Water, of course! Water parks have huge pumps that pump the water to the top of the slides. The rushing water runs down the slides, making them slippery. Then the fun begins. Slip! Slide! Splash!

Fill in the blanks on each water slide to explain how they work. Find the answers in the pool below.

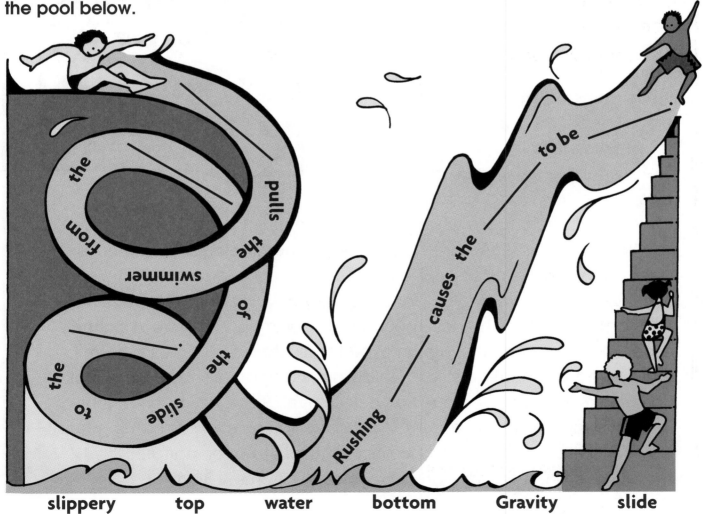

the — from — swimmer — pulls the — of the — slide — to — to be — causes the — Rushing

| slippery | top | water | bottom | Gravity | slide |

Nonfiction: A Biography

A **biography** is the history of a person's life. You have probably read biographies of presidents or famous people in history. The following biography is about one of the most popular zookeepers of our time.

Steve Irwin

Have you ever seen **Steve Irwin**, the **Crocodile Hunter,** on TV? Steve is a **reptile** specialist and zoo director in Queensland, **Australia**.

Steve's parents, Bob and Lyn Irwin, owned a reptile park. Steve grew up learning about and handling reptiles, as well as many other kinds of **animals**. When Steve was six years old, his father gave him a snake called a scrub **python**. Steve named it **Fred**. Steve's dad taught him all about the **wildlife** of Australia and took him on field trips to study about it. Steve often begged to go on these field trips rather than going to school. He caught his first crocodile when he was only nine years old.

Now Steve runs the Australia **Zoo**. He is a **herpetologist**. That means he is a reptile **expert**. His mission in life is to educate people about animals, teaching them to treat even dangerous animals with **respect**. Steve never hurts animals. In fact, he has rescued many animals that were in **danger**, especially crocodiles. Steve is an expert snake handler. He holds them by the tail and lets them go safely. He always warns others, though, that picking up a **snake** is very dangerous. Sometimes even Steve has been bitten!

Steve married an American who was visiting his zoo. Her name is **Terri**. Now Terri helps Steve handle the animals, and she often narrates the TV show. Steve and Terri have one daughter. Her name is **Bindi**.

Scholastic Professional Books

Look at the bolded words in the story. Find each word in the puzzle and circle it. The words may go up, down, forward, backward, or diagonally.

```
G  P  R  Z  T  R  E  P  X  E  Y  L  F
X  Y  R  E  S  P  E  C  T  U  V  M  R
S  T  W  H  G  D  C  B  S  T  E  V  E
P  H  A  H  O  N  I  N  Z  L  K  W  D
Q  O  F  U  I  L  A  N  I  M  A  L  S
J  N  O  W  S  K  V  D  W  X  H  L  K
H  E  R  P  E  T  O  L  O  G  I  S  T
U  I  D  Q  M  C  R  T  S  B  C  N  E
N  J  Z  O  O  E  K  A  X  Z  Y  O  R
T  B  U  R  E  P  T  I  L  E  V  H  R
E  P  C  U  I  O  A  Q  B  I  N  D  I
R  X  E  F  I  L  D  L  I  W  A  Z  F
```

List two facts about Steve Irvin.

1. _____

2. _____

Find the biography section in the library. Check out a biography about someone who had a career that interests you.

Acrostic Poems

*Acrostic poetry is fun. An **acrostic poem** starts with a word that is the subject of the whole poem. The word is written vertically. Then words or phases about that subject are written using each letter. Look at the examples below.*

Sleeping late
Under the ceiling fan
May we go to the pool?
My, it's hot!
Eating watermelon
Relaxing on vacation

Do you have a fever?
Open wide!
Checks for sore throat
Talks to the nurse
Orders some medicine
Ready for the next patient

Now it is your turn! Finish each acrostic poem below by writing something about the word that is written vertically, using each letter of the word.

T _____

E lementary school

A _____

C _____

H elps me learn

E _____

R _____

H _____

O ats for dinner

R _____

S _____

E _____

S addle them up!

On another piece of paper, make an acrostic poem about yourself. Start by writing your name vertically.

Scholastic Professional Books

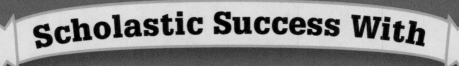

Scholastic Success With

TESTS: READING

Reading Skills Practice Test 1

READING COMPREHENSION

Read each story. Then fill in the circle that best completes each sentence or answers each question.

SAMPLE

Imagine drinking 500 cups of water at once. Believe it or not, that's what camels do! In the desert, water is hard to find. When a camel finds water, it drinks as much as it can. Because a camel has a big stomach, it can *gulp* down 30 gallons. That's nearly 500 cups. Then it can go for 10 months without another drink.

1. What is the best title for this story?
    - ○ **A.** "Why Water Is Good for You"
    - ○ **B.** "Life in the Desert"
    - ◉ **C.** "Thirsty Camels"
    - ○ **D.** "Water Pollution"

2. In the story, the word **gulp** means
    - ○ **A.** throw.
    - ◉ **B.** drink.
    - ○ **C.** watch.
    - ○ **D.** walk.

A. Have you ever heard of the Man in the Moon? Many people say they can see a man's face on the surface of the moon. It's not really a face, of course. Instead, the "face" is a pattern made by *craters* and mountains on the moon's surface. When the moon is full and the sky is clear, we see some of those holes and hills.

1. What is the best title for this story?
    - ○ **A.** "The Moon and Stars"
    - ○ **B.** "A Full Moon"
    - ○ **C.** "People Land on the Moon"
    - ◉ **D.** "The Man in the Moon"

2. In this story, the word **craters** means
    - ◉ **A.** holes.
    - ○ **B.** moons.
    - ○ **C.** mountains.
    - ○ **D.** nights.

3. You can see the Man in the Moon best when the moon is
    - ○ **A.** hidden.
    - ○ **B.** new.
    - ◉ **C.** full.
    - ○ **D.** flat.

4. You would probably find this story in a
    - ◉ **A.** science book.
    - ○ **B.** dictionary.
    - ○ **C.** poetry book.
    - ○ **D.** travel guide.

B. A fire can be serious. But these few simple tips can help keep you safe:
1.   Put a smoke detector on every level of your home. Check the batteries once a month.
2.   Make an escape plan with your family. Plan two ways to get out of each room in case of fire. Pick a spot to meet outside. Then practice!
3.   If your city does not have 911, know the phone number for the fire department.
4.   If there is a fire, feel a door before opening it. If it is warm, do not open it. Use another way out.
5.   Crawl low under smoke.
6.   If your clothes catch fire, stop and drop to the ground. Roll around to put out the flames.

1.   This story is mainly about
   ○ **A.** how most fires start.
   ◉ **B.** how to stay safe from fire.
   ○ **C.** how to fix a smoke detector.
   ○ **D.** what firefighters do.

2.   You should check the batteries in a smoke detector
   ○ **A.** once a year.
   ○ **B.** twice a year.
   ○ **C.** when you think of it.
   ◉ **D.** once a month.

3.   You can guess from the story that a warm door means
   ○ **A.** the fire is over.
   ◉ **B.** the fire is close by.
   ○ **C.** firefighters are on the way.
   ○ **D.** the fire is small.

4.   If your clothes catch fire, what should you do first?
   ○ **A.** Stop.
   ○ **B.** Cry.
   ◉ **C.** Roll.
   ○ **D.** Run.

C. The President of the United States has one of the toughest jobs in the world. He also has one of the nicest homes.

The President lives in the White House, in Washington, D.C. This *mansion* has 132 rooms, 32 bathrooms, and 3 elevators. It has a swimming pool, a bowling alley, and a movie theater. It even has its own doctor's office and barbershop! That means the President can do a lot without leaving home.

The President's home is so beautiful, it used to be called the "President's Palace." President Theodore Roosevelt named it the White House in 1901.

Do you wish you owned a home like the White House? You already do! According to the U.S. Constitution, the President does not own the White House. The American people do!

1.   What is the best title for this story?
   ○ **A.** "Beautiful Homes"
   ○ **B.** "A New President"
   ◉ **C.** "The President's Home"
   ○ **D.** "Write to the President"

2.   In this story, the word **mansion** means a big
   ○ **A.** job.   ○ **C.** car.
   ○ **B.** pool.   ◉ **D.** home.

3.   Which of these is an **opinion** about the White House?
   ○ **A.** It's in Washington, D.C.
   ○ **B.** It has 132 rooms.
   ◉ **C.** It's the nicest house in the world.
   ○ **D.** It has a barbershop.

D. One African folktale tells why some spiders have bald heads. In the tale, Dog, Elephant, and other animals were having a festival to honor their parents. Anansi the spider bragged to the other animals. He said he had the best way to honor his parents. He would go a whole week without eating! The other animals groaned. They knew Anansi was a show-off.

That week, the other animals ate and ate. But Anansi got hungrier and hungrier. One day, he spotted a pot full of beans. "I will take a tiny taste," thought Anansi. "No one will know."

So Anansi took off his hat and filled it with beans. He had just begun to eat when he heard a noise. The other animals were coming! Quickly, Anansi put the hat on his head. But he forgot the hat was full of beans. The hot beans burned all the hair off Anansi's head. The other animals laughed. "Maybe this will teach Anansi to stop bragging," they said.

1. Which happened first?
   ○ **A.** Anansi ate the beans.
   ○ **B.** The beans burned Anansi's head.
   ○ **C.** Anansi saw the pot.
   ○ **D.** Anansi filled his hat.

2. The author created this story to tell
   ○ **A.** that it is good to show off.
   ○ **B.** how to cook beans.
   ○ **C.** that it is wrong to brag.
   ○ **D.** that beans are tasty.

E. Much of our planet is covered by water. This water is always on the move. It makes a journey called the *water cycle.*

The water cycle starts when the sun's heat warms Earth's oceans and rivers. The heat makes tiny drops of water rise into the air. These tiny drops are called *water vapor.*

Next, the tiny drops of water gather together. They form clouds. When the clouds get too heavy, water spills out of them. The water falls back down to Earth as rain or snow. Then, the water begins its journey again.

1. In this story, the word rise means
   ○ **A.** move up.
   ○ **B.** move over.
   ○ **C.** fall.
   ○ **D.** break.

2. What is the best title for this story?
   ○ **A.** "Let It Snow!"
   ○ **B.** "Earth's Oceans"
   ○ **C.** "The Water Cycle"
   ○ **D.** "Types of Clouds"

3. You can guess from the story that
   ○ **A.** Earth has very little water.
   ○ **B.** snow is made of water.
   ○ **C.** clouds are made of salt.
   ○ **D.** water never moves.

4. Which of these is a **fact**?
   ○ **A.** Everyone hates rain.
   ○ **B.** Snow is better than rain.
   ○ **C.** Science is boring.
   ○ **D.** Drops of water form clouds.

Vocabulary

Synonyms

Read the underlined word in each phrase. Mark the word below it that has the same (or close to the same) meaning.

Sample:

roam around
- **A.** play
- **B.** wander
- **C.** read
- **D.** see

1. speak loudly
   - **A.** laugh
   - **B.** look
   - **C.** talk
   - **D.** bend

2. allow her in
   - **A.** turn
   - **B.** let
   - **C.** stand
   - **D.** call

3. a terrible day
   - **A.** slow
   - **B.** awful
   - **C.** early
   - **D.** old

4. the correct answer
   - **A.** right
   - **B.** first
   - **C.** blue
   - **D.** wrong

5. create artwork
   - **A.** none
   - **B.** buy
   - **C.** drop
   - **D.** make

6. the fearful boy
   - **A.** gentle
   - **B.** scared
   - **C.** silly
   - **D.** kind

7. finish the chore
   - **A.** play
   - **B.** pet
   - **C.** job
   - **D.** day

Antonyms

Read the underlined word in each phrase. Mark the word below it that means the opposite or nearly the opposite.

Sample:

a strong person
- **A.** smart
- **B.** new
- **C.** healthy
- **D.** weak

1. a narrow hall
   - **A.** wide
   - **B.** shiny
   - **C.** cool
   - **D.** dry

2. a noisy crowd
   - **A.** neat
   - **B.** lost
   - **C.** quiet
   - **D.** big

3. load the truck
   - **A.** lonely
   - **B.** unload
   - **C.** pack
   - **D.** reload

4. many friends
   - **A.** real
   - **B.** my
   - **C.** few
   - **D.** all

5. a fancy coat
   - **A.** plain
   - **B.** short
   - **C.** soft
   - **D.** cold

6. a useful tool
   - **A.** powerful
   - **B.** wonderful
   - **C.** used
   - **D.** useless

7. a rare animal
   - **A.** common
   - **B.** ugly
   - **C.** wild
   - **D.** oily

Reading Skills Practice Test 2

READING COMPREHENSION

Read each story. Then fill in the circle that best completes each sentence or answers each question.

SAMPLE

Did you ever hear someone say, "I'd do it at the drop of a hat"? The person means he or she would do it right away. This saying started hundreds of years ago. Back then, people would drop a hat in order to start a race. When the hat touched the ground, the runners would take off. Today, we use the phrase "at the drop of a hat" when a person does something suddenly or eagerly.

1. What is the best title for this story?
   ○ **A.** "Races of Long Ago"
   ○ **B.** "At the Drop of a Hat"
   ○ **C.** "Hat Styles"
   ○ **D.** "Who Will Win?"

2. In this story, the word phrase means
   ○ **A.** runner.
   ○ **B.** hat.
   ○ **C.** saying.
   ○ **D.** name.

A. To a bat, the world must seem topsy-turvy. That's because this creature spends a good part of its day hanging upside down! A bat has five sharp claws on each of its short *hind* legs. It uses the claws to hang upside down from tree branches, caves, and city bridges. A bat hangs for many hours each day—even while it is sleeping, eating, and washing itself. In fact, the only time this flying mammal is right side up is when it is fetching insects, fruit, or other meals.

1. This story is mainly about
   ○ **A.** how bats find food.
   ○ **B.** how bats hang upside down.
   ○ **C.** bats and other mammals.
   ○ **D.** all kinds of caves.

2. In this story, the word **hind** means
   ○ **A.** flying.
   ○ **B.** imaginary.
   ○ **C.** dry.
   ○ **D.** back.

3. Bats are right side up when they
   ○ **A.** find food.
   ○ **B.** sleep.
   ○ **C.** wash themselves.
   ○ **D.** eat.

4. You can guess from the story that bats
   ○ **A.** never leave their caves or trees.
   ○ **B.** are very dirty animals.
   ○ **C.** eat only insects.
   ○ **D.** live in the city and the country.

B. In the 1620s, Pilgrim children had plenty of work to do in the new settlement. They studied, hunted for food, prepared meals, and helped care for younger brothers and sisters. But these early American kids had some time for fun, too. One of their favorite games was called Puss in the Middle. Would you like to play this Pilgrim game? Just follow the directions below:

1. Gather four friends. Have one child stand in the middle of the room. He or she is Puss.
2. Have the other four children stand in the corners of the room.
3. The corner players must change places without giving Puss a chance to grab a corner spot.
4. When Puss gets a corner spot, the child who lost his or her spot becomes the next Puss. The game starts all over again!

1. This story is mainly about
   ○ **A.** how to play a Pilgrim game.
   ○ **B.** how the Pilgrims came to America.
   ○ **C.** foods the Pilgrims ate.
   ○ **D.** what Pilgrim kids studied.

2. Pilgrim children played Puss in the
   ○ **A.** 1800s.   ○ **C.** 1500s.
   ○ **B.** 1600s.   ○ **D.** 1900s.

3. To play Puss in the Middle, what should you do first?
   ○ **A.** Try to change places.
   ○ **B.** Stand in the corners.
   ○ **C.** Have Puss stand in the middle.
   ○ **D.** Gather four friends.

4. Which of these is an opinion about Pilgrim children?
   ○ **A.** They played silly games.
   ○ **B.** They helped prepare meals.
   ○ **C.** They lived in the Colonies.
   ○ **D.** They hunted for food.

C. For many kids, there is nothing like a good action movie. They love seeing their favorite stars *leap* across rooftops or drive at high speeds in a thrilling chase. What they may not know is that, behind every dangerous scene, there is a stunt person. Stunt people look like the real movie stars, but they are specially trained to perform daring tricks. They practice dangerous scenes over and over again. And they wear thick padding on their backs, arms, and shoulders to protect themselves.

Stunt people use other safety tricks, too. When they must fall during a scene, they often land on a mattress or trampoline. When a car window explodes in the stunt person's face, it is made of fake glass that will not cut the skin. Although you can't see these tricks on camera, they sure help keep you glued to the screen!

1. What is the best title for this story?
   ○ **A.** "Kids' Favorite Movie Stars"
   ○ **B.** "Dangerous Jobs"
   ○ **C.** "How Stunt People Work"
   ○ **D.** "Action Movies"

2. In this story the word **leap** means
   ○ **A.** jump.   ○ **C.** land.
   ○ **B.** skip.   ○ **D.** practice.

3. Movie makers use fake glass because
   ○ **A.** it is cheaper than real glass.
   ○ **B.** it breaks easily.
   ○ **C.** it won't cut the skin.
   ○ **D.** it is easy to get.

4. You might find this story in
   ○ **A.** a book about movies.
   ○ **B.** an encyclopedia.
   ○ **C.** a nature guide.
   ○ **D.** a book about planes.

Scholastic Professional Books

Name _____

D. One African folktale tells how Leopard got his spots. According to the tale, Leopard and some other animals had a funeral march for their friend Ant. As the animals walked, Leopard's stomach rumbled. He was hungry!

As the animals passed a farm, Leopard noticed some baskets filled with fresh eggs. He tossed one egg after another into his mouth. Soon he had eaten an entire basket! Satisfied, he returned to the other animals.

When the farmer saw the empty basket, he chased after the animals. "Who stole my eggs?" he asked. All of the animals denied it. Then the farmer had an idea. He asked all the animals to jump over a bonfire. He said the animal who had eaten the eggs would fall in. One by one, the creatures leaped over the flames. When it was Leopard's turn, he took a deep breath, jumped, and landed in the fire. "Aha!" said the farmer. "It was you!"

Leopard climbed out of the fire, but his coat was burned in spots as a reminder of his greed.

1. Which happened last?
   ○ **A.** Leopard ate the eggs.
   ○ **B.** Leopard burned his coat.
   ○ **C.** Leopard was hungry.
   ○ **D.** The farmer saw the empty basket.

2. The author created this story to tell
   ○ **A.** that it is bad to steal.
   ○ **B.** how to make music.
   ○ **C.** how leopards live.
   ○ **D.** all about Africa.

3. You can guess that
   ○ **A.** African animals can talk.
   ○ **B.** this event never really happened.
   ○ **C.** ants are very smart.
   ○ **D.** leopards are allergic to eggs.

E. To author Joanna Cole, writing about science is a dream come true. When Cole was growing up in New Jersey, she explored nature. She grew gardens and caught bugs in her yard.

When Cole grew up, she became a teacher. One day, she saw an article about cockroaches. She learned that these bugs are older than dinosaurs. She thought kids would like to learn about roaches, too. She decided to write a book about them. Later, Cole wrote books about fish, fleas, frogs, dogs, and more. Of course, some of Cole's most famous books are the *Magic School Bus* science stories.

No matter what she is writing about, Cole says that two things are important to her. One is research. Cole reads many books and talks to experts to make sure her facts are *correct*. The second thing is a sense of humor. She says even science should be funny!

1. In this story, the word correct means
   ○ **A.** fix.   ○ **C.** funny.
   ○ **B.** new.   ○ **D.** right.

2. This story would probably go on to talk about
   ○ **A.** the success of Cole's books.
   ○ **B.** cockroaches and dinosaurs.
   ○ **C.** kids' hobbies.
   ○ **D.** using the library.

3. What is the best title for this story?
   ○ **A.** "Cockroaches: Ancient Bugs"
   ○ **B.** "Joanna Cole: Science Writer"
   ○ **C.** "The *Magic School Bus* Books"
   ○ **D.** "How to Write a Funny Story"

4. Which of these is a **fact**?
   ○ **A.** Cole is the best author ever.
   ○ **B.** Roaches are gross.
   ○ **C.** Cole grew up in New Jersey.
   ○ **D.** Science is more interesting than art.

Vocabulary

Synonyms

Read the underlined word in each phrase. Mark the word below it that has the same (or close to the same) meaning.

Sample:
> nibble the food
> ○ **A.** see   ○ **C.** fill
> ○ **B.** bite   ○ **D.** leave

1. a joyful day
   ○ **A.** long   ○ **C.** sad
   ○ **B.** new   ○ **D.** happy

2. complete the work
   ○ **A.** forget   ○ **C.** finish
   ○ **B.** know   ○ **D.** try

3. an ache in her ear
   ○ **A.** drop   ○ **C.** noise
   ○ **B.** way   ○ **D.** pain

4. a foolish idea
   ○ **A.** large   ○ **C.** silly
   ○ **B.** old   ○ **D.** great

5. plead for food
   ○ **A.** beg   ○ **C.** drive
   ○ **B.** run   ○ **D.** look

6. vanish without a trace
   ○ **A.** appear   ○ **C.** cry
   ○ **B.** disappear ○ **D.** laugh

7. permit him to go
   ○ **A.** rush   ○ **C.** allow
   ○ **B.** stop   ○ **D.** forbid

Antonyms

Read the underlined word in each phrase. Mark the word below it that means the opposite or nearly the opposite.

Sample:
> an ill person
> ○ **A.** small   ○ **C.** healthy
> ○ **B.** kind   ○ **D.** sick

1. refuse to go
   ○ **A.** say   ○ **C.** read
   ○ **B.** agree   ○ **D.** fail

2. the worst thing
   ○ **A.** best   ○ **C.** first
   ○ **B.** last   ○ **D.** scariest

3. beneath the table
   ○ **A.** under   ○ **C.** above
   ○ **B.** near   ○ **D.** off

4. a slow trickle
   ○ **A.** drip   ○ **C.** gush
   ○ **B.** line   ○ **D.** day

5. a lively show
   ○ **A.** dull   ○ **C.** fun
   ○ **B.** expensive ○ **D.** short

6. a difficult test
   ○ **A.** tricky   ○ **C.** planned
   ○ **B.** exciting   ○ **D.** easy

7. an enormous creature
   ○ **A.** quiet   ○ **C.** wild
   ○ **B.** tiny   ○ **D.** fierce

Reading Skills Practice Test 3

READING COMPREHENSION

Read each story. Then fill in the circle that best completes each sentence or answers each question.

SAMPLE

Red-knee tarantula spiders are in trouble. Some people take these spiders from the wild and sell them as pets. Now, scientists hope to save the red-knee tarantula. They think the spider's *venom,* or poison, might be used to cure some diseases.

1. What is the best title for this story?
   ○ **A.** "The Spider's Knees"
   ○ **B.** "A Terrific Pet"
   ○ **C.** "Save the Spiders"
   ○ **D.** "How to Catch a Spider"

2. In the story, the word **venom** means
   ○ **A.** poison.
   ○ **B.** red knee.
   ○ **C.** tarantula.
   ○ **D.** disease.

A. Imagine a world where countries work together to solve problems. A group called the United Nations works to make that dream come true. The United Nations, or UN, is made up of 189 countries. It was formed in 1945, after World War II. The countries that started the UN wanted to *prevent* another big war from happening.

Today, the UN still tries to stop wars, but it has other jobs, too. UN workers bring food to people in poor countries. They try to wipe out deadly diseases. They even look for ways to help the environment.

1. The best title for this story is
   ○ **A.** "All About World War II."
   ○ **B.** "All About the UN."
   ○ **C.** "How to Help the Earth."
   ○ **D.** "How to Stop Wars."

2. Which of these happened last?
   ○ **A.** The UN was formed.
   ○ **B.** World War II ended.
   ○ **C.** World War II started.
   ○ **D.** The UN began to help poor people.

3. In the story, the word **prevent** means
   ○ **A.** help.
   ○ **B.** hungry.
   ○ **C.** stop.
   ○ **D.** begin.

4. You can guess from the story that
   ○ **A.** the UN started World War II.
   ○ **B.** peace is important to the UN.
   ○ **C.** the United States does not belong to the UN.
   ○ **D.** every country in the world belongs to the UN.

B. In the rain forest, orangutans swing from tree to tree all day. Now, they can feel right at home at the National Zoo in Washington, D.C. The zoo has set up a pretend forest. Instead of trees, it has tall towers. Wires called *cables* run between the towers. Orangutans can swing from the cables—just like they would from branches. The zoo's six orangutans swing around the exhibit. Visitors sit in the middle and watch the apes swing overhead.

1. This story is mainly about
   ○ **A.** what orangutans eat.
   ○ **B.** how to build a pretend forest.
   ○ **C.** how the National Zoo has made orangutans feel at home.
   ○ **D.** what visitors can buy at the National Zoo.

2. Instead of trees, the orangutan exhibit has
   ○ **A.** towers.
   ○ **B.** flowers.
   ○ **C.** apes.
   ○ **D.** buildings.

3. In the story, the word **cables** means
   ○ **A.** wires.
   ○ **B.** forests.
   ○ **C.** pretend.
   ○ **D.** monkeys.

4. Which sentence is an opinion about orangutans?
   ○ **A.** They swing from tree to tree.
   ○ **B.** They live in forests.
   ○ **C.** They are cute.
   ○ **D.** Six of them live at the National Zoo.

C. He was born in Italy more than 500 years ago. He is known as one of the world's greatest artists. But Leonardo da Vinci might also be one of the smartest people who ever lived.

People who have studied Leonardo's notebooks can't believe what they've found. Leonardo's drawings show that he was a scientist, an astronomer, and an engineer. He had ideas about how waves form, why the moon shines, and how flying machines might work. Though no one knows why, Leonardo wrote all his ideas down backward! You need a mirror to read his writing.

1. The main idea of the story is that Leonardo da Vinci
   ○ **A.** liked watching the moon.
   ○ **B.** may be one of the smartest people who ever lived.
   ○ **C.** lived a very long time ago.
   ○ **D.** was an astronomer.

2. Leonardo da Vinci was born in
   ○ **A.** Italy.　　○ **C.** England.
   ○ **B.** the U.S.　○ **D.** France.

3. You need a mirror to read Leonardo's writing because
   ○ **A.** he had messy handwriting.
   ○ **B.** he wrote by moonlight.
   ○ **C.** he wrote in pictures instead of words.
   ○ **D.** he wrote backward.

4. You can guess from the story that
   ○ **A.** Leonardo da Vinci could fly.
   ○ **B.** Italy ruled the world 500 years ago.
   ○ **C.** there were no airplanes 500 years ago.
   ○ **D.** people were smarter 500 years ago than they are now.

Scholastic Professional Books

D. Thousands of years ago, people in Egypt preserved the bodies of their dead and wrapped them in cloth called *linen*. Today, these mummies can tell scientists about how the Egyptians lived. However, scientists have always had a big problem when they tried to study mummies. If they unwrapped a mummy, they would damage it.

Now, scientists have a way to study mummies without unwrapping them. An X-ray machine called a CAT scanner takes pictures of mummies right through their wraps.

The first mummy that scientists scanned was a female Egyptian mummy. The scanner took pictures of her from different angles. Then, a computer put all the pictures together to form a complete image.

1. In the story, the word **linen** means
   ○ **A.** old.   ○ **C.** machine.
   ○ **B.** cloth.   ○ **D.** scientist.

2. Which of these happened first?
   ○ **A.** Scientists used CAT scanners to study mummies.
   ○ **B.** Scientists had trouble unwrapping mummies.
   ○ **C.** People in Egypt preserved dead bodies.
   ○ **D.** Egyptian mummies were discovered.

3. This story would probably go on to talk about
   ○ **A.** what scientists learned about the mummies they scanned.
   ○ **B.** how the CAT scanner was invented.
   ○ **C.** machines in ancient Egypt.
   ○ **D.** different kinds of cloth.

4. Which of these is a fact?
   ○ **A.** Mummies are disgusting.
   ○ **B.** CAT scanners are a great invention.
   ○ **C.** Mummies are boring.
   ○ **D.** Mummies can teach scientists about how people lived.

E. Once there was a very fast rabbit. He bragged loudly to all the town about his speed.

Frog was annoyed by Rabbit's bragging. He challenged Rabbit to a race through some swamp grass down to the town pond. Rabbit agreed.

On the day of the race, Frog played a trick. Several of his frog friends were *concealed* in the swamp grass, one big leap apart from one another.

Rabbit ran as fast as he could through the grass, but no matter how fast he ran, Frog was always one jump ahead of him. By the time Rabbit got to the pond, he was running too fast to stop. He fell right into the pond, just as Frog leaped up from behind a rock and shouted, "I am the fastest!"

And that was that.

1. Frog's friends hid
   ○ **A.** in grass.   ○ **C.** on a rock.
   ○ **B.** under a log.   ○ **D.** in a pond.

2. In this story, the word **concealed** probably means
   ○ **A.** sleeping. ○ **C.** hidden.
   ○ **B.** swamp.   ○ **D.** all.

3. You would probably find this story in
   ○ **A.** a book about frogs.
   ○ **B.** a book of folktales.
   ○ **C.** a book about running.
   ○ **D.** a book about swamp life.

4. This story was probably created to tell
   ○ **A.** where frogs live.
   ○ **B.** why bragging is a bad idea.
   ○ **C.** a few facts about rabbits.
   ○ **D.** all about ponds.

Scholastic Professional Books

Vocabulary

Synonyms

Read the underlined word in each phrase. Mark the word below it that has the same (or close to the same) meaning.

Sample:

damage the building
- ○ **A.** hurt
- ○ **B.** give
- ○ **C.** paint
- ○ **D.** roof

1. enormous balloon
   - ○ **A.** shiny
   - ○ **B.** red
   - ○ **C.** huge
   - ○ **D.** instant

2. wild blizzard
   - ○ **A.** storm
   - ○ **B.** sunset
   - ○ **C.** monster
   - ○ **D.** candy

3. angry child
   - ○ **A.** smile
   - ○ **B.** happy
   - ○ **C.** kid
   - ○ **D.** mad

4. sly thief
   - ○ **A.** angry
   - ○ **B.** sneaky
   - ○ **C.** quick
   - ○ **D.** robber

5. appear instantly
   - ○ **A.** disappear
   - ○ **B.** work
   - ○ **C.** climb
   - ○ **D.** show up

6. awoke late
   - ○ **A.** away
   - ○ **B.** woke up
   - ○ **C.** ran
   - ○ **D.** let out

7. choose wisely
   - ○ **A.** never
   - ○ **B.** eat
   - ○ **C.** think
   - ○ **D.** pick

8. the entire time
   - ○ **A.** dinner
   - ○ **B.** lost
   - ○ **C.** whole
   - ○ **D.** wasted

Antonyms

Read the underlined word in each phrase. Mark the word below it that means the opposite or nearly the opposite.

Sample:

silent evening
- ○ **A.** noisy
- ○ **B.** quiet
- ○ **C.** patient
- ○ **D.** perfect

1. rare coin
   - ○ **A.** unusual
   - ○ **B.** money
   - ○ **C.** common
   - ○ **D.** copper

2. lead the troops
   - ○ **A.** hire
   - ○ **B.** metal
   - ○ **C.** mail
   - ○ **D.** follow

3. expensive jewels
   - ○ **A.** cheap
   - ○ **B.** sparkly
   - ○ **C.** diamond
   - ○ **D.** precious

4. narrow path
   - ○ **A.** rocky
   - ○ **B.** trail
   - ○ **C.** dirt
   - ○ **D.** wide

5. foolish person
   - ○ **A.** funny
   - ○ **B.** smart
   - ○ **C.** wealthy
   - ○ **D.** human

6. darkened room
   - ○ **A.** living
   - ○ **B.** lighted
   - ○ **C.** painted
   - ○ **D.** small

7. danger signs
   - ○ **A.** stop
   - ○ **B.** funny
   - ○ **C.** safety
   - ○ **D.** animal

8. beneath the ground
   - ○ **A.** above
   - ○ **B.** near
   - ○ **C.** beside
   - ○ **D.** walk

Reading Skills Practice Test 4

READING COMPREHENSION

Read each story. Then fill in the circle that best completes each sentence or answers each question.

SAMPLE

Your nose and mouth are an open door to germs. But your tonsils stop germs before they get too far. Tonsils are like little sponges inside your throat. They soak up and *destroy* germs.

1. What is the best title for this story?
   - ○ **A.** "How to Be Healthy"
   - ○ **B.** "Keep Your Nose Clean"
   - ○ **C.** "How Your Tonsils Help You"
   - ○ **D.** "Germs Are Bad for You"

2. In this story, the word **destroy** means
   - ○ **A.** hide.
   - ○ **B.** kill.
   - ○ **C.** see.
   - ○ **D.** run.

A. Manatees are large water mammals. They have lived in the ocean near Florida for millions of years. But today, manatees are in danger of dying out. Many manatees get hit by motorboats. Some get tangled in fishing nets. Other manatees get sick in the winter when the water turns cold. Some scientists in Florida want to save the manatees. They have set up a special center where they take care of sick and *injured* manatees. They also rescue baby manatees whose mothers have died.

1. What is the main idea of this story?
   - ○ **A.** Manatees are in danger of dying out.
   - ○ **B.** Some baby manatees need mothers.
   - ○ **C.** Winter makes the ocean turn cold.
   - ○ **D.** Manatees are friendly.

2. Manatees are sometimes hit by
   - ○ **A.** scientists.
   - ○ **B.** fishing poles.
   - ○ **C.** ocean waves.
   - ○ **D.** motorboats.

3. In this story, the word **injured** means
   - ○ **A.** wet.
   - ○ **B.** hurt.
   - ○ **C.** playful.
   - ○ **D.** healthy.

Scholastic Professional Books

B. Who Has Seen the Wind?

Who has seen the wind?
　　Neither I nor you:
But when the leaves hang *trembling*
　　The wind is passing through.

Who has seen the wind?
　　Neither you nor I:
But when the trees bow down their heads,
　　The wind is passing by.

By Christina Rossetti

1. In this poem, the word **trembling** means
   ○ **A.** shaking.　　○ **C.** falling.
   ○ **B.** green.　　　 ○ **D.** still.

2. The leaves tremble because
   ○ **A.** they are afraid.
   ○ **B.** the wind is blowing on them.
   ○ **C.** they are cold.
   ○ **D.** they are about to dry up and fall off the tree.

3. In the poem, the trees bow down their
   ○ **A.** leaves.　　○ **C.** trunks.
   ○ **B.** tops.　　　 ○ **D.** roots.

4. You would probably find this poem in
   ○ **A.** a book about weather.
   ○ **B.** a book of poetry.
   ○ **C.** a science book.
   ○ **D.** a book about trees.

C. Chief Crazy Horse was a Native American hero. In the 1870s, he protected his people from settlers who tried to take their land. Many years after Crazy Horse died, some Native Americans decided to honor him. They hired an artist to carve a giant sculpture of Chief Crazy Horse.

In 1948, the artist started carving the sculpture. He carved into a mountain in South Dakota, using a drill and dynamite. The artist died in 1982. His sculpture of Crazy Horse was not finished. But his family and other workers are finishing the sculpture.

When it is done, it will probably be the largest sculpture in the world.

1. What is the best title for this story?
   ○ **A.** "Mountains of South Dakota"
   ○ **B.** "Native American Chiefs"
   ○ **C.** "A Clay Sculpture"
   ○ **D.** "Sculpture of a Hero"

2. Who began carving the sculpture?
   ○ **A.** Chief Crazy Horse
   ○ **B.** an artist
   ○ **C.** the chief's grandchild
   ○ **D.** a mountain climber

3. Which happened last?
   ○ **A.** Crazy Horse died.
   ○ **B.** An artist began carving a sculpture of Crazy Horse.
   ○ **C.** Some Native Americans decided to honor Crazy Horse.
   ○ **D.** The artist died.

4. Which of these is an *opinion* about Chief Crazy Horse?
   ○ **A.** He protected his people from settlers.
   ○ **B.** He was Native American.
   ○ **C.** He was the bravest chief of all.
   ○ **D.** He was alive during the 1870s.

D. One fine summer day, some ants were hauling grain into their anthill. They were working hard to store enough grain for winter. A *merry* grasshopper came along, hopping and jumping around. He laughed at the ants. "Why are you working on such a nice day?" he asked. "You should be playing like me."

Soon, winter came. The ants had plenty to eat. One day, the grasshopper came along, looking very sad. He asked the ants to give him some grain. But the ants just laughed. "Why should we?" they said. "You played all summer while we worked hard. Now you'll go hungry while we eat."

1. In this story, the word **merry** means
    ○ **A.** sad.
    ○ **B.** ugly.
    ○ **C.** happy.
    ○ **D.** funny.

2. What is the main idea of this story?
    ○ **A.** All ants are hard workers.
    ○ **B.** Working hard and planning ahead are important.
    ○ **C.** Ants and grasshoppers don't get along very well.
    ○ **D.** It's important to have fun in the summertime.

3. You can guess from this story that
    ○ **A.** the grasshopper was lazy.
    ○ **B.** the ants didn't like to have fun.
    ○ **C.** real ants eat nothing but grain.
    ○ **D.** grasshoppers live in meadows.

4. What happened first?
    ○ **A.** Winter came.
    ○ **B.** The ants stored grain.
    ○ **C.** The ants laughed at the grasshopper.
    ○ **D.** The grasshopper asked the ants for some grain.

E. Most people agree that trees look nice. But trees can also help cities save money. A few years ago, the U.S. Forest Service studied trees in Chicago, Illinois. They learned that just one tree can save a city $402 over the tree's lifetime.

One way trees save money is by helping us save energy. Trees shade buildings from the summer sun. They also block the winter wind. That cuts down on the energy needed to heat and cool homes and offices. Saving energy means lower bills.

Here is another way trees can help a city save money. When it rains, a city's sewers fill up with water. Cities spend lots of money to clean that water. But trees' leaves and roots soak up rainwater before it gets to the dirty sewers. With the help of trees, there is less water to clean.

1. What is the main idea of this story?
    ○ **A.** Trees are pretty.
    ○ **B.** Trees block winter wind.
    ○ **C.** Air pollution costs money.
    ○ **D.** Trees help save money.

2. This story would probably go on to talk about
    ○ **A.** how to plant flowers.
    ○ **B.** how to get cities to plant more trees.
    ○ **C.** the best way to chop down a tree.
    ○ **D.** forest fires.

3. Which is a *fact* about trees?
    ○ **A.** Trees look nice.
    ○ **B.** The tallest trees are found in cities.
    ○ **C.** Trees can shade sun and block wind.
    ○ **D.** People should plant more trees.

Vocabulary

Synonyms

Read the underlined word in each phrase. Mark the word below it that has the same (or close to the same) meaning.

Sample:

sip lemonade
- ○ **A.** pour
- ○ **B.** drink
- ○ **C.** make
- ○ **D.** sweet

1. speed away
- ○ **A.** race
- ○ **B.** walk
- ○ **C.** far
- ○ **D.** fast

2. gentle touch
- ○ **A.** sharp
- ○ **B.** cold
- ○ **C.** soft
- ○ **D.** finger

3. grumpy neighbor
- ○ **A.** friendly
- ○ **B.** tall
- ○ **C.** grouchy
- ○ **D.** woman

4. steam carrots
- ○ **A.** chop
- ○ **B.** rabbit
- ○ **C.** eat
- ○ **D.** cook

5. loud groan
- ○ **A.** sound
- ○ **B.** laugh
- ○ **C.** moan
- ○ **D.** odor

6. enormous building
- ○ **A.** big
- ○ **B.** tired
- ○ **C.** urban
- ○ **D.** dark

7. moist washcloth
- ○ **A.** purple
- ○ **B.** shower
- ○ **C.** damp
- ○ **D.** dirty

Antonyms

Read the underlined word in each phrase. Mark the word below it that means the opposite or nearly the opposite.

Sample:

huge truck
- ○ **A.** large
- ○ **B.** red
- ○ **C.** fast
- ○ **D.** tiny

1. begin reading
- ○ **A.** finish
- ○ **B.** read
- ○ **C.** hard
- ○ **D.** start

2. pleasant weather
- ○ **A.** nice
- ○ **B.** sunny
- ○ **C.** outdoors
- ○ **D.** stormy

3. feel grief
- ○ **A.** sadness
- ○ **B.** comfortable
- ○ **C.** happiness
- ○ **D.** winter

4. shallow water
- ○ **A.** fresh
- ○ **B.** deep
- ○ **C.** pool
- ○ **D.** cold

5. hind leg
- ○ **A.** back
- ○ **B.** furry
- ○ **C.** front
- ○ **D.** arm

6. visible stain
- ○ **A.** messy
- ○ **B.** invisible
- ○ **C.** cold
- ○ **D.** new

7. sink in the water
- ○ **A.** trip
- ○ **B.** run
- ○ **C.** bathe
- ○ **D.** float

Scholastic Professional Books

Reading Skills Practice Test 5

READING COMPREHENSION

Read each story. Then fill in the circle that best completes each sentence or answers each question.

SAMPLE

Weather experts use information from space to predict the weather on Earth. How? Satellites in space take pictures of Earth's atmosphere. The pictures show experts where storms are *brewing*.

1. The story is mainly about
   - ○ **A.** serious hurricanes.
   - ○ **B.** weather satellites.
   - ○ **C.** our solar system.
   - ○ **D.** rockets.

2. In the story, the word **brewing** means
   - ○ **A.** finishing.
   - ○ **B.** learning.
   - ○ **C.** forming.
   - ○ **D.** dripping.

A. Do you know how the states got their names? Many names come from Native American words. The word Utah comes from "Ute," the name of a Native American *tribe*. The name Wyoming comes from a Native American word meaning "large prairie."

Other states have names that tell how the states got started. For example, Georgia was named after King George II of England. He started the colony that became Georgia.

1. The best title for this story is
   - ○ **A.** "King George II."
   - ○ **B.** "Native American Tribes."
   - ○ **C.** "Wyoming's Prairie Land."
   - ○ **D.** "How States Got Their Names."

2. In the story, the word **tribe** means
   - ○ **A.** state.
   - ○ **B.** name.
   - ○ **C.** group.
   - ○ **D.** person.

3. You can guess from the story that
   - ○ **A.** the Ute people lived in the area we now call Utah.
   - ○ **B.** there are 48 states.
   - ○ **C.** the name Georgia comes from a Native American word for "king."
   - ○ **D.** the word Florida is French.

4. The story would probably go on to talk about
   - ○ **A.** rivers in the United States.
   - ○ **B.** other ways states were named.
   - ○ **C.** the kings and queens of England.
   - ○ **D.** languages of the world.

B.   Do your feet stink after you exercise? The bad smell comes from microbes, or living things that grow on your skin. Microbes are very small. You can only see them with a microscope. But they have big names. One is called *corybacteria.*

Microbes are all over your body. But they grow best on skin that is sweaty and warm. That's why feet smell after you exercise.

1. This story is mainly about
   ○ **A.** why you exercise.
   ○ **B.** why feet smell.
   ○ **C** . how to use a microscope.
   ○ **D.** how microbes are named.

2. **Corybacteria** is a kind of
   ○ **A.** sneaker.   ○ **C** kid.
   ○ **B.** exercise.   ○ **D.** microbe.

3. Your feet smell because
   ○ **A.** microbes grow on them.
   ○ **B.** you use old soap.
   ○ **C.** they are too big.
   ○ **D.** they are funny looking.

4. You can guess from the story that
   ○ **A.** exercise is bad for your health.
   ○ **B.** there are microbes on your face and hands.
   ○ **C** you should wash your feet three times a day.
   ○ **D.** microbes are green and slimy.

C.   Once, only kids at private schools wore uniforms. Now, many public schools ask students to wear uniforms. It has caused a big debate.

Many students like wearing uniforms. They say it is easy to get dressed in the morning. And families have to buy only one or two uniforms, instead of a closet full of clothes.

Not everyone likes school uniforms, though. Some people say it's not fair to make kids wear the same thing.

1. The main idea of the story is that school uniforms
   ○ **A.** are more expensive than regular clothes.
   ○ **B.** are less expensive than regular clothes.
   ○ **C** have caused a big debate.
   ○ **D.** look nice.

2. Today, uniforms are worn
   ○ **A.** only at private schools.
   ○ **B.** only at public schools.
   ○ **C.** at many private and public schools.
   ○ **D.** only in other countries.

3. The author probably wrote this story to
   ○ **A.** persuade students to wear uniforms.
   ○ **B.** give both sides of the uniform debate.
   ○ **C.** stop children from wearing uniforms.
   ○ **D.** help schools create new uniforms.

Scholastic Professional Books

D.   The story of Paul Bunyan is a famous American legend. It was first told in the early 1900s.

According to the legend, Paul Bunyan was a giant. Paul's parents knew he was going to be big right from the start. When he was only one week old, he wore his father's clothes! He would eat 40 bowls of porridge at one meal.

For his first birthday, Paul got a *huge* blue ox named Babe. Babe and Paul played in the woods. They were so heavy that their footprints formed lakes.

When Paul grew up, he became a lumberjack. He could cut down a whole forest by himself. Once, he formed the Grand Canyon by dragging his tools behind him!

1. In the story, the word **huge** means
   ○ **A.** large.   ○ **C.** blue.
   ○ **B.** hungry.   ○ **D.** smart.

2. Which of these happened first?
   ○ **A.** Paul became a lumberjack.
   ○ **B.** Paul wore his father's clothes.
   ○ **C.** Paul formed the Grand Canyon.
   ○ **D.** Paul got a blue ox.

3. You can guess that
   ○ **A.** Paul Bunyan lived in Florida.
   ○ **B.** Paul Bunyan lived in 1850.
   ○ **C.** the legend is not really true.
   ○ **D.** footprints can form lakes.

4. Which of these is a fact?
   ○ **A.** Paul Bunyan was cool.
   ○ **B.** Legends are very interesting.
   ○ **C.** It would be fun to have an ox.
   ○ **D.** A legend is a story.

E. Riding a bike can be fun, but it's important to stay safe. Here are some tips for safe cycling:
- Always wear a bicycle helmet that fits your head. If you fall, it can protect your head from serious injuries.
- Never ride a bike after dark.
- If you are under age 10, do not ride in the street without an adult. When you do ride in the street, use hand signals to show where you are going. Obey stop signs and other traffic rules.
- Wear bright clothing when you ride so that drivers, walkers, and other bicyclists can spot you.
- Do not ride a bike that is too large for you, or one that is not in good working order.

1. The story is mainly about
   ○ **A.** traffic rules.   ○ **C.** bike safety.
   ○ **B.** tricycles.   ○ **D.** sports.

2. Bike riders should wear clothes that are
   ○ **A.** bright.   ○ **C.** loose.
   ○ **B.** tight.   ○ **D.** dark.

3.   In the story, the word spot means
   ○ **A.** see.   ○ **C.** dog.
   ○ **B.** mark.   ○ **D.** help.

4. You would probably find this story in a book about
   ○ **A.** driving.
   ○ **B.** safety.
   ○ **C.** a dictionary.
   ○ **D.** folk tales.

Vocabulary

Synonyms

Read the underlined word in each phrase. Mark the word below it that has the same (or close to the same) meaning.

Sample:

<u>speak</u> loudly
- ○ **A.** look
- ○ **B.** fly
- ○ **C.** talk
- ○ **D.** cry

1. <u>shut</u> the door
   - ○ **A.** ring
   - ○ **B.** knock
   - ○ **C** open
   - ○ **D.** close

2. <u>giant</u> creature
   - ○ **A.** tiny
   - ○ **B.** scary
   - ○ **C** large
   - ○ **D.** animal

3. <u>reply</u> soon
   - ○ **A.** return
   - ○ **B.** swim
   - ○ **C** answer
   - ○ **D.** mind

4. <u>shall</u> go
   - ○ **A.** will
   - ○ **B.** never
   - ○ **C** please
   - ○ **D.** back

5. <u>intelligent</u> student
   - ○ **A.** new
   - ○ **B.** smart
   - ○ **C** alone
   - ○ **D.** old

6. <u>wander</u> around
   - ○ **A.** fold
   - ○ **B.** roam
   - ○ **C** soak
   - ○ **D.** let

7. <u>shred</u> paper
   - ○ **A.** raise
   - ○ **B.** news
   - ○ **C** rip
   - ○ **D.** draw

8. <u>chuckle</u> quietly
   - ○ **A.** laugh
   - ○ **B.** drink
   - ○.**C.** whistle
   - ○ **D.** wash

Antonyms

Read the underlined word in each phrase. Mark the word below it that means the opposite or nearly the opposite.

Sample:

<u>lay</u> asleep
- ○ **A.** fast
- ○ **B.** worried
- ○ **C** still
- ○ **D.** awake

1. <u>straight</u> line
   - ○ **A.** nice
   - ○ **B.** crooked
   - ○ **C** dark
   - ○ **D.** lost

2. <u>wrong</u> answer
   - ○ **A.** check
   - ○ **B.** mark
   - ○ **C** right
   - ○ **D.** last

3. <u>sweet</u> taste
   - ○ **A.** sugary
   - ○ **B.** sour
   - ○ **C** chocolate
   - ○ **D.** cold

4. <u>terrible</u> day
   - ○ **A.** great
   - ○ **B.** bad
   - ○ **C** long
   - ○ **D.** early

5. <u>frown</u> on her face
   - ○ **A.** spill
   - ○ **B.** mad
   - ○ **C** smile
   - ○ **D.** nose

6. <u>tight</u> coat
   - ○ **A.** loose
   - ○ **B.** blue
   - ○ **C** warm
   - ○ **D.** small

7. <u>worst</u> thing
   - ○ **A.** stop
   - ○ **B.** best
   - ○ **C** kind
   - ○ **D.** past

8. <u>true</u> story
   - ○ **A.** false
   - ○ **B.** long
   - ○ **C** mine
   - ○ **D.** near

Scholastic Professional Books

Reading Skills Practice Test 6

READING COMPREHENSION

Read each story. Then fill in the circle that best completes each sentence or answers each question.

SAMPLE

You can guess the meaning of some words by the way the words sound. For example, the word "squeak" sounds like a squeak. The word "cackle" sounds like a person cackling. These words are called "sound words." It is fun to use sound words when you write.

1. The best title for this story is
   - ○ **A.** "Be a Good Writer."
   - ○ **B.** "Using a Dictionary."
   - ○ **C.** "Sound Words."
   - ○ **D.** "Rhyming Words."

2. You can guess from the story that _____ is a sound word.
   - ○ **A.** "hiss"
   - ○ **B.** "plant"
   - ○ **C** "spoon"
   - ○ **D.** "sister"

A. Everyone knows about the telephone, the car, and the electric light. People use these inventions every day. But there are other inventions that few people have heard of. For example, one inventor *created* a twirling fork to make it easier to eat spaghetti. Another invented diapers for pet birds. And someone else invented a sleeping bag with leg holes. Why? The holes let a camper run away when a bear comes along!

1. A good title for this story is
   - ○ **A.** "More Spaghetti!"
   - ○ **B.** "Unusual Inventions."
   - ○ **C.** "Famous Inventions."
   - ○ **D.** "Pet Supplies."

2. In the story, the word **created** means
   - ○ **A.** ate.
   - ○ **B.** ran away.
   - ○ **C** twirled.
   - ○ **D.** made.

3. You can guess from the story that
   - ○ **A.** more people own cars than twirling forks.
   - ○ **B.** most people have twirling forks.
   - ○ **C.** all campers hate bears.
   - ○ **D.** the person who invented bird diapers is famous.

4. Which of these is an *opinion*?
   - ○ **A.** People use telephones and cars.
   - ○ **B.** Someone invented a twirling fork.
   - ○ **C.** It's silly to make diapers for pets.
   - ○ **D.** Some sleeping bags have leg holes.

Name _____

B. Imagine giving stitches to sheep or taking a tiger's temperature. That's what a veterinarian, or animal doctor, does.

There are 60,000 veterinarians in the United States. Some take care of pets like dogs, cats, and hamsters. Others care for farm animals like horses and cows. Still other vets work at zoos. They get to work with elephants, zebras, gorillas, and other unusual creatures.

Being a vet is not easy. Veterinarians go to college for at least eight years to learn about animals. They often work more than 50 hours a week. But many animal doctors say that their *career* is exciting and fun.

1. How many veterinarians are in the U.S.?
   ○ **A.** 12,000
   ○ **B.** 40,000
   ○ **C.** 60,000
   ○ **D.** 90,000

2. In the story, the word **career** means
   ○ **A.** job.
   ○ **B.** cat.
   ○ **C.** patient.
   ○ **D.** stitches.

3. Being a vet is hard because a vet often
   ○ **A.** does not go to college.
   ○ **B.** works many hours a week.
   ○ **C.** does not earn any money.
   ○ **D.** hates dogs and cats.

C. In February of 1962, John Glenn made space history. This American astronaut climbed aboard a tiny space capsule called the *Friendship 7*. He traveled 160 miles above Earth. Glenn orbited the planet three times, then safely returned to Earth. He had become the first American astronaut to circle the Earth.

In October of 1998, John Glenn made history again. At the age of 77, Glenn became the oldest person ever to fly in space. Glenn blasted into space on board the space shuttle *Discovery*. Glenn's adventure showed space scientists how space travel affects older people.

1. This story is mostly about
   ○ **A.** space missions of the 1960s.
   ○ **B.** astronauts of today.
   ○ **C.** John Glenn's space flights.
   ○ **D.** different kinds of spacecraft.

2. When did Glenn travel on the *Friendship 7*?
   ○ **A.** October of 1962
   ○ **B.** October of 1998
   ○ **C.** February of 1962
   ○ **D.** February of 1998

3. Which happened last?
   ○ **A.** Glenn traveled on the *Discovery*.
   ○ **B.** Glenn climbed on board the *Friendship 7*.
   ○ **C.** Glenn became the first American to orbit the Earth.
   ○ **D.** Glenn flew in space for the first time.

Scholastic Professional Books

D. Crayons have been around for more than a hundred years. But they have changed a lot.

The first crayons were all black. Workers in shipyards used them to label crates. Then, in the early 1900s, the Crayola company decided to make colorful crayons for kids. The first box had eight colors: black, brown, red, blue, purple, orange, yellow, and green. The box cost just five cents.

Today, there are hundreds of crayon colors, from "tickle me pink" to "tropical rain forest." Scientists keep blending different colors to come up with new shades. Then the scientists show the new color to kids to see if they will use it. Crayon companies have also asked children to help name new crayon colors.

1. This story is mostly about
   ○ **A.** rain forests.
   ○ **B.** scientists.
   ○ **C.** rainbows.
   ○ **D.** crayons.

2. You can guess from the story that
   ○ **A.** a box of crayons costs more than five cents today.
   ○ **B.** crayon companies no longer make plain red crayons.
   ○ **C.** no one uses crayons anymore.
   ○ **D.** "tropical rain forest" is a shade of blue.

3. This story would probably go on to talk about
   ○ **A.** shipyard workers.
   ○ **B.** kids' favorite crayon colors.
   ○ **C.** the history of paper.
   ○ **D.** the first crayons.

E. Respect Them, Protect Them

Splish, splash! Splish, splash!
Fish frolic in the seas.
Swish, swoosh! Swish, swoosh!
Birds fly in the breeze.

Scritch, scratch! Scritch, scratch!
Crabs dig in the sand.
Romp, stomp! Romp, stomp!
Animals roam the land.

Seas, breeze, sand, land.
There are creatures everywhere.
Respect them, protect them
On this planet that we share.

By Karen Kellaher

1. In the poem, the word protect means
   ○ **A.** keep safe.
   ○ **B.** see.
   ○ **C.** know.
   ○ **D.** dig.

2. You'd probably find this poem in a
   ○ **A.** book of autumn poems.
   ○ **B.** book of animal poems.
   ○ **C.** book of New Year's poems.
   ○ **D.** book of Halloween poems.

3. The poet probably wrote the poem
   ○ **A.** to convince kids to study hard in school.
   ○ **B.** to teach people about crabs.
   ○ **C.** to celebrate winter.
   ○ **D.** to convince people to help animals.

Scholastic Professional Books

Vocabulary

Which Word Is Missing?

In each of the following paragraphs, a word is missing. First, read the paragraph. Then find the missing word in the list of words beneath the paragraph. Fill in the circle next to the word that is missing.

Sample:

I have a lot of homework, so I should get started on it _____.

- ○ **A.** someday
- ○ **B.** maybe
- ○ **C.** soon
- ○ **D.** later

There was a pie-eating contest at the fair. Jonathan entered the contest and ate four pies. He won first _____.

- ○ **A.** prize
- ○ **B.** day
- ○ **C.** pie
- ○ **D .** stop

1. Icy Antarctica is not an easy place to live. In summer, this continent has an average temperature of zero degrees. In winter, the temperature can drop to 100 degrees below zero! Brrrr! Few creatures can live in such _____ conditions.
   - ○ **A.** cold
   - ○ **B.** warm
   - ○ **C.** strange
   - ○ **D.** ugly

2. However, penguins do not seem to mind the cold. These birds live along Antarctica's coast. They spend some of their time on land. But they spend most of their time in the chilly _____ around Antarctica.
   - ○ **A.** birds
   - ○ **B.** feathers
   - ○ **C.** lands
   - ○ **D** waters

3. How do penguins stay warm? They have a thick layer of fat called blubber. And they have oily black and white _____ to keep the icy water away from their skin.
   - ○ **A.** windows
   - ○ **B.** head
   - ○ **C.** feathers
   - ○ **D.** eyes

4. Penguins cannot _____ like most birds. Instead, they waddle around on two feet. Sometimes they slide on the ice on their stomachs.
   - ○ **A.** read
   - ○ **B.** fly
   - ○ **C.** eat
   - ○ **D.** see

5. In the ocean, penguins can dive _____ under the water. They swim by opening and closing their wings and paddling their feet.
   - ○ **A** never
   - ○ **B.** late
   - ○ **C.** deep
   - ○ **D.** walk

6. Penguins live in groups. Mothers lay their eggs in a spot called a rookery. There can be thousands of penguins in one rookery. Even in the ocean, penguins stick _____.
   - ○ **A** home
   - ○ **B.** together
   - ○ **C.** alone
   - ○ **D.** cousin

7. Penguins don't eat a lot. They usually munch on fish and tiny creatures called krill. When they are very _____, they might eat a squid.
   - ○ **A.** hungry
   - ○ **B.** tired
   - ○ **C.** cold
   - ○ **D.** gone

Scholastic Professional Books

Reading Skills Practice Test 7

READING COMPREHENSION

Read each story. Then fill in the circle that best completes each sentence or answers each question.

SAMPLE

A dolphin is a sea animal. However, it is not a fish and cannot breathe in water. It is a type of whale. It must come up to the surface to breathe air. Dolphins travel through the sea in large groups.

1. What is the best title for this story?
   ○ **A.** "Breathing"
   ○ **B.** "Fish"
   ○ **C.** "Dolphins"
   ○ **D.** "Animals"

2. In this story, the word surface means
   ○ **A.** the top of the water.
   ○ **B.** the bottom of the sea.
   ○ **C.** an ocean rock.
   ○ **D.** a sea plant.

A. Sojourner Truth was born into slavery in New York in 1797. When she was 9 years old, Sojourner's owner separated her from her mother and sold her to another slave owner. Sojourner remained a slave until she was 30. After she was set free, she spent the rest of her life traveling and speaking out against slavery. She even met with President Abraham Lincoln.

1. This story is mainly about
   ○ **A.** Abraham Lincoln.
   ○ **B.** slavery.
   ○ **C.** New York.
   ○ **D.** Sojourner Truth.

2. You would probably find this story in a book about
   ○ **A.** New York City.
   ○ **B.** famous women.
   ○ **C.** Presidents.
   ○ **D.** speeches.

3. Which happened first?
   ○ **A.** Sojourner met Lincoln.
   ○ **B.** Sojourner was set free.
   ○ **C.** Sojourner was taken from her mother.
   ○ **D.** Sojourner spoke out against slavery.

B. Many people think spiders are creepy. But some scientists say we can learn a lot from these eight-legged creatures. Scientists are studying the sticky strands of silk that spiders use to weave their webs. The silk is very strong. Scientists are trying to make thread in their labs that is just like spider silk, only thicker. They hope this thick "spider silk" can be turned into strong cables that can be used to hold up bridges.

1. Scientists hope to use thread that is like spider silk to make
   ○ **A.** webs.   ○ **C.** cables.
   ○ **B.** steel.   ○ **D.** rugs.

2. The author wrote this story to
   ○ **A.** tell a scary story.
   ○ **B.** show the value of spider silk.
   ○ **C.** explain why bridges are strong.
   ○ **D.** tell how cloth is made.

C. Venus is sometimes called Earth's "sister" or "twin." That's because it is the planet *nearest* to Earth. It's also about the same size as Earth.

   But Venus is different from Earth in many ways. Venus is much hotter than Earth. It is about 850 degrees on Venus's surface! The air, or atmosphere, around Venus is thick and heavy. It's so thick you can't even see through it. This air traps the sun's heat.

1. What is the best title for this story?
   ○ **A.** "Nine Planets"
   ○ **B.** "Hot Air"
   ○ **C.** "Sisters"
   ○ **D.** "Earth's Hot Twin"

2. One reason Venus is called Earth's twin is because
   ○ **A.** they are both planets.
   ○ **B.** they are both very hot.
   ○ **C.** they are about the same size.
   ○ **D.** they have the same air.

3. In this story, the word **nearest** means
   ○ **A.** hottest.
   ○ **B.** closest.
   ○ **C.** driest.
   ○ **D.** roundest.

D. The way dogs act around human families has a lot to do with how their wild ancestors lived. Wolves and other wild dogs live in groups or packs with one leader. Today, a pet dog still acts as if it lives in a pack. It *behaves* as if its owner is its pack leader. That makes it easy for people to train dogs.

1. In this story, the word **behaves** means
   ○ **A.** eats.
   ○ **B.** plays.
   ○ **C.** acts.
   ○ **D.** leads.

2. You can guess from this story that
   ○ **A.** dogs are difficult to train.
   ○ **B.** dogs are related to wolves.
   ○ **C.** all dogs want to be a pack leader.
   ○ **D.** dogs like to live alone.

Scholastic Professional Books

E. Each year in Japan, children celebrate Undokai, or Sports Day. On this special day, schools compete against each other in relay races and other track events. One favorite race is the daruma. In this event, runners race in pairs. One runner in the pair wears something over his or her head, making it impossible to see. This runner is *guided* by his or her partner, who carries a small ball on a scoop. If the ball drops, the pair of runners must start the race over!

1. What is the best title for this story?
   - ○ **A.** "Races Through History"
   - ○ **B.** "Sports Day in Japan"
   - ○ **C.** "Japan Today"
   - ○ **D.** "Teams"

2. Who competes on Sports Day?
   - ○ **A.** children
   - ○ **B.** parents
   - ○ **C.** professional athletes
   - ○ **D.** teachers

3. In this story, the word **guided** means
   - ○ **A.** won.
   - ○ **B.** led.
   - ○ **C.** followed.
   - ○ **D.** driven.

F. A bike helmet is made of hard foam. The foam absorbs the force of a fall so that the hard ground does not hurt your head. But your helmet won't protect your head if it doesn't fit right. Here are some tips for *selecting* the best helmet.

- Try on helmets at a bike store. Pick one that isn't too tight. But make sure it isn't so big that it rocks back and forth.
- Most helmets come with soft pads. Stick the pads on the inside of the helmet to make it fit just right.
- Keep the front of your helmet just above your eyebrows when you ride.
- Make sure the chin strap fits snugly under your chin. The strap holds the helmet on if you are in an accident.

1. In this story, the word **selecting** means
   - ○ **A.** wearing.
   - ○ **B.** riding.
   - ○ **C.** choosing.
   - ○ **D.** cleaning.

2. You can guess from the story that
   - ○ **A.** loose helmets might slip off.
   - ○ **B.** chin straps often break.
   - ○ **C.** it hurts to wear a helmet.
   - ○ **D.** bike riding is always safe.

3. Bike helmets are needed because
   - ○ **A.** all bike riders go too fast.
   - ○ **B.** kids are careless.
   - ○ **C.** they protect your head.
   - ○ **D.** they keep your head warm.

4. Which of these is an opinion about helmets?
   - ○ **A.** They are made of hard foam.
   - ○ **B.** They must fit correctly.
   - ○ **C.** They have chin straps.
   - ○ **D.** They are attractive.

Vocabulary

Synonyms

Read the underlined word in each phrase. Mark the word below it that has the same (or close to the same) meaning.

Sample:

mend the sweater
- ○ **A.** rip
- ○ **B.** raise
- ○ **C.** wear
- ○ **D.** fix

1. discover treasure
   - ○ **A.** bury
   - ○ **B.** find
   - ○ **C.** golden
   - ○ **D.** pirate

2. false alarm
   - ○ **A.** loud
   - ○ **B.** long
   - ○ **C.** mistaken
   - ○ **D.** true

3. receive a gift
   - ○ **A.** get
   - ○ **B.** give
   - ○ **C.** lose
   - ○ **D.** wrap

4. old custom
   - ○ **A.** trunk
   - ○ **B.** clothes
   - ○ **C.** money
   - ○ **D.** tradition

5. long silence
   - ○ **A.** quiet
   - ○ **B.** storm
   - ○ **C.** light
   - ○ **D.** package

6. complete the test
   - ○ **A.** finish
   - ○ **B.** fail
   - ○ **C.** lose
   - ○ **D.** write

7. scent of roses
   - ○ **A.** field
   - ○ **B.** store
   - ○ **C.** color
   - ○ **D.** smell

Multiple Meanings

Read each set of sentences. Mark the word that makes sense in both sentences.

Sample:

The doctor put the girl's broken leg in a _____.
The _____ of that TV show is very talented.
- ○ **A.** cast
- ○ **B.** sling
- ○ **C.** actor
- ○ **D.** station

1. Can you help me _____ a shirt?
   The machine is made of _____.
   - ○ **A.** steel
   - ○ **B.** wash
   - ○ **C.** iron
   - ○ **D.** find

2. I would love another _____ of stew.
   He is known for _____ others.
   - ○ **A.** share
   - ○ **B.** plate
   - ○ **C.** teaching
   - ○ **D.** helping

3. Mom wrote a _____ to pay for the groceries.
   The teacher wants us to _____ our homework.
   - ○ **A.** check
   - ○ **B.** do
   - ○ **C.** bill
   - ○ **D.** note

4. There is a _____ on your shirt.
   If you _____ a parking space, let me know.
   - ○ **A.** stain
   - ○ **B.** spot
   - ○ **C.** see
   - ○ **D.** button

Scholastic Professional Books.

Reading Skills Practice Test 8

READING COMPREHENSION

Read each story. Then fill in the circle that best completes each sentence or answers each question.

SAMPLE

Mars is called the "Red Planet." That's because the soil on Mars has a lot of rust. Rust is the same substance that forms on a bicycle left out in the rain. The rusty dirt makes Mars look red.

1. The best title for this story is
   ○ **A.** "Mars: The Orange Planet."
   ○ **B.** "Mars: The Red Planet."
   ○ **C.** "Take Care of Your Bike."
   ○ **D.** "Plants on Mars."

2. In the story, the word soil means
   ○ **A.** air.
   ○ **B.** bike.
   ○ **C.** dirt.
   ○ **D.** red.

A. Imagine a music group that has no guitars, pianos, or drums. Instead, its members make music with brooms, trash cans, and pot lids!

Believe it or not, this *odd* group really exists. It is called *Stomp*. *Stomp* started in England in 1991. Since then, it has performed all over the world. It is famous for its lively music and funny shows.

1. The best title for this story is
   ○ **A.** "Playing the Piano."
   ○ **B.** "The History of Music."
   ○ **C.** "*Stomp's* Unusual Music."
   ○ **D.** "English Musicians."

2. The members of *Stomp* play
   ○ **A.** guitars.   ○ **C.** flutes.
   ○ **B.** trash cans.   ○ **D.** pianos.

3. In the story, the word **odd** means
   ○ **A.** helpful.
   ○ **B.** lost.
   ○ **C.** old.
   ○ **D.** unusual.

4. You would probably find this story
   ○ **A.** in a magazine about music.
   ○ **B.** in a history book.
   ○ **C.** in a book about pianos.
   ○ **D.** in a geography book.

5. Which of these is an opinion?
   ○ **A.** *Stomp* started in England.
   ○ **B.** *Stomp's* music is too loud.
   ○ **C.** *Stomp* does not use drums.
   ○ **D.** *Stomp* began in 1991.

B. In the 1800s, American women were not allowed to vote. Many people fought to change that. They were called suffragists.

One famous suffragist was Elizabeth Cady Stanton. In 1848, she planned a meeting called the Seneca Falls Convention. More than 100 people met to talk about women's rights. Stanton *spoke* to them. She said that "men and women are created equal."

In 1878, lawmakers finally listened to Stanton and the other suffragists. They started talking about changing the law to give women the right to vote. The law finally changed 42 years later.

1. This story is mainly about
   ○ **A.** Susan B. Anthony.
   ○ **B.** Elizabeth Cady Stanton.
   ○ **C.** the history of the United States.
   ○ **D.** many famous women.

2. The Seneca Falls Convention was in
   ○ **A.** 1800.   ○ **C.** 1848.
   ○ **B.** 1828.   ○ **D.** 1878.

3. In the story, the word **spoke** means
   ○ **A.** talked.
   ○ **B.** found.
   ○ **C.** a part of a wheel.
   ○ **D.** helped.

4. You can guess from this story that
   ○ **A.** Stanton didn't think men should have the right to vote.
   ○ **B.** Stanton was very rich.
   ○ **C.** American women can vote today.
   ○ **D.** lawmakers did not like Stanton.

C.   Do you love to ride on a racing roller coaster? You are not alone. Roller coasters have been thrilling riders for hundreds of years!

Roller coasters got their start in Russia 600 years ago. Back then, there were no lightning-fast loops. Instead, riders just slid down icy mountains. By 1700, people were making rides that used tracks and wheels instead of ice.

The first American coaster was built in Coney Island, New York, in 1884. It was the Switchback Railway. It looked like a train going down a mountain. Soon, other parks made similar rides, and roller coasters really took off!

1. The first American roller coaster was called the
   ○ **A.** Loop-A-Rama.
   ○ **B.** Coney Island.
   ○ **C.** Superdrop.
   ○ **D.** Switchback Railway.

2. Which of these happened **first**?
   ○ **A.** An American coaster was built.
   ○ **B.** Russian people slid down icy mountains.
   ○ **C.** Coasters started using wheels.
   ○ **D.** The Switchback Railway opened.

3. The story would probably go on to talk about
   ○ **A.** today's roller coasters.
   ○ **B.** weather in Russia.
   ○ **C.** where Coney Island is located.
   ○ **D.** railroads of the world.

Scholastic Professional Books

D.   Most people have never heard of Patty Smith Hill. But almost everyone knows this songwriter's famous work!

Patty Smith Hill was a teacher who lived in Kentucky more than 100 years ago. In 1893, she was *searching* for songs for children to sing at school. She decided to write one of her own. She wrote words to a song and called it "Good Morning to All." Smith's sister, Mildred, wrote some music to go with the words.

Schoolchildren loved the sisters' song. In 1924, the Smiths added a new verse to the song. It was called, "Happy Birthday to You." Sound familiar? It's now one of the most famous songs in the world!

1. This story is mostly about
   ○ **A.** the history of a popular song.
   ○ **B.** children around the world.
   ○ **C.** living in Kentucky.
   ○ **D.** how people can work together.

2. Patty Smith Hill wrote the "Happy Birthday" song with her
   ○ **A.** father.   ○ **C.** brother.
   ○ **B.** mother.   ○ **D.** sister.

3. In the story, the word **searching** means
   ○ **A.** singing.   ○ **C.** driving.
   ○ **B.** looking.   ○ **D.** knowing.

4. The author probably wrote the story
   ○ **A.** to get readers to sing.
   ○ **B.** to celebrate his or her birthday.
   ○ **C.** to make Patty Smith Hill happy.
   ○ **D.** to give readers some history.

E.   For six states in the middle of our country, springtime brings more than birds and flowers. It also brings tornadoes.

Tornadoes, or twisters, can strike almost anywhere. But many tornadoes happen in Texas, Oklahoma, Kansas, Nebraska, Iowa, and Missouri. These states are called "Tornado Alley."

A tornado is a spinning column of air that forms in the middle of a thunderstorm. Inside a tornado, air spins at nearly 300 miles per hour. The spinning air acts like a vacuum. It can pull trees from the ground and make cars fly through the sky.

The United States has hundreds of tornadoes every year. Luckily, only a few of them are strong enough to cause damage.

1. You can guess from the story that
   ○ **A.** most tornadoes happen in fall.
   ○ **B.** "twister" is another word for tornado.
   ○ **C.** Iowa gets more tornadoes than Kansas does.
   ○ **D.** Missouri does not get tornadoes.

2. A tornado's spinning air can cause
   ○ **A.** thunderstorms to begin.
   ○ **B.** flowers to bloom.
   ○ **C.** springtime to start early.
   ○ **D.** cars to fly through the sky.

3. Which of these is a *fact* about tornadoes?
   ○ **A.** They are scarier than blizzards.
   ○ **B.** They are interesting to study.
   ○ **C.** They often happen in spring.
   ○ **D.** They should be called "spinners."

Vocabulary

Synonyms

Read the underlined word in each phrase. Mark the word below it that has the same (or close to the same) meaning.

Sample:

a huge <u>feast</u>
- ○ **A.** letter
- ○ **B.** wish
- ○ **C.** lawn
- ○ **D.** meal

1. <u>frighten</u> him
   - ○ **A.** ask
   - ○ **B.** scare
   - ○ **C.** draw
   - ○ **D.** pull

2. a long <u>battle</u>
   - ○ **A.** year
   - ○ **B.** bag
   - ○ **C.** fight
   - ○ **D.** nail

3. a fire <u>blazed</u>
   - ○ **A.** cleaned
   - ○ **B.** stopped
   - ○ **C.** fell
   - ○ **D.** burned

4. a feeling of <u>joy</u>
   - ○ **A.** fear
   - ○ **B.** happiness
   - ○ **C.** anger
   - ○ **D.** sadness

5. don't <u>disturb</u> her
   - ○ **A.** bother
   - ○ **B.** let
   - ○ **C.** smile
   - ○ **D.** grow

6. <u>calm</u> sea
   - ○ **A.** peaceful
   - ○ **B.** my
   - ○ **C.** far
   - ○ **D.** locked

7. famous <u>author</u>
   - ○ **A.** meal
   - ○ **B.** driver
   - ○ **C.** eat
   - ○ **D.** writer

8. he <u>declared</u>
   - ○ **A.** dreamed
   - ○ **B.** truck
   - ○ **C.** said
   - ○ **D.** moved

Multiple Meanings

Read each set of sentences. Mark the word that makes sense in both sentences.

Sample:

Margaret is a stylish _____.
I have a new _____ in my bedroom.
- ○ **A.** painting
- ○ **B.** bed
- ○ **C.** dresser
- ○ **D.** door

1. I was so hungry, I felt like I might _____.
   We could see very _____ numbers on the old mailbox.
   - ○ **A.** starve
   - ○ **B.** faint
   - ○ **C.** low
   - ○ **D.** many

2. I _____ my spelling book at school.
   Gregory writes with his _____ hand.
   - ○ **A.** right
   - ○ **B.** leave
   - ○ **C.** bought
   - ○ **D.** left

3. My neighbor asked me to _____ her dog while she's on vacation.
   Katie looked like something was on her _____.
   - ○ **A.** shirt
   - ○ **B.** mind
   - ○ **C.** keep
   - ○ **D.** feed

4. I like steak cooked until it is well done, but my brother likes it _____.
   That rain forest bird is very _____.
   - ○ **A.** burned
   - ○ **B.** colorful
   - ○ **C.** beautiful
   - ○ **D.** rare

5. The runners jog around the _____.
   Our teacher told us to keep _____ of how much we read each night.
   - ○ **A.** school
   - ○ **B.** records
   - ○ **C.** track
   - ○ **D.** street

Scholastic Professional Books

Reading Skills Practice Test 9

READING COMPREHENSION

Read each story. Then fill in the circle that best completes each sentence or answers each question.

SAMPLE

What does your last name say about you? If you lived in England in the 1100s, it told others what you did for a living. For example, people in the Parker family were park keepers, and the Baker *clan* actually baked bread and cakes! The Walls were builders, while the Smiths were blacksmiths. If your family's name is one of these, you may have a clue about how your ancestors earned a living!

1. What is the best title for this story?
   ○ **A.** "Make a Family Tree"
   ○ **B.** "Names Tell Stories"
   ○ **C.** "How to Choose a Job"
   ○ **D.** "Builders of Long Ago"

2. In this story, the word **clan** means
   ○ **A.** time.
   ○ **B.** clue.
   ○ **C.** family.
   ○ **D.** bread.

A. Here's some good news for pizza lovers! Pizza is not just tasty, it also provides important nutrients your body needs. Tomatoes, cheese, and wheat crust all contain vitamins to keep your body healthy and strong. Add some mushrooms or peppers on top, and you'll pack in even more vitamins. Pizza cheese has protein, which your body uses to grow and repair cells. Pizza dough has plenty of carbohydrates—the nutrients that give you energy to play and learn. And, last but not least, the cheese and oil on pizza have fats, which your body needs to store energy over time. Of course, too much fat is bad for your heart, so it's smart to save pizza for a special treat.

1. This story is mainly about
   ○ **A.** ways to serve pizza.
   ○ **B.** kids' favorite pizza toppings.
   ○ **C.** the invention of pizza.
   ○ **D.** the nutrients in pizza.

2. In this story, the word repair means
   ○ **A.** fix.　　○ **C.** eat.
   ○ **B.** lose.　　○ **D.** cook.

3. Cheese and oil both contain
   ○ **A.** protein.　○ **C.** pizza.
   ○ **B.** fat.　　　○ **D.** carbohydrates.

4. You can guess from the story that
   ○ **A.** you should never eat pizza.
   ○ **B.** you should not eat pizza every day.
   ○ **C.** pizza is very hard to make.
   ○ **D.** pizza has 20 different ingredients.

B. In dinosaur movies and TV shows, dinos hiss, hoot, screech, and roar. But in real life, paleontologists, or dinosaur experts, don't know what kinds of sounds dinosaurs made. These experts do believe that dinosaurs made some type of noise, however. And they can make some guesses based on studies of dinosaur skulls. For example, paleontologists say that many dinos had pointy crests on their heads. These hollow crests would have filled with air when the dinosaur breathed. As air moved through the crest, the dinosaur probably made a deep bellowing or roaring sound.

Experts also say that dinosaurs probably had good reasons to make noise. Like other creatures, dinos probably made sounds to warn fellow dinosaurs away from danger, to find mates, and to communicate with their young.

1. This story is mainly about
   ○ **A.** how paleontologists work.
   ○ **B.** dinosaur skeletons.
   ○ **C.** how dinosaurs breathed.
   ○ **D.** the noises dinosaurs made.
2. According to the story, which of these is probably *not* a reason for dinosaurs to have made noise?
   ○ **A.** to warn fellow dinos from danger
   ○ **B.** to find mates
   ○ **C.** to entertain each other
   ○ **D.** to communicate with their young
3. Air moving through a dinosaur's crest would have caused
   ○ **A.** a deep bellowing noise.
   ○ **B.** a low rumbling noise.
   ○ **C.** hisses, hoots, and screeches.
   ○ **D.** breathing problems.
4. Which of these is a *fact* about dinosaurs?
   ○ **A.** Dinosaurs made frightening sounds.
   ○ **B.** Many dinosaurs had crests.
   ○ **C.** Dinosaurs are dull.
   ○ **D.** Dinosaurs are interesting.

C. If you like talking to people and writing stories, being a news reporter may be the job for you. It is challenging, though! Reporters work hard and face tough deadlines. They follow four steps to finish a news story:
1. Do research. When reporters learn about a news event, they gather facts. They *interview* people involved in the event and take careful notes. They try to answer the questions who, what, when, where, why, and how.
2. Write the lead. The lead of a news story is the first sentence or several sentences. The lead tells the most important idea of the story and makes the reader want to keep reading.
3. Write the body of the story. The body, or main part, of the story, gives details that support the lead sentence. Sometimes, the body contains quotes from the people interviewed by the reporter.
4. Write a headline. A headline is the title of a news story. It should summarize the main idea of the story and grab the reader's attention.

1. What is the best title for this story?
   ○ **A.** "This Week's Top News"
   ○ **B.** "How Reporters Write Stories"
   ○ **C.** "Writing Good Headlines"
   ○ **D.** "The Research Process"
2. In this story the word **interview** means
   ○ **A.** talk to.   ○ **C.** share.
   ○ **B.** read to.   ○ **D.** summarize.
3. To write a news story, what should you do first?
   ○ **A.** Write the body.
   ○ **B.** Write the lead.
   ○ **C.** Write the headline.
   ○ **D.** Do research.
4. The first sentence or sentences of a news story is called the
   ○ **A.** body.   ○ **C.** lead.
   ○ **B.** interview.   ○ **D.** caption.

D. The Robin

The north wind doth blow,
And we *shall* have snow,
And what will the robin do then,
     Poor thing?
He'll sit in a barn,
And keep himself warm,
And hide his head under his wing,
     Poor thing!

1. Another good title for this poem
   might be
   ○ **A.** "A Robin's Nest."
   ○ **B.** "A Robin in Winter."
   ○ **C.** "The North Wind."
   ○ **D.** "Snow Is on the Way."

2. In this poem, the word **shall** means
   ○ **A.** flies.
   ○ **B.** hope.
   ○ **C.** will.
   ○ **D.** did.

3. The poet probably created this
   rhyme to
   ○ **A.** entertain people.
   ○ **B.** entertain robins.
   ○ **C.** explain snowfall.
   ○ **D.** celebrate springtime.

4. You can guess from the poem that
   ○ **A.** robins only live where it's cold.
   ○ **B.** robins enjoy cold weather.
   ○ **C.** the poet feels sorry for robins.
   ○ **D.** the poet dislikes robins.

E. Loch Ness is a lake in northern
Scotland. It is also home to a famous
story—the *legend* of the Loch Ness
Monster.

    The legend began 1,500 years ago.
That's when people near the lake first
began talking about a strange sea beast.
Then, in 1933, a couple said they saw a
giant creature tossing and turning in the
lake. Newspapers all over the world
reported the strange event.

    Since then, about 4,000 people have
claimed to see the creature in the lake.
They have even given it a name—Nessie.
Some people say they saw Nessie's huge
head. Others say they saw its neck or tail.
But no one has ever been able to prove
that the creature really exists.

    In 1987, scientists wanted to find out if
there was truth behind the legend. They
used special equipment to search for
living things in the lake. They found a lot of
salmon and other fish, but no monster.

1. In this story, the word **legend** means
   ○ **A.** country.
   ○ **B.** creature.
   ○ **C.** lake.
   ○ **D.** story.

2. The best title for this story is
   ○ **A.** "Lakes of Scotland."
   ○ **B.** "The Legend of Nessie."
   ○ **C.** "Monster Stories."
   ○ **D.** "Scientists Find Loch Ness
        Monster."

3. You can guess from the story that
   ○ **A.** the Loch Ness Monster is red.
   ○ **B.** Scotland has only one lake.
   ○ **C.** many people don't believe in
        the Loch Ness Monster.
   ○ **D.** there really is a monster in the
        lake.

Vocabulary

Synonyms

Read the underlined word in each phrase. Mark the word below it that has the same (or close to the same) meaning.

Sample:

glance over
- ○ **A.** look
- ○ **B.** try
- ○ **C.** return
- ○ **D.** share

1. the calm ocean
   - ○ **A.** cold
   - ○ **B.** deep
   - ○ **C.** rough
   - ○ **D.** peaceful

2. the final game
   - ○ **A.** hardest
   - ○ **B.** last
   - ○ **C.** first
   - ○ **D.** best

3. stumble over it
   - ○ **A.** trip
   - ○ **B.** fight
   - ○ **C.** hear
   - ○ **D.** leap

4. a timid boy
   - ○ **A.** intelligent
   - ○ **B.** tired
   - ○ **C.** shy
   - ○ **D.** happy

5. reply quickly
   - ○ **A.** pull
   - ○ **B.** answer
   - ○ **C.** draw
   - ○ **D.** lock

6. twist the top
   - ○ **A.** touch
   - ○ **B.** turn
   - ○ **C.** close
   - ○ **D.** lift

7. trembling like a leaf
   - ○ **A.** falling
   - ○ **B.** shaking
   - ○ **C.** growing
   - ○ **D.** living

Multiple Meanings

Read each set of sentences. Mark the word that makes sense in both sentences.

Sample:

George lost his new _____ at the park.
I want to _____ the sun set tonight.
- ○ **A.** book
- ○ **B.** watch
- ○ **C.** see
- ○ **D.** pen

1. The kids lined up in alphabetical _____ .
   May I take your _____?" he asked.
   - ○ **A.** line
   - ○ **B.** coat
   - ○ **C.** name
   - ○ **D.** order

2. Hillary threw the ball with all her _____ .
   The Joneses _____ stop by for a visit.
   - ○ **A.** strength
   - ○ **B.** did
   - ○ **C.** might
   - ○ **D.** may

3. _____ blew air around the room.
   The team's _____ applauded every play.
   - ○ **A.** fans
   - ○ **B.** wind
   - ○ **C.** coach
   - ○ **D.** they

4. All people have a _____ to food and shelter.
   Do you know the _____ answer?
   - ○ **A.** next
   - ○ **B.** right
   - ○ **C.** need
   - ○ **D.** best

5. The man helped his mother _____ the bus.
   The students made a bulletin _____ for winter.
   - ○ **A.** board
   - ○ **B.** ride
   - ○ **C.** catch
   - ○ **D.** poster

Scholastic Professional Books

Name _____

Reading Skills Practice Test 10

READING COMPREHENSION

Read each story. Then fill in the circle that best completes each sentence or answers each question.

SAMPLE

Is your smile full of holes these days? You are not alone. Most kids your age are losing their baby teeth. Baby teeth fall out to make room for permanent teeth. Baby teeth fall out when their roots *shrink*. The roots are what hold the teeth in the jawbone.

1. The best title for this story is
   ○ **A.** "Goodbye, Baby Teeth."
   ○ **B.** "How Cavities Form."
   ○ **C.** "How to Care for Teeth."
   ○ **D.** "The Tooth Fairy."

2. In the story, the word **shrink** means
   ○ **A.** grow.
   ○ **B.** get sick.
   ○ **C.** get smaller.
   ○ **D.** appear.

A. Before money was invented, people *exchanged* one kind of goods for another. For example, long ago, people used shells, beans, or beads to buy food. Later, people began to make coins out of valuable materials like silver and gold.

Today, we use paper money and coins to buy things. Our money is not made of precious materials, but it is valuable all the same. Each bill or coin is worth the amount printed or stamped on it.

1. The best title for this story is
   ○ **A.** "How to Make Money."
   ○ **B.** "The History of Money."
   ○ **C.** "Rare Coins."
   ○ **D.** "Working at a Bank."

2. What do we use for money today?
   ○ **A.** gold   ○ **C.** bills and coins
   ○ **B.** shells   ○ **D.** beans and beads

3. In the story, the word **exchanged** means
   ○ **A.** helped. ○ **C.** lost.
   ○ **B.** traded. ○ **D.** made.

4. Which of these happened first?
   ○ **A.** Silver coins were invented.
   ○ **B.** Gold coins were invented.
   ○ **C.** Paper money was invented.
   ○ **D.** People used beads to buy food.

5. You can guess from the story that
   ○ **A.** beads have been around a long time.
   ○ **B.** people have always used paper money.
   ○ **C.** money was invented in the U.S.
   ○ **D.** shells are more valuable than coins.

B. On January 20, 1951, a snowstorm hit the village of Andermatt, Switzerland. For many hours, snow fell on the village and the tall mountains nearby.

Suddenly, around 2 p.m., a giant slab of snow rolled down a mountain onto Andermatt. It was an avalanche. Within hours, three more avalanches fell on the village. The avalanches crushed homes and buried the village's main street.

Rescuers worked quickly to help the villagers. Rescue dogs helped too. They used their strong noses to sniff out people who were *trapped* in the snow.

1. This story is mainly about
   ○ **A.** Europe.
   ○ **B.** snowstorms.
   ○ **C.** dogs.
   ○ **D.** avalanches in a village in Switzerland.

2. How many avalanches fell on Andermatt on January 20, 1951?
   ○ **A.** one   ○ **C.** three
   ○ **B.** two   ○ **D.** four

3. In the story, the word trapped means
   ○ **A.** stuck.   ○ **C.** sniffed.
   ○ **B.** playing.   ○ **D.** helped.

4. Which sentence is an opinion about avalanches?
   ○ **A.** They can happen suddenly.
   ○ **B.** They are the worst kinds of disaster.
   ○ **C.** They can crush a village.
   ○ **D.** They happen when snow falls down a mountain.

C. Hundreds of years ago, grasslands called prairies covered the middle part of the United States. The prairie land stretched from southern Canada to northern Mexico. Prairie dogs, buffalo, and other animals roamed the prairie and ate the wild grasses.

In the 1800s, the number of people in our country began to grow. All those people needed somewhere to live. Many of them built homes and farms where the prairie used to be. Most of the prairie disappeared.

Today, some people are working to bring back pieces of the prairie. First, they find a piece of land that used to be a prairie. Then they plant prairie grass seeds and wait patiently for the wild grass to come back.

1. One example of a prairie animal is a
   ○ **A.** buffalo. ○ **B.** bear.
   ○ **C.** monkey. ○ **D.** squirrel.

2. The best title for this passage is
   ○ **A.** "Prairie Animals."
   ○ **B.** "Prairies: Then and Now."
   ○ **C.** "Where to Find Prairie Grass."
   ○ **D.** "Growth of Our Country."

3. The prairies disappeared because
   ○ **A.** people built homes and farms.
   ○ **B.** prairie dogs ate all the grass.
   ○ **C.** the prairie grasses all died.
   ○ **D.** Canada took over the prairie land.

4. You can guess from the story that
   ○ **A.** the prairie used to be very large.
   ○ **B.** there are no more prairie dogs.
   ○ **C.** prairie grass is ugly.
   ○ **D.** prairie land turned into forest land.

Scholastic Professional Books

D. For a hundred years, people have told he tale of John Henry, one of the strongest men who ever lived.

According to *legend,* John Henry was born with a hammer in his hand. When John Henry grew up, he took a job with the railroad. He used his hammer to chip away mountains so the train tracks could pass through.

One day, a man with a fancy new drilling machine challenged John Henry to a contest. For nine hours, both men would chip away at the mountain. The man who carved farther into the mountain would be the winner.

As John Henry worked, sweat poured from his body. But his strong arms kept hammering. Finally, a judge measured how far each man had gone. John Henry won. With his simple hammer, he had chipped away 20 feet of rock—and beat a fancy machine!

1. What tool did John Henry use?
   ○ **A.** a hammer   ○ **C.** a drill
   ○ **B.** a saw   ○ **D.** a tractor

2. In the story, the word **legend** means
   ○ **A.** a story handed down from long ago.
   ○ **B.** a special kind of hammer.
   ○ **C.** a mountain made of rock.
   ○ **D.** a strong person.

3. Which of these did John Henry do last?
   ○ **A.** He joined a contest.
   ○ **B.** He was born.
   ○ **C.** He chipped away 20 feet of rock.
   ○ **D.** He got a job with the railroad.

4. Next, the story would probably talk about
   ○ **A.** John Henry's mom and dad.
   ○ **B.** John Henry's next adventure.
   ○ **C.** how to build a railroad.
   ○ **D.** other types of hammers.

E. Guide dogs are a big help to blind people. A guide dog helps its owner cross the street and do many other things. But it is not easy to become a guide dog. Here's what a dog must do to get the job:
1. When the dog is a puppy, trainers watch the dog to make sure it is friendly and calm.
2. For one year, the dog goes to live with a family. The family teaches the dog some *simple* commands, like "Sit!" and "Stay!"
3. Then the dog goes to school, where trainers teach the dog to lead a person. The dog must learn to steer clear of cars and other dangers.
4. The trainers take the dog into town to practice going into stores and banks.
5. If the dog has done well at school, it is ready to meet its blind owner. Now they will work as a team.

1. In this story, the word **simple** means
   ○ **A.** easy.   ○ **C.** hidden.
   ○ **B.** happy.   ○ **D.** loving.

2. You would probably find this story in
   ○ **A.** a book about families.
   ○ **B.** a book of folktales.
   ○ **C.** a book about working animals.
   ○ **D.** a travel book.

3. This story was probably created to
   ○ **A.** explain how guide dogs are trained.
   ○ **B.** tell people to get pet dogs.
   ○ **C.** compare dogs to other pets.
   ○ **D.** help blind people find the right pet.

4. Which of these is a *fact* from the story?
   ○ **A.** It is fun to train a dog.
   ○ **B.** Dogs are cute.
   ○ **C.** Guide dogs must be calm.
   ○ **D.** All dogs should be guide dogs.

Vocabulary

Synonyms

Read the underlined word in each phrase. Mark the word below it that has the same (or close to the same) meaning.

Sample:

receive the package
- ○ **A.** send
- ○ **B.** get
- ○ **C.** paint
- ○ **D.** file

1. create art
   - ○ **A.** make
   - ○ **B.** buy
   - ○ **C.** learn
   - ○ **D.** sight

2. stomachache
   - ○ **A.** order
   - ○ **B.** pill
   - ○ **C.** belly
   - ○ **D.** pain

3. imaginary place
   - ○ **A.** school
   - ○ **B.** pretend
   - ○ **C.** sad
   - ○ **D.** nice

4. a beautiful area
   - ○ **A.** place
   - ○ **B.** person
   - ○ **C.** store
   - ○ **D.** song

5. beneath the desk
   - ○ **A.** sit
   - ○ **B.** under
   - ○ **C.** use
   - ○ **D.** over

6. cellar door
   - ○ **A.** attic
   - ○ **B.** knob
   - ○ **C.** open
   - ○ **D.** basement

7. delicious feast
   - ○ **A.** meal
   - ○ **B.** time
   - ○ **C.** eat
   - ○ **D.** great

8. a long battle
   - ○ **A.** bell
   - ○ **B.** day
   - ○ **C.** fight
   - ○ **D.** jail

Multiple Meanings

Read each set of sentences. Mark the word that makes sense in both sentences.

Sample:

I have a complete _____ of sports cards.
My dad asked me to _____ the table.
- ○ **A.** move
- ○ **B.** set
- ○ **C.** box
- ○ **D.** collection

1. The crossing _____ helps me across the street.
   Will you _____ my bike while I run into the library?
   - ○ **A.** ride
   - ○ **B.** watch
   - ○ **C.** light
   - ○ **D.** guard

2. I can't _____ to put this book down.
   We saw a _____ running in the woods.
   - ○ **A.** deer
   - ○ **B.** man
   - ○ **C.** bear
   - ○ **D.** stand

3. Let's _____ the listings for a movie.
   Ask your mom to write a _____ for your soccer uniform.
   - ○ **A.** read
   - ○ **B.** check
   - ○ **C.** look
   - ○ **D.** letter

4. It's hot, so we turned on the _____.
   I am a big basketball _____.
   - ○ **A.** fan
   - ○ **B.** air
   - ○ **C.** cold
   - ○ **D.** player

5. The teacher asked the class to _____ a straight line.
   Write your name on the _____.
   - ○ **A.** run
   - ○ **B.** blank
   - ○ **C.** form
   - ○ **D.** paper

Reading Skills Practice Test 11

READING COMPREHENSION

Read each story. Then fill in the circle that best completes each sentence or answers each question.

SAMPLE

Octopuses live in the world's warm oceans. Their bodies are soft and boneless, but they have tough skin called a *mantle* to protect them. Octopuses have eight arms. Their arms are called tentacles. They use their tentacles to catch lobsters, shrimps, clams, and crabs.

1. What is the best title for this story?
   ○ **A.** "Life Under the Sea"
   ○ **B.** "What Fish Eat for Dinner"
   ○ **C.** "The Octopus"
   ○ **D.** "How to Catch a Lobster"

2. In this story, the word **mantle** means
   ○ **A.** tough skin.
   ○ **B.** tentacle.
   ○ **C.** boneless.
   ○ **D.** arm.

A. There are five steps to writing a story. The first step is called pre-writing. That's when you choose a subject and learn all you can about it. The next step is to write a rough draft of your story. It does not have to be perfect. Then you revise your draft. That means you find ways to make it better. Now you are ready for the fourth step, editing. To edit a story, you correct any mistakes. Finally, you publish, or share, your story. You might read the story aloud or give it to a friend.

1. What is the best title for this story?
   ○ **A.** "My Favorite Subject"
   ○ **B.** "Read to a Friend"
   ○ **C.** "How to Write a Story"
   ○ **D.** "How to Write a Letter"

2. What should you do first?
   ○ **A.** Write a rough draft.
   ○ **B.** Choose a subject.
   ○ **C.** Publish your story.
   ○ **D.** Look for mistakes.

3. To publish a story, you
   ○ **A.** share it with others.
   ○ **B.** collect information.
   ○ **C.** write a rough draft.
   ○ **D.** edit it.

4. You can guess from this story that
   ○ **A.** ough drafts must be perfect.
   ○ **B.** all stories have lots of spelling mistakes.
   ○ **C.** even kids can publish stories.
   ○ **D.** only grown-ups can publish stories.

B. When the Earth travels in its *orbit* around the Sun, it takes 365 1/4 calendar days to make the trip. But it would be strange to see 1/4 of a day on your calendar! So, for three years we save up that 1/4 day. By the fourth year, it adds up to a whole day! Then we add that extra day to the month of February. When February has 29 days instead of 28, we call that a "leap year."

1. This article is mainly about
   ○ **A.** why we have leap year.
   ○ **B.** the seasons of the year.
   ○ **C.** who invented the calendar.
   ○ **D.** why February is cold.

2. The Earth travels around the Sun in
   ○ **A.** 365 days.   ○ **C.** 365 1/4 days.
   ○ **B.** 366 days.   ○ **D.** 366 1/4 days.

3. In this article, the word **orbit** means
   ○ **A.** ship.   ○ **C.** quickly.
   ○ **B.** path.   ○ **D.** slowly.

4. Which of the following is an *opinion* about February 29?
   ○ **A.** It comes once every four years.
   ○ **B.** It's a special day.
   ○ **C.** It comes during a leap year.
   ○ **D.** It follows February 28.

C. Digging through old garbage probably doesn't sound fun to you. But that's exactly what a "garbologist" does. A garbologist goes to landfills, where trash is buried. The garbologist digs up the trash to find out how long different things take to decompose, or break down into soil. He or she also looks to see what kinds of trash people throw away.

Why do garbologists care so much about other people's trash? They know that too much garbage is bad for the earth. They want to teach people how to *create* less trash.

1. What is the main idea of this article?
   ○ **A.** It's not fun to dig through garbage.
   ○ **B.** "Garbologist" is a silly job name.
   ○ **C.** Garbologists study garbage to teach people how to make less trash.
   ○ **D.** Trash is taken to landfills.

2. A landfill is a place where people
   ○ **A.** live.
   ○ **B.** bury trash.
   ○ **C.** recycle trash.
   ○ **D.** grow food.

3. In this story the word **create** means
   ○ **A.** make.
   ○ **B.** dig up.
   ○ **C.** break down.
   ○ **D.** decompose.

4. Garbologists dig up trash to
   ○ **A.** look for buried treasure.
   ○ **B.** find objects they can sell.
   ○ **C.** see what kind of trash is there and how long it takes to decompose.
   ○ **D.** spy on people.

5. You can guess from this story that
   ○ **A.** garbologists earn a lot of money.
   ○ **B.** most trash is made of plastic.
   ○ **C.** landfills can never get too big.
   ○ **D.** people throw away a lot of garbage.

Scholastic Professional Books

D. Anansi the spider thought that if he had a jar full of wisdom, he would be wiser than everybody else. So he walked through his village with a jar, asking the wisest people he knew to put some wisdom in it.

When the jar was full, Anansi decided to hide the jar high up in a tree. He tied a belt around his middle and tucked the jar in front. Then he tried to climb the tree, but the jar kept getting in his way.

Just then Anansi's baby son came along. "Father," he asked, "shouldn't you tuck the jar in the back of the belt?"

Anansi was annoyed. He had a jar full of wisdom, but even a baby was wiser than he was. So after he climbed to the top of the tree, he threw the jar down and smashed it. The wisdom scattered all over the earth. And that is how people got wisdom.

1. The author told this story to tell
   - **A.** a few facts about spiders.
   - **B.** how people got wisdom.
   - **C.** why jars are good for holding things.
   - **D.** how people can become smarter.

2. Which happened last?
   - **A.** Anansi smashed the jar.
   - **B.** Anansi collected wisdom in a jar.
   - **C.** Anansi tucked the jar behind him.
   - **D.** Anansi climbed the tree.

3. You would probably find this story in
   - **A.** a book about spiders.
   - **B.** a book about the brain.
   - **C.** a book of folktales.
   - **D.** a nature guide.

E. If you think that computers don't belong on a farm, think again! Over the past few years, people have found new ways to make work faster and easier on farms. Here are some of their ideas:

- Farmers need to know how much their animals eat. If the animals don't get enough to eat, they won't be healthy. Now, a farmer can put a special collar on each animal. The collar hooks up to a computer that will *alert* the farmer if the animal is not eating enough.

- It can take dairy farmers hours to milk their cows. But a Dutch company has invented a robot that does all the work. When a cow is ready to be milked, it stands next to the robot. A gate closes, and the robot does the milking.

1. In this story, the word **alert** means
   - **A.** warn.   **C.** shout.
   - **B.** hide.   **D.** ignore.

2. This story would probably go on to talk about
   - **A.** farm animals in different countries.
   - **B.** more inventions to help farmers.
   - **C.** how to milk a cow by hand.
   - **D.** what cows eat.

3. What is the main idea of this story?
   - **A.** Milking cows is hard work.
   - **B.** Computers don't belong on a farm.
   - **C.** Inventions make farm work easier.
   - **D.** Farm animals eat a lot.

4. Which is a **fact**?
   - **A.** Every farmer in America should have a computer.
   - **B.** Cows can be milked by robots.
   - **C.** Farmers love new inventions.
   - **D.** People are better than robots at milking cows.

Vocabulary

Synonyms

Read the underlined word in each phrase. Mark the word below it that has the same (or close to the same) meaning.

Sample:

creep across the floor
- ○ **A.** far
- ○ **B.** sneak
- ○ **C.** run
- ○ **D.** stomp

1. burst the bubble
   - ○ **A.** blow
   - ○ **B.** float
   - ○ **C.** soap
   - ○ **D.** pop

2. a loud giggle
   - ○ **A.** sob
   - ○ **B.** sneeze
   - ○ **C.** noise
   - ○ **D.** laugh

3. my favorite author
   - ○ **A.** color
   - ○ **B.** writer
   - ○ **C.** story
   - ○ **D.** singer

4. bright student
   - ○ **A.** shiny
   - ○ **B.** tall
   - ○ **C.** smart
   - ○ **D.** silly

5. fry a hamburger
   - ○ **A.** eat
   - ○ **B.** cook
   - ○ **C.** share
   - ○ **D.** taste

6. rotating earth
   - ○ **A.** turning
   - ○ **B.** falling
   - ○ **C.** slowing
   - ○ **D.** glowing

7. challenging problem
   - ○ **A.** ugly
   - ○ **B.** hard
   - ○ **C.** easy
   - ○ **D.** new

Antonyms

Read the underlined word in each phrase. Mark the word below it that means the opposite or nearly the opposite.

Sample:

cheerful child
- ○ **A.** happy
- ○ **B.** pretty
- ○ **C.** sleepy
- ○ **D.** sad

1. calm lake
   - ○ **A.** dry
   - ○ **B.** large
   - ○ **C.** stormy
   - ○ **D.** quiet

2. chilly breeze
   - ○ **A.** warm
   - ○ **B.** strong
   - ○ **C.** slight
   - ○ **D.** icy

3. contest champion
   - ○ **A.** umpire
   - ○ **B.** loser
   - ○ **C.** player
   - ○ **D.** winner

4. enjoy the movie
   - ○ **A.** watch
   - ○ **B.** show
   - ○ **C.** like
   - ○ **D.** dislike

5. recall her name
   - ○ **A.** forget
   - ○ **B.** remember
   - ○ **C.** say
   - ○ **D.** listen

6. shrinking in size
   - ○ **A.** shopping
   - ○ **B.** teasing
   - ○ **C.** changing
   - ○ **D.** growing

7. wobbly legs
   - ○ **A.** young
   - ○ **B.** short
   - ○ **C.** sturdy
   - ○ **D.** old

Scholastic Professional Books

Reading Skills Practice Test 12

READING COMPREHENSION

Read each story. Then fill in the circle that best completes each sentence or answers each question.

SAMPLE

John Chapman loved apple trees. He walked hundreds of miles around the country. He always carried a bag of apple seeds with him. He gave farmers seeds to *plant*. John also planted seeds as he walked. He was called Johnny Appleseed.

1. What is the best title for this story?
   - ○ **A.** "How to Plant Seeds"
   - ○ **B.** "Johnny Appleseed"
   - ○ **C.** "A Tall Apple Tree"
   - ○ **D.** "Fruits of the World"

2. In this story, the word **plant** means
   - ○ **A.** a factory.
   - ○ **B.** a young tree.
   - ○ **C.** to put in the ground.
   - ○ **D.** fields.

A. Can you imagine wearing an outfit made of garbage? It could happen! A few companies across the country are making clothes from things people throw away. For example, one company makes sweaters from old soda bottles. First, plastic bottles are cut into small pieces. The pieces are melted. Then the melted plastic is stretched into long, thin yarn. The yarn is used to make fluffy sweaters. Many people think these new "recycled" clothes can help us cut down on trash.

1. What can be used to make sweaters?
   - ○ **A.** bags
   - ○ **B.** bottles
   - ○ **C.** cups
   - ○ **D.** shoes

2. What happens first?
   - ○ **A.** Pieces are melted.
   - ○ **B.** Sweaters are sold.
   - ○ **C.** Bottles are cut up.
   - ○ **D.** Yarn is made.

3. The author wrote this story to
   - ○ **A.** sell clothes.
   - ○ **B.** explain how yarn is made.
   - ○ **C.** show how trash can be recycled.
   - ○ **D.** tell why plastic is harmful.

B. Large parts of southern California are dry, desert areas. Very little rain falls there. Only northern California gets much rain or snow.

Most people in California live in big cities in the south. So people have found ways to move water from the north to these dry *locations*. They collect rainwater in man-made lakes called reservoirs. Then they use waterways and large pipes to move the water across long distances.

1. This story is mainly about
   ○ **A.** water in California.
   ○ **B.** lakes in California.
   ○ **C.** how to build waterways.
   ○ **D.** rainfall in the U.S.

2. In this story, the word **locations** means
   ○ **A.** states.   ○ **C.** rivers.
   ○ **B.** places.   ○ **D.** people.

3. You can guess that
   ○ **A.** California is very small.
   ○ **B.** California is large.
   ○ **C.** California has few cities.
   ○ **D.** it is easy to move water.

C. Long ago in Persia, a man owned 117,000 books. He took his books everywhere. But it was not easy. He had to stack them on the backs of 400 camels! The camels carried the books in alphabetical order across deserts and through small towns. When the man wanted a new book, he paid townspeople to find one for him.

1. What is the best title for this story?
   ○ **A.** "Desert Camels"
   ○ **B.** "The Traveling Library"
   ○ **C.** "Persia Today"
   ○ **D.** "How to Find Books"

2. How many books did the man in the story own?
   ○ **A.** 400
   ○ **B.** 100,000
   ○ **C.** 17,000
   ○ **D.** 117,000

D. Firefighters risk their lives to save others. When an alarm sounds, these brave workers rush to the scene of a fire. They put out the flames by shooting water from long hoses. They crawl into burning buildings to save trapped people. They even cut through roofs and walls to get at the fire.

1. You can guess from this story that
   ○ **A.** firefighters have important jobs.
   ○ **B.** smoking causes all fires.
   ○ **C.** most fires happen in houses.
   ○ **D.** water does not help to put out fires.

2. Which of these is an **opinion** about firefighters?
   ○ **A.** They use hoses.
   ○ **B.** They save people's lives.
   ○ **C.** They ride on fire trucks.
   ○ **D.** They have fun jobs.

Scholastic Professional Books

E. Many years ago, the U.S. Navy put microphones on the ocean floor. The microphones picked up noises in the water. Scientists listened to the sounds to try to figure out what kinds of ships were in the water. But the scientists *detected* other noises too. Some of the noises were made by whales!

Whales make noises to "talk" to each other. Each kind of whale makes a different noise. Now scientists are using microphones to study whales. They are listening to the whale noises to count how many whales are in the oceans. The scientists want to find out which kinds of whales are endangered.

1. This story's main idea is that
   ○ **A.** hunters kill whales.
   ○ **B.** the Navy watches ships.
   ○ **C.** oceans have many animals.
   ○ **D.** microphones are being used to study whales.

2. In this story, the word **detected** means
   ○ **A.** saw.   ○ **C.** heard.
   ○ **B.** sent.   ○ **D.** added.

3. You can guess that
   ○ **A.** whales talk to people.
   ○ **B.** some kinds of whales are in danger.
   ○ **C.** microphones are new.
   ○ **D.** whales are afraid of ships.

F. Taking care of your teeth is important. It can help prevent tooth decay and gum disease. Good tooth care includes brushing and flossing every day, visiting your dentist, and eating healthful foods. To brush your teeth, follow these steps:
1. Get a toothbrush with soft bristles.
2. Place a small amount of toothpaste on the brush. A toothpaste with fluoride is best.
3. Place the toothbrush against your teeth at an angle.
4. To brush the front and back of your teeth, move the brush back and forth or in small circles.
5. Scrub back and forth on the part of your teeth you use to chew.
6. Brush your tongue to remove tiny *particles* of food.
7. Rinse your mouth with water or mouthwash.

1. In this story, the word **particles** means
   ○ **A.** colors.   ○ **C.** bites.
   ○ **B.** pieces.   ○ **D.** eats.

2. Before brushing, you should
   ○ **A.** rinse with mouthwash.
   ○ **B.** wash your face.
   ○ **C.** drink cold water.
   ○ **D.** get fluoride toothpaste.

3. Poor tooth care can cause
   ○ **A.** a bad diet.
   ○ **B.** soft bristles on your toothbrush.
   ○ **C.** healthy teeth.
   ○ **D.** gum disease.

4. This story would probably go on to talk about
   ○ **A.** visiting the dentist.
   ○ **B.** taking care of your ears.
   ○ **C.** cleaning your sink.
   ○ **D.** how animals chew.

Scholastic Professional Books

Study Skills

Reading a Table of Contents

This table of contents is from a book called **Maple City**. The table tells what you will find in the book.

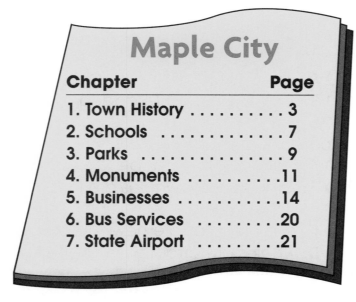

Maple City

Chapter	Page
1. Town History	3
2. Schools	7
3. Parks	9
4. Monuments	11
5. Businesses	14
6. Bus Services	20
7. State Airport	21

1. This book is about
   ○ **A.** history. ○ **C.** Maple City.
   ○ **B.** parks.   ○ **D.** buses.

2. Chapter 3 starts on
   ○ **A.** page 7. ○ **C.** page 11.
   ○ **B.** page 9. ○ **D.** page 14.

3. How many pages are in chapter 5?
   ○ **A.** three   ○ **C.** five
   ○ **B.** four   ○ **D.** six

4. When was Maple City first built? You might find out on
   ○ **A.** pages 3–6.
   ○ **B.** pages 11–13.
   ○ **C.** pages 14–19.
   ○ **D.** page 21.

Reading a Pictograph

This pictograph shows how many dogs and cats live in Maple City.

Pets in Maple City

Street	Cats	Dogs
Oak Street	🐱 🐱	🐶
Elm Street	🐱 🐱	🐶 🐶
Walnut Street		🐶
Pine Street	🐱	🐶

Key:	🐱 = 5 Cats	🐶 = 5 Dogs

1. The number of pets on Elm Street is
   ○ **A.** 4.   ○ **C.** 10.
   ○ **B.** 5.   ○ **D.** 20.

2. The street with 15 pets is
   ○ **A.** Pine.   ○ **C.** Oak.
   ○ **B.** Walnut. ○ **D.** Elm.

3. The street with fewer than 10 pets is
   ○ **A.** Pine.   ○ **C.** Oak.
   ○ **B.** Walnut. ○ **D.** Elm.

4. In Maple City, there are
   ○ **A.** the same number of cats as dogs.
   ○ **B.** more cats than dogs.
   ○ **C.** more dogs than cats.
   ○ **D.** too many cats and dogs.

Reading Skills Practice Test 13

READING COMPREHENSION

Read each story. Then fill in the circle that best completes each sentence or answers each question.

SAMPLE

Did you ever wonder why your mouth waters when you smell supper cooking or spot a fresh-baked batch of cookies? When you smell or see the food, your senses send a signal to your brain that it's time to eat. Then your brain tells your mouth to start making watery saliva. When you finally take a bite of food, this saliva will make the food *moist*. Wet food is easier to chew and swallow.

1. What is the best title for this story?
   ○ **A.** "How to Bake Cookies"
   ○ **B.** "How Your Brain Works"
   ○ **C.** "Why Your Mouth Waters"
   ○ **D.** "Tasty Treats Around the World"

2. In this story, the word **moist** means
   ○ **A.** wet.
   ○ **B.** spicy.
   ○ **C.** cold.
   ○ **D.** hot.

A. Police dogs have an important role in fighting crime. Each dog works closely with one police officer. Together, the dog and the officer go through four months of difficult training. Once the training is complete, the dog uses its super-powerful nose to help the officer track down criminals, search for stolen property, and sniff out drugs and other illegal substances. A police dog and its human partner always work as a team. In most cases, a dog even lives at home with its human partner! This helps to keep the *bond* between them strong.

1. This story is mainly about
   ○ **A.** fighting crime.
   ○ **B.** police dogs.
   ○ **C.** dogs' sense of smell.
   ○ **D.** which dogs make the best pets.

2. In this story, the word **bond** means
   ○ **A.** battle.
   ○ **B.** job.
   ○ **C.** connection.
   ○ **D.** house.

3. A police dog does not
   ○ **A.** track down criminals.
   ○ **B.** live at the police station.
   ○ **C.** sniff out drugs.
   ○ **D.** go through training.

4. You can guess from the story that
   ○ **A.** dogs' noses are stronger than humans'.
   ○ **B.** all police officers have police dogs.
   ○ **C.** police-dog training is easy.
   ○ **D.** police officers and their dogs get tired of one another.

B. Spring comes every year—and so do insects! Each year when the weather gets warmer, gardens, meadows, fields, and forests fill with bugs. There are at least one million different species of insects—more than any other kind of animal. Some of them are as big as the palm of your hand, while others are too small to be seen without a microscope.

Despite their differences, all insects share a few important characteristics. For example, they all have six legs and three body parts—a head, a thorax, and an abdomen. They also all have an *exoskeleton*, or skeleton on the outside of their body instead of on the inside. This exoskeleton looks like a hard shell. Its job is to protect an insect's delicate digestive system and other internal organs.

1. This story is mainly about
   ○ **A.** using a microscope.
   ○ **B.** characteristics of insects.
   ○ **C.** spring weather.
   ○ **D.** insects in fields and forests.

2. You can guess from the story that an eight-legged spider is
   ○ **A.** a large insect.   ○ **C.** a forest insect.
   ○ **B.** not an insect.   ○ **D.** very rare.

3. An insect needs an exoskeleton because
   ○ **A.** it has only three body parts.
   ○ **B.** it lives in extremely hot places.
   ○ **C.** its legs are long.
   ○ **D.** its internal organs are delicate.

4. Which of these is an **opinion** about insects?
   ○ **A.** They can live in fields.
   ○ **B.** They come in many sizes.
   ○ **C.** They are very creepy.
   ○ **D.** They have six legs.

C. A family vacation is a lot of fun, but getting to your vacation spot can be boring! There's nothing like sitting in a car for hours at a time to make a person grouchy and groggy. The next time your family takes a long road trip, try playing one of these traditional travel games. Families have been enjoying them for decades!

- License Plate Game: To play this game, give each player a pencil and pad of paper. Then try to spot license plates from different states. Whoever finds the most states wins.
- Beep: Pick a certain *model* of car (for example, pickup trucks or station wagons) at the start of your trip. Each time you spot that type of car, say "beep" and the color of the vehicle you saw. The first person to say "beep" gets one point. The first person to get 10 points wins the game.

1. What is the best title for this story?
   ○ **A.** "License Plates"
   ○ **B.** "Fun Travel Games"
   ○ **C.** "Long Road Trips"
   ○ **D.** "How to Win at "Beep"

2. In this story the word **model** means
   ○ **A.** beauty.   ○ **C.** type.
   ○ **B.** size.   ○ **D.** truck.

3. To play the license-plate game, what should you do first?
   ○ **A.** Pick a type of car.
   ○ **B.** Get one point.
   ○ **C.** Look for plates from different states.
   ○ **D.** Give out pencils and paper.

4. A person wins at "Beep" when he or she
   ○ **A.** gets 1 point.
   ○ **B.** gets 10 points.
   ○ **C.** gets more states than everyone else.
   ○ **D.** gets all 50 states.

D. Monday

I overslept and missed my bus.
I didn't have time to eat.
I wore plaid pants with polka dots
And my sneakers on the wrong feet.
I *trudged* to school in the rain
And got there just in time
To hear the teacher announce a test
On math chapters one through nine.
When teacher asked if we had questions,
I raised my hand and said,
"I'm not quite ready for today.
May I please go back to bed?"

By Karen Kellaher

1. Another good title for this poem might be
   ○ **A.** "Math Test."
   ○ **B.** "My Bad Day."
   ○ **C.** "I Missed the Train."
   ○ **D.** "Saturday Morning."

2. In this poem, the word **trudged** means
   ○ **A.** few.   ○ **C.** dressed.
   ○ **B.** overslept.   ○ **D.** walked.

3. The poet probably created this rhyme to
   ○ **A.** entertain children.
   ○ **B.** make teachers angry.
   ○ **C.** complain about weekends.
   ○ **D.** celebrate a holiday.

4. You can guess that the child in the poem
   ○ **A.** is not hungry for breakfast.
   ○ **B.** needs to buy new sneakers.
   ○ **C.** didn't study for the math test.
   ○ **D.** looks good in plaid.

E.   Today, many doctors are women, but that was not always the case. Until the middle of the 19th century, only men were permitted to become doctors. A determined woman named Elizabeth Blackwell thought that was unfair—and changed the course of history.

Elizabeth Blackwell was born in England in 1821. She moved to the United States with her family when she was a teenager. When she was 23 years old, Blackwell decided to become a doctor. The smart young woman applied to many medical schools, but was told "no" again and again. Finally, three years later, a small school in New York accepted Blackwell. Professors at the school never believed she would show up for classes. But Blackwell showed up and studied hard. She graduated at the head of her class.

Once she had her medical degree, Blackwell cared for many patients. She even opened a special hospital for women and children. Years later, she moved back to England and helped women there break into the medical field.

1. What did Blackwell do last?
   ○ **A.** She opened a hospital.
   ○ **B.** She applied to medical school.
   ○ **C.** She moved to England.
   ○ **D.** She moved to the U.S.

2. This story would probably go on to talk about
   ○ **A.** Elizabeth Blackwell's family.
   ○ **B.** how things have changed for female doctors.
   ○ **C.** how to get into medical school.
   ○ **D.** why Blackwell decided to become a doctor.

3. Which of these is a **fact** about Blackwell?
   ○ **A.** She was an amazing woman.
   ○ **B.** She was a doctor.
   ○ **C.** She was smarter than most male doctors.
   ○ **D.** She was probably not very bright.

4. You might find this story in
   ○ **A.** an atlas.
   ○ **B.** a nature encyclopedia.
   ○ **C.** a book of biographies.
   ○ **D.** a book of poems.

Vocabulary
Which Word Is Missing?

In each of the following paragraphs, a word is missing. First, read the paragraph. Then find the missing word in the list of words beneath the paragraph. Fill in the circle next to the word that is missing.

Sample:

When I awoke Saturday morning, I had hoped to spend the day in the park. Then I glanced out the window and saw the day was rainy and _____ . So much for my big plans!

○ **A.** sunny   ○ **C.** foggy
○ **B.** long   ○ **D.** bright

Instead, I decided to stay inside. I put some water in the _____ to make a cup of tea and settled down with a good book.

○ **A.** window   ○ **C.** sink
○ **B.** kettle   ○ **D.** tub

1. Everyone knows that manners are important, but sometimes we all need a reminder. Here are some simple things you can do to be _____ .
    ○ **A.** polite   ○ **C.** rude
    ○ **B.** first   ○ **D.** sweet

2. At the dinner table, you should always use a fork, spoon, and knife to eat your food. And keep in mind that chewing with your mouth open is _____ !
    ○ **A.** difficult   ○ **C.** tasty
    ○ **B.** lovely   ○ **D.** impolite

3. If you would like a dish that is at the other end of the table, it is better not to reach for it yourself. Kindly ask someone else to pass the item to you. And don't forget to say "thank you" _____ .
    ○ **A.** loudly   ○ **C.** first
    ○ **B.** afterward   ○ **D.** slowly

4. When answering the telephone at home, don't just pick up the line and mutter, "yo." Instead, _____ the person in a cheerful voice and ask who is calling.
    ○ **A.** request   ○ **C.** greet
    ○ **B.** mind   ○ **D.** dismiss

5. Good manners are important at school, too. When the teacher or another student is speaking, let him or her finish before you respond. No one likes to be _____ .
    ○ **A.** boring   ○ **C.** sad
    ○ **B.** answered   ○ **D.** interrupted

6. If you accidentally bump into someone in line in the cafeteria, make sure the person is not hurt. Also, remember to say, "_____ me." This will show that you did not mean to be rude.
    ○ **A.** watch   ○ **C.** excuse
    ○ **B.** embarrass   ○ **D.** dear

7. These pointers tell you what to do in a variety of situations. But above all, keep in mind that having good manners means being considerate of others around you. If you remember that, you'll find that others will truly enjoy your _____ .
    ○ **A.** jokes   ○ **C.** stories
    ○ **B.** company   ○ **D.** smile

Scholastic Professional Books

Reading Skills Practice Test 14

READING COMPREHENSION

Read each story. Then fill in the circle that best completes each sentence or answers each question.

Thanksgiving has been around for over 350 years. That's when Pilgrims and Native Americans *dined* together. But this holiday has changed a lot! For example, potatoes are a hit today. But the Pilgrims had never even heard of potatoes! And apples were not yet grown in America, so there was no apple pie.

1. What is the best title for this story?
   ○ **A.** "Thanksgiving Then and Now"
   ○ **B.** "Favorite Foods of the Pilgrims"
   ○ **C.** "Why Thanksgiving Has Always Been the Same"
   ○ **D.** "Home for the Holidays"

2. In this story, the word **dined** means
   ○ **A.** worked.
   ○ **B.** planted.
   ○ **C.** ate.
   ○ **D.** sang.

A. Students at Table Mound Elementary in Iowa knew all about recycling and other ways to help the Earth. So, they decided to teach the rest of their community about Earth Day. First, they borrowed 500 big brown paper bags from a local food store. Then, they decorated the bags with Earth Day messages and pictures. Later, the kids *returned* the bags to the store. Shoppers used the bags to take home their groceries.

1. This story is mainly about
   ○ **A.** ways to save money on groceries.
   ○ **B.** Earth Day celebrations around the country.
   ○ **C.** one school's Earth Day project.
   ○ **D.** art projects using brown bags.

2. In this story, the word **returned** means
   ○ **A.** took back.
   ○ **B.** sold.
   ○ **C.** took away.
   ○ **D.** shopped.

3. What happened first?
   ○ **A.** Students decorated brown bags.
   ○ **B.** Students borrowed bags from a store.
   ○ **C.** Shoppers used the decorated bags.
   ○ **D.** Students returned bags to the store.

4. You can guess from the story that
   ○ **A.** People in Iowa buy lots of groceries.
   ○ **B.** Students at Table Mound Elementary are good artists.
   ○ **C.** The bags taught shoppers about Earth Day.
   ○ **D.** Shoppers in Iowa love the Earth.

B. An area called Patagonia, in Argentina, was home to some of the largest dinosaurs that ever lived. Fernando Novas is a scientist who studies dinosaur bones. He says, "The giants of all giants lived here." One of them, the Giganotosaurus, was a meat-eating monster. It was about 45 feet long and weighed 8 to 10 tons. Another huge dinosaur was called the Argentinosaurus. It was about 100 feet long and weighed 100 tons. It was no meat-eating monster, though. The Argentinosaurus was an *herbivore*. In other words, it ate only plants.

1. Which is the name of a giant dinosaur?
   ○ **A.** Patagonia ○ **C.** Argentina
   ○ **B.** Argentinosaurus ○ **D.** Novas

2. What is the main idea of this story?
   ○ **A.** Some of the largest dinosaurs ever lived in Patagonia.
   ○ **B.** Fernando Novas is a scientist who studied dinosaur bones.
   ○ **C.** The Giganotosaurus ate huge amounts of meat.
   ○ **D.** Some dinosaurs were quite small.

3. In this story, the word **herbivore** means
   ○ **A.** meat eater. ○ **C.** scientist.
   ○ **B.** giant dinosaur. ○ **D.** plant eater.

4. How large was the Giganotosaurus?
   ○ **A.** about 100 feet long
   ○ **B.** over 500 feet long
   ○ **C.** about 45 feet long
   ○ **D.** less than 30 feet long

C. It's amazing what you can create from a field of maize, or corn. One summer, a farmer in Walden, New York, turned his cornfield into a giant maze! To make the maze, farmer Richard Hodgson planted rows and rows of corn. Then, when the corn was about 10 inches high, farm workers carefully pulled out some of the corn plants. That made a maze pattern in the fields. By late summer, the corn maze was 8 feet high and ready for visitors.

Hundreds of people explored Hodgson's maze. Most people took a whole hour to find their way out. Each group of explorers was given a tall flag. If they got lost, they waved the flag and someone went to help. The maze shut down at the end of the summer. The corn was used to feed farm animals.

1. What is the best title for this story?
   ○ **A.** "How to Grow Tall Corn"
   ○ **B.** "A Farm in New York"
   ○ **C.** "What to Feed Farm Animals"
   ○ **D.** "An Amazing Maze of Maize"

2. The maze was ready for visitors when the corn was
   ○ **A.** about 10 inches high.
   ○ **B.** about 8 feet high.
   ○ **C.** waving tall flags.
   ○ **D.** planted in rows.

3. Which happened last?
   ○ **A.** Hodgson pulled out some corn plants.
   ○ **B.** Hodgson planted rows of corn.
   ○ **C.** The corn was fed to farm animals.
   ○ **D.** The corn plants grew 10 inches high.

4. You can guess from the story that
   ○ **A.** few visitors came to the maze.
   ○ **B.** the maze was pretty hard to go through.
   ○ **C.** the maze was really simple.
   ○ **D.** everyone who entered the maze got lost.

Scholastic Professional Books

D. The next time you munch on a peanut-butter sandwich, say thanks to George Washington Carver. This African-American scientist invented hundreds of products, including everyone's favorite sandwich spread.

Carver was born around 1860. He became an expert in science and farming. In 1897, he learned that farmers in the Southern U.S. were having a problem. These farmers grew a lot of cotton, and the cotton plants were ruining their *soil.*

Carver offered to help. He discovered that planting peanuts every other year would make the soil rich again. Southern farmers began planting peanuts, and the problem was solved.

But soon, there was a new problem. The farmers fed the peanuts to their cows, but there were still many peanuts left over. Carver got to work. He invented 325 different ways to use peanuts. Soon, people were using peanuts to make everything from cooking oil to ink—and, of course, peanut butter!

1. In the story, the word **soil** means
    ○ **A.** peanut.   ○ **C.** cotton.
    ○ **B.** dirt.   ○ **D.** plant.

2. Farmers started growing many peanuts because peanut plants
    ○ **A.** grew very quickly.
    ○ **B.** were easy to find.
    ○ **C.** were good for the soil.
    ○ **D.** were cheaper than cotton.

3. Which of these is an *opinion*?
    ○ **A.** Peanut butter is delicious.
    ○ **B.** Carver was born around 1860.
    ○ **C.** Farmers fed peanuts to their cows.
    ○ **D.** Peanuts grow on plants.

E. Way back when, the Sun and the Moon were very good friends with the Sea. Every day, Sun and Moon visited Sea. They talked and laughed and had a good time. But Sea never visited Sun and Moon, and that hurt their feelings.

Finally, Sun and Moon asked Sea why he never visited. "Your house is not big enough," said Sea. "You would need to build a very, very, big house for me to visit."

So Sun and Moon built a huge house. It was so big that it took a whole day to walk from one end to the other. Sun and Moon felt *confident* that Sea would fit.

The next day, Sea visited. He flowed into the house until the water was waist high. "Should I stop?" he asked.

"No, no," said Sun and Moon. "Come on in." So Sea kept flowing. Soon, he reached the ceiling. Sun and Moon had to sit on the roof. Finally, the whole house was underwater, including the roof. Sun and Moon had to leap onto a cloud floating by. And that's how Sun and Moon came to live in the sky.

1. In this story, the word **confident** means
    ○ **A.** scared.   ○ **C.** huge.
    ○ **B.** sure.   ○ **D.** ocean.

2. Sun and Moon leaped onto a cloud
    ○ **A.** because they were angry at Sea.
    ○ **B.** because their new house was too big.
    ○ **C.** to stay above water.
    ○ **D.** to visit friends in the sky.

3. This story might go on to tell about
    ○ **A.** the biggest house in the world.
    ○ **B.** tips for water safety.
    ○ **C.** more adventures of Sun and Moon.
    ○ **D.** eclipses.

Vocabulary
Which Word Is Missing?

In each of the following paragraphs, a word is missing. First, read the paragraph. Then find the missing word in the list of words beneath the paragraph. Fill in the circle next to the word that is missing.

Sample:

I'm going to take a walk in the rain. But first, I'll grab my _____. I don't want to get wet.

○ **A.** book   ○ **C.** umbrella
○ **B.** sweater   ○ **D.** socks

I had a really large lunch today. I ate two sandwiches, an apple, and a ____ slice of cake. I felt very full by the time I finished all that cake.

○ **A.** tiny   ○ **C.** fruit
○ **B.** thick   ○ **D.** piece

1. Some tigers live in zoos around the world. But tigers in the wild are found only in Asia. In the wild, tigers live in grassy, wooded areas. At one time, about 100,000 tigers roamed the _____ of Asia.

○ **A.** cities   ○ **C.** forests
○ **B.** China   ○ **D.** deserts

2. The Siberian tiger is the world's _____ tiger. It weighs about 500 pounds and is over eight and a half feet tall. The smallest tiger is the Sumatran tiger. It weighs about 250 pounds and is eight feet long.

○ **A.** largest   ○ **C.** fastest
○ **B.** pounds   ○ **D.** heavy

3. Today, tigers are _____ in number. There are only 7,500 tigers left in the wild. In fact, tigers are in danger of dying out.

○ **A.** size   ○ **C.** dead
○ **B.** growing   ○ **D.** shrinking

4. What's happening to the mighty tiger? One problem is that tigers are losing their _____. People have built villages and farms on the land where tigers lived. They have destroyed tiger habitats.

○ **A.** homes   ○ **C.** stripes
○ **B.** speed   ○ **D.** cubs

5. Another problem is hunters. They kill the tigers to make medicine from their bones and to sell the beautiful tiger skins. It is _____ to hunt tigers. But many people break the law.

○ **A.** exciting   ○ **C.** scary
○ **B.** illegal   ○ **D.** boring

6. Who caused the tiger problem? People caused it. Now, it is up to people to ____ the problem. If we don't do something to help tigers they will surely become extinct.

○ **A.** cause   ○ **C.** fix
○ **B.** hide   ○ **D.** write

7. Tiger experts around the world want to help tigers. They had a big meeting in Texas to talk about ways to stop tigers from dying out. School children are also working to keep tigers safe. Schools in the U.S. have raised thousands of dollars to _____ tigers.

○ **A.** hunt   ○ **C.** spend
○ **B.** pet   ○ **D.** save

Scholastic Professional Books

Reading Skills Practice Test 15

READING COMPREHENSION

Read each story. Then fill in the circle that best completes each sentence or answers each question.

SAMPLE

Some vegetables, such as broccoli, contain nutrients that may help to *prevent* diseases. But many kids don't like to eat these vegetables. Now researchers are looking for ways to make veggies fun. They are trying to create doughnuts and other snacks that contain vegetables.

1. What is the best title for this story?
   ○ A. "My Favorite Vegetables"
   ○ B. "Making Veggies Fun"
   ○ C. "Doughnuts Are Delicious"
   ○ D. "Why Broccoli Tastes Bad"

2. In this story, the word **prevent** means
   ○ A. eat.
   ○ B. fry.
   ○ C. keep away.
   ○ D. melt.

A. Are you scared of heights? Fifteen-year-old Merrick Johnston is not. In 1995, she climbed Mount McKinley—a 20,320-foot mountain in Alaska. She became the youngest person ever to reach the mountain's *peak*! Merrick climbed with her mom and a guide. They each carried a backpack full of supplies. The team faced icy slopes and rough weather. It took 26 days to reach the top.

1. What is the main idea of this story?
   ○ A. Merrick reached a tough goal at a young age.
   ○ B. Fear of heights is a serious problem.
   ○ C. Merrick carried a backpack.
   ○ D. Weather can be a problem for mountain climbers.

2. In this story, the word **peak** means
   ○ A. bottom.
   ○ B. rocky.
   ○ C. top.
   ○ D. snow.

3. Mount McKinley is
   ○ A. less than 20,000 feet tall.
   ○ B. 26 days old.
   ○ C. a mountain in Alabama.
   ○ D. more than 20,000 feet tall.

4. You can guess from the story that
   ○ A. Mount McKinley is the world's tallest mountain.
   ○ B. the weather is usually mild on Mount McKinley.
   ○ C. Merrick's guide was older than she was.
   ○ D. Merrick's guide was 13 years old.

B. People have been flying kites for 3,000 years. During that time, kites have served many purposes. The Chinese were the first kite makers. One story says that Chinese soldiers attached bamboo pipes to their kites. As wind passed through the pipes, it made a whistling sound that scared away enemies! In 1752, Ben Franklin used a kite to study lightning. And in the early 1900s, the Wright brothers used kites to help design the first airplane.

1. What did Chinese soldiers attach to their kites?
   ○ **A.** lightning rods
   ○ **B.** bamboo pipes
   ○ **C.** silver flutes
   ○ **D.** box kites

2. This story is mostly about
   ○ **A.** kites as weapons of war.
   ○ **B.** the history of bamboo.
   ○ **C.** the many ways kites have been used.
   ○ **D.** Ben Franklin.

3. Which happened last?
   ○ **A.** The Wright brothers used kites.
   ○ **B.** The Chinese began making kites.
   ○ **C.** Ben Franklin studied lightning.
   ○ **D.** Chinese soldiers used kites in battle.

4. You can guess from this story that
   ○ **A.** Chinese soldiers won many battles.
   ○ **B.** kites have always been just for kids.
   ○ **C.** kites have had many uses.
   ○ **D.** Ben Franklin owned many kites.

C. Long ago, an Ojibway Indian named Wenibojo went on a long trip to the forest. When he got hungry, he dug up the roots of a bush and ate them. The roots tasted good, but they made him sick.

Wenibojo looked for something better to eat. Suddenly he heard the sound of ducks nearby. He followed the sounds to a beautiful lake, where the ducks were eating plants. Wenibojo tasted one. It was wild rice! He returned to his village to tell the people there about the special food.

The Ojibway still harvest rice today, but only as much as they need. They always leave some so that the ducks can eat.

1. Wenibojo was led to the lake by the
   ○ **A.** sound of ducks nearby.
   ○ **B.** smell of wild rice cooking.
   ○ **C.** sight of ducks eating plants.
   ○ **D.** sound of waves crashing.

2. What is the best title for this story?
   ○ **A.** "Wenibojo's Adventures in the Forest"
   ○ **B.** "Why Ducks Like Wild Rice"
   ○ **C.** "How the Ojibway Discovered Wild Rice"
   ○ **D.** "The Eating Habits of the Ojibway"

3. The author probably told this story
   ○ **A.** to warn people about eating roots.
   ○ **B.** to tell about a part of the Ojibway heritage.
   ○ **C.** to tell people to eat more wild rice.
   ○ **D.** to tell people to be nice to ducks.

4. You can guess from this story that
   ○ **A.** wild rice grows on plants.
   ○ **B.** wild rice is harvested from the roots of a bush.
   ○ **C.** ducks are smarter than people.
   ○ **D.** the Ojibway people eat wild rice only on special occasions.

Scholastic Professional Books

D. Frogs have lived on this planet for millions of years. But recently, scientists have noticed that certain types of frogs are disappearing. Some species have even become extinct. What's the problem? Experts have two *theories:*

• Ruined homes: Many frogs live in ponds or other wet areas. People have dried up these areas in order to build roads or buildings. Some other frogs live in forests. Many forests have been destroyed so that people can use the land. That leaves fewer places for frogs to live.

• Pollution: Chemicals get into the ponds and lands where many frogs live. Some scientists say the chemicals make frogs sick.

1. In this story, the word **theories** means
   ○ **A.** scientists.   ○ **C.** habitats.
   ○ **B.** lily pads.   ○ **D.** ideas.

2. This story is mostly about
   ○ **A.** why frogs are disappearing.
   ○ **B.** where frogs live.
   ○ **C.** scientists who study frogs.
   ○ **D.** pollution.

3. Frogs have fewer places to live because
   ○ **A.** scientists have chased them away.
   ○ **B.** oceans have dried up.
   ○ **C.** people have destroyed their homes.
   ○ **D.** too many baby frogs have been born.

4. Which of these is an *opinion*?
   ○ **A.** Some frogs lose their homes when ponds are dried up.
   ○ **B.** People should never destroy frogs' homes.
   ○ **C.** Some types of frogs have become extinct.
   ○ **D.** Some frogs live in forests.

E.   The Old Lady Who Swallowed a Fly

I know an old lady who swallowed a fly.
I don't know why she swallowed a fly.
Perhaps she'll die.

I know on old lady who swallowed a spider.
It wiggled, and jiggled, and tickled inside her.
She swallowed the spider to catch the fly.
I don't know why she swallowed the fly.
Maybe she'll die.

I know an old lady who swallowed a bird.
How absurd to swallow a bird!
She swallowed the bird to catch the spider
That wiggled, and jiggled, and tickled inside her.

She swallowed the spider to catch the fly.
I don't know why she swallowed the fly.
I guess she'll die.

1. In this song, the word **perhaps** means
   ○ **A.** definitely.   ○ **C.** unlikely.
   ○ **B.** maybe.   ○ **D.** always.

2. The second item the old lady swallowed was
   ○ **A.** a bird.   ○ **C.** a spider.
   ○ **B.** a fly.   ○ **D.** a rat.

3. The next verse will probably tell
   ○ **A.** why the old lady swallowed the fly.
   ○ **B.** where the old lady lived.
   ○ **B.** what the lady ate to catch the bird.
   ○ **D.** what flies and spiders eat.

4. You would probably find this song in
   ○ **A.** a book of rock songs.
   ○ **B.** a book about insects.
   ○ **C.** a children's songbook.
   ○ **D.** a cookbook.

Vocabulary
Which Word Is Missing?

In each of the following paragraphs, a word is missing. First, read the paragraph. Then find the missing word in the list of words beneath the paragraph. Fill in the circle next to the word that is missing.

Sample:

I want to go for a bike ride. But first, I'll put on my _____ . It is not safe to ride without one.

○ **A.** book ○ **C.** shoes
○ **B.** raincoat ○ **D.** helmet

It can be hard work to ride a bicycle uphill. Yesterday, I rode up a very _____ hill. I was really tired when I finally got to the top.

○ **A.** short ○ **C.** heavy
○ **B.** steep ○ **D.** fast

1. Cheetahs live on the plains of Africa. Like the lion and the _____ , the cheetah is a cat. But don't be fooled: Cheetahs are a lot bigger and faster than your pet kitten at home!

○ **A.** dog ○ **C.** house
○ **B.** leopard ○ **D.** zebra

2. Cheetahs are meat eaters. That means they have to _____ and kill smaller animals to survive. Cheetahs often hunt gazelles.

○ **A.** wash ○ **C.** stalk
○ **B.** ride ○ **D.** defend

3. The gazelle is an animal that looks a little like a deer. Gazelles are very fast runners. Luckily for the cheetah, it is even more _____ than a gazelle. Once a cheetah gets close to a gazelle, it can easily catch the creature and eat it.

○ **A.** hungry ○ **C.** swift
○ **B.** pretty ○ **D.** spotted

4. In fact, the cheetah is the fastest land animal in the world—faster than a grizzly bear or an Olympic athlete. At top speed, a cheetah runs even faster than some people drive their cars. Luckily, drivers don't have to deal with cheetahs racing down the _____ .

○ **A.** cabin ○ **C.** lawn
○ **B.** highway ○ **D.** river

5. Another big cat—the lion—is sometimes called the King of Beasts. It lives in Africa, too. Although cheetahs are faster than lions, lions are much bigger and more powerful. What they lack in speed, they make up for in _____ . The lion really uses its muscles.

○ **A.** strength ○ **C.** humor
○ **B.** smell ○ **D.** brains

6. A lion's big _____ might mean that it's showing you its teeth. Or, it might be just tired. To stay as strong as they are, lions need a lot of rest. Sometimes, they sleep 21 hours a day!

○ **A.** mane ○ **C.** muscle
○ **B.** yawn ○ **D.** cage

7. Leopards are not as strong as lions, or as fast as cheetahs. But they have their own secret weapon. The leopard's spots help it to hunt! The spots help to hide the leopard from other animals. That way, the _____ beast can easily sneak up on its unsuspecting prey.

○ **A.** funny ○ **C.** huge
○ **B.** sly ○ **D.** wet

Scholastic Success With

CONTEMPORARY CURSIVE

Name ____________________

Aa

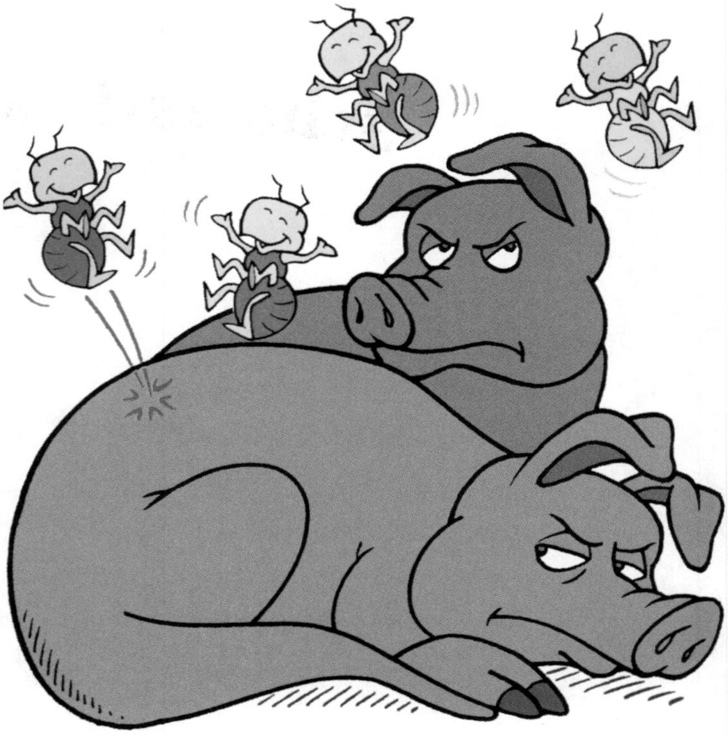

Trace and write.

A A

a a

Aa

Atlantic

ape apple

Active ants awaken

angry Asian aardvarks.

Bb

Trace and write.

$B\ B$

$b\ b$

Bb

Baltimore

baby   boy

Beautiful baboons blow

bubbles in a bathtub.

Cc

Trace and write.

C C

c c

Cc

Cincinnati

candy   case

Confident camels carry

cute, cuddly cats.

Dd

Trace and write.

D D

d d

Dd

Detroit

dandy   *dirt*

Daring dogs decide

to drive to Dallas.

Name ________________________________ **Ee**

Ee

Trace and write.

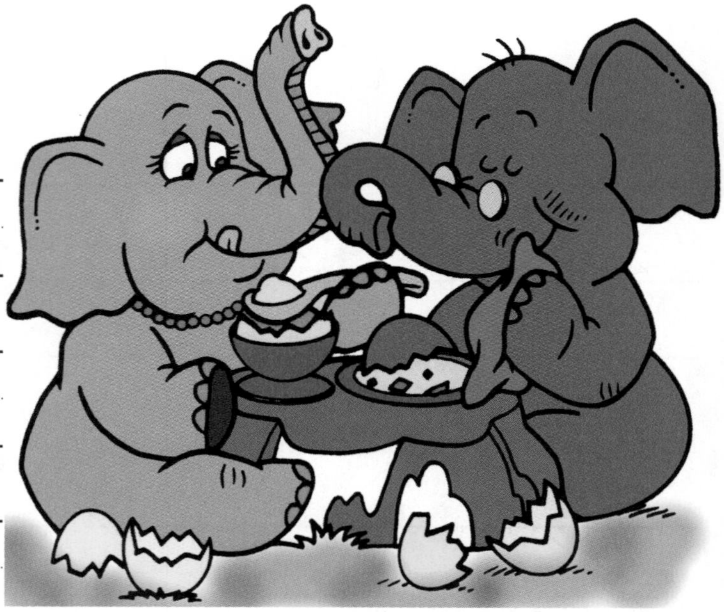

E E

e e

Ee

Erie

ever *eye*

Elderly, elegant elephants

eagerly eat eggs.

Name ____________________

Ff

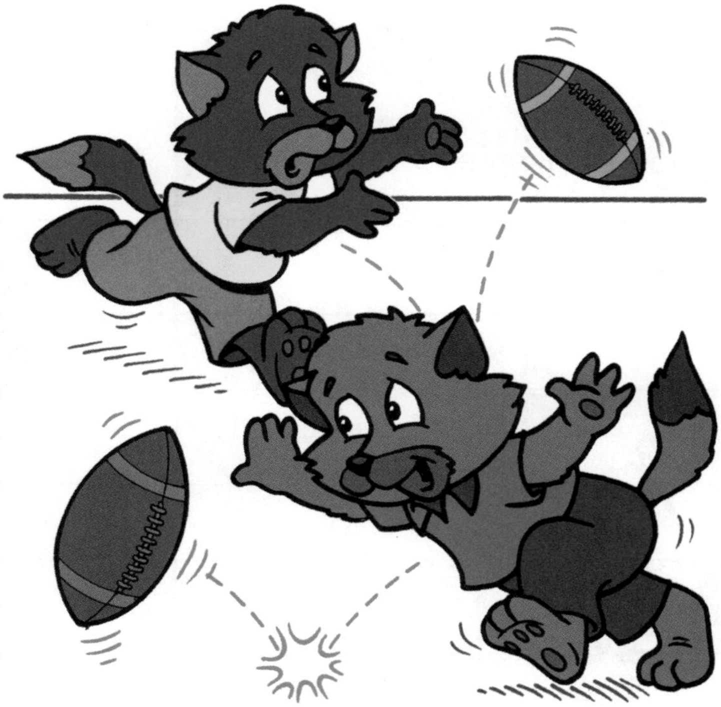

Trace and write.

F F

f f

F f

Fenton

five fast

Frisky foxes frequently

fumble footballs.

$\mathcal{G}g$

Trace and write.

$\mathcal{G}$ $\mathcal{G}$

g g

$\mathcal{G}g$

Green Bay

gauge   grate

Giggling geese gobble

giant green gumballs.

Scholastic Professional Books

Name ____________________

Hh

Trace and write.

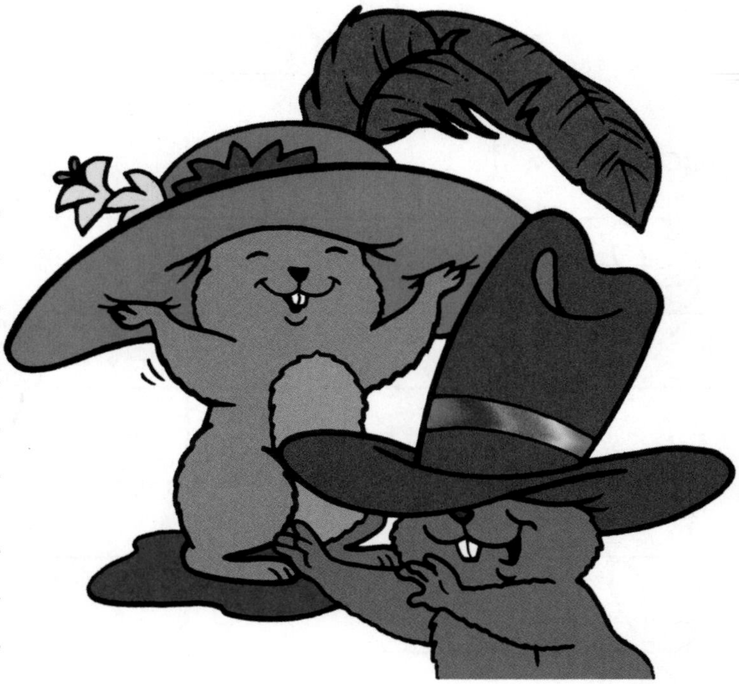

H H

h h

Hh

Hanover

honor *halt*

Happy hamsters have huge, hilarious hats.

Ii

Trace and write.

l l

i i

Ii

Inglewood

ink   ill

Idle inchworms ignore

irate insects in Iowa.

$\mathcal{J}\,j$

Trace and write.

$\mathcal{J}\quad\mathcal{J}$

$j\quad j$

$\mathcal{J}\,j$

Joliet

jump   jet

Jaguars juggle jars of

jelly beans in January.

Kk

Trace and write.

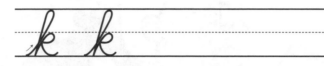

K K

k k

Kk

Kenosha

kite   kick

Kind kangaroos knit

knickers for kids.

L l

Trace and write.

L L

l l

L l

Littleton

lock   little

Large, lazy lobsters

lounge leisurely.

M m

Trace and write.

M M

m m

M m

Missoula

miss   movie

Many merry mice

make mushy meatballs.

Scholastic Professional Books

Nn

Trace and write.

n n

m m

Nn

Newton

navy   next

Nine nocturnal newts

navigate north nightly.

Oo

Trace and write.

O O

o o

Oo

Omaha

over   oblong

Odorous otters order

olive oil over oysters.

Pp

Trace and write.

P P

p p

Pp

Princeton

pipe   parrot

Pretty pigs pop popcorn

perfectly in Pittsburgh.

Qq

Trace and write.

Q Q

q q

Qq

Quincy

quick   *quit*

Quaint queens quilt

quickly and quietly.

Scholastic Professional Books

Name ______________________________

Rr

Trace and write.

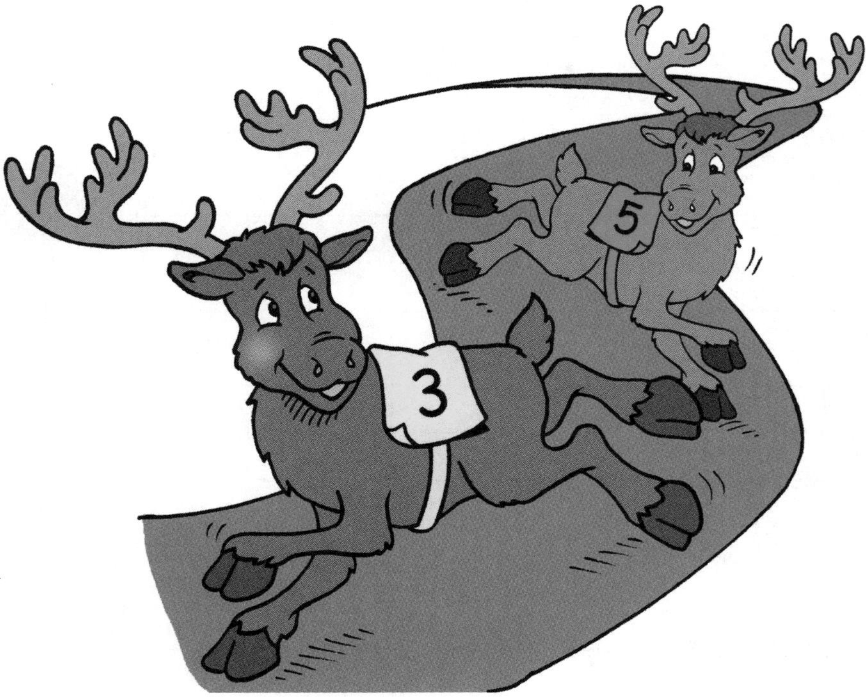

R R

r r

Rr

Rochester

rich rear

Restless reindeer run

races rapidly in Reno.

Ss

Trace and write.

S S

s s

Ss

Seattle

sense   safe

Sleepy spiders sell

smelly skunk soap.

Scholastic Professional Books

Name ____________________ Tt

Tt

Trace and write.

T T

t t

Tt

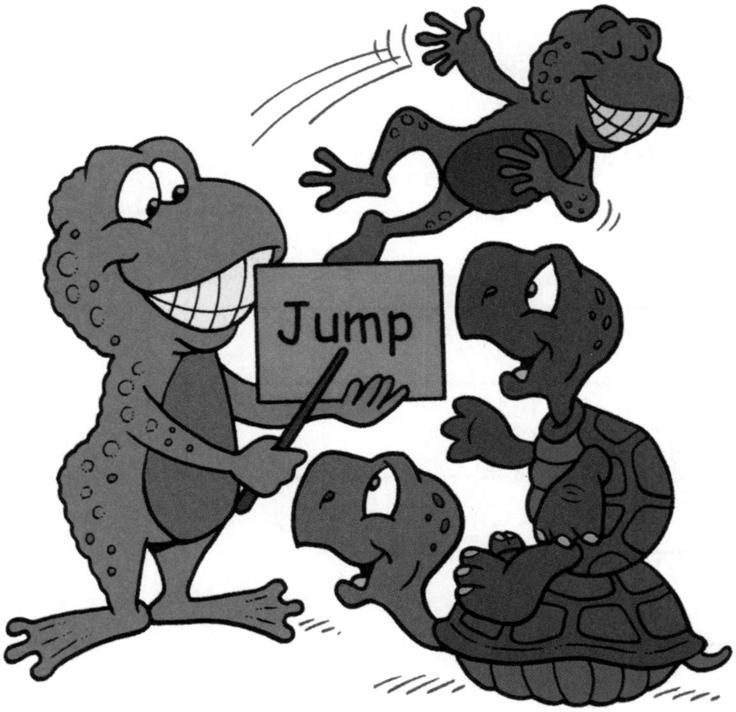

Texarkana

total tea

Talented, toothy toads

teach talkative turtles.

Uu

Trace and write.

U U

u u

Uu

Urbana

utter   use

Uniformed umpires

usher upset unicorns.

Vv

Trace and write.

V V

v v

Vv

Vancouver

vivid   *vase*

Vain vultures

vacuum vigorously.

Scholastic Professional Books

Ww

Trace and write.

W W

w w

Ww

Westover

women   *wow*

Wiggly worms wander

westward with whistles.

Name ______________________________

Xx

Trace and write.

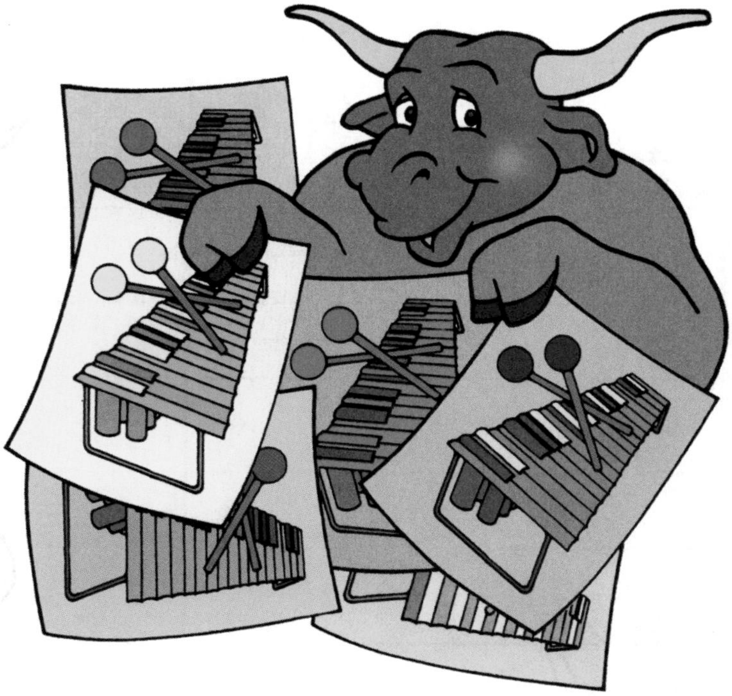

X X

x x

Xx

Xenia

axis exit

Xavier Ox x-rayed

six extra xylophones.

$\mathcal{Y}y$

Trace and write.

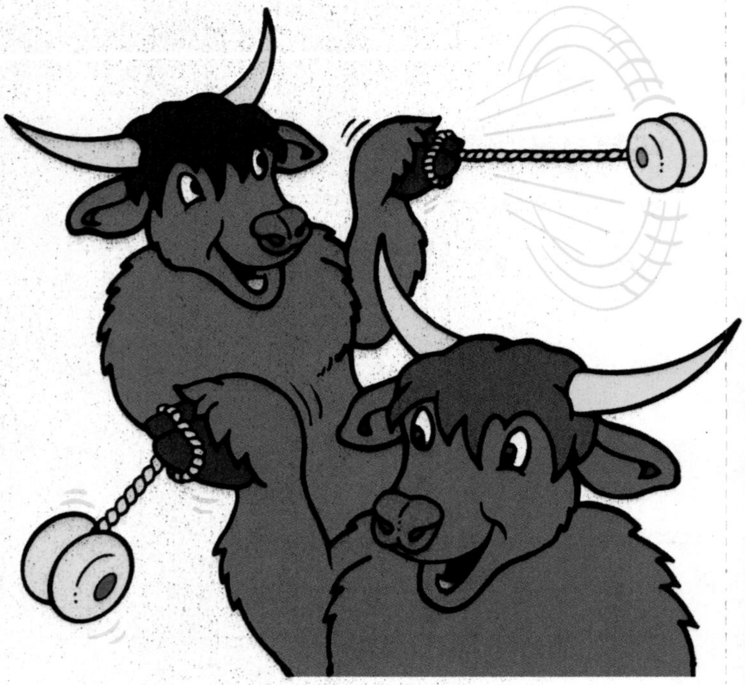

$\mathcal{Y}$ $\mathcal{Y}$

y y

$\mathcal{Y}y$

Yorktown

yacht   yet

Youthful yaks yell,

"Yeah, yellow yo-yos!"

Name ____________________

Z z

Trace and write.

Z Z

z z

Z z

Zanesville

zipper zero

Zany zebras zigzag

zestfully to Zimbabwe.

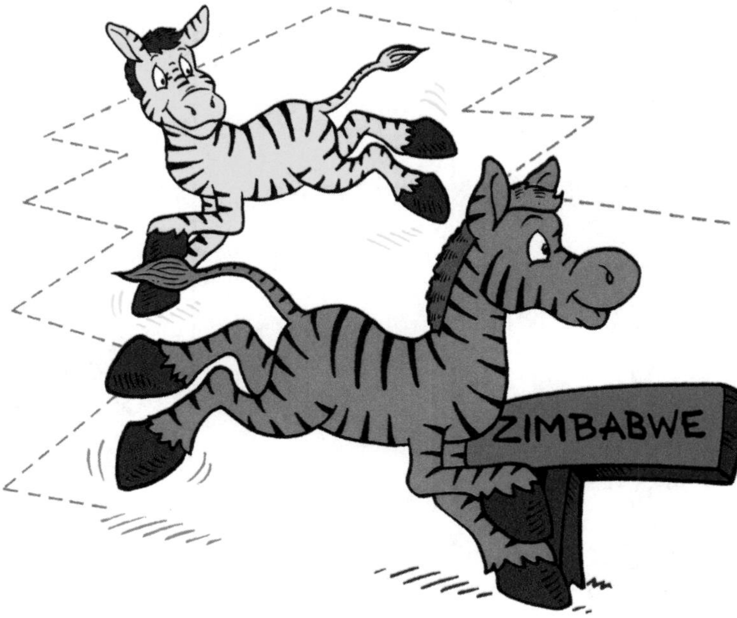

A–Z

A B C D E F G

H I J K L M

N O P Q R S T

U V W X Y Z

Write.

_____

_____

_____

_____

a–z

a   b   c   d   e   f   g

h   i   j   k   l   m

n   o   p   q   r   s   t

u   v   w   x   y   z

Write.

_____
- -
_____

_____
- -
_____

_____
- -
_____

_____
- -
_____

Numbers 0-9

Trace and write.

0   0   0

1   1   1

2   2   2

3   3   3

4   4   4

5   5   5

6   6   6

7   7   7

8   8   8

9   9   9

Our Solar System

The sun is the center of our solar system. It is the only star in our solar system. The nine planets and their moons all orbit the sun. The sun provides heat and light to the planets and their moons.

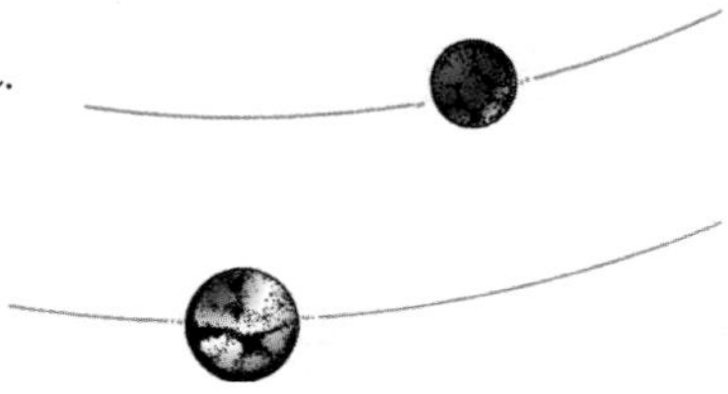

Write.

_____

_____

_____

_____

_____

_____

_____

_____

_____

_____

_____

Ancient Astronomers

People who study the sun, moon, planets, and stars are called astronomers. Cave people were some of the first astronomers. They drew the different shapes of the moon on walls of their caves. Long ago, sailors studied the stars to help them travel. The ancient Greeks discovered many of the planets.

Write.

_____

_____

_____

_____

_____

_____

_____

_____

_____

_____

_____

_____

What Is a Year?

A year is the time it takes for a planet to orbit the sun. A year on Earth is 365 days. It only takes Mercury 88 days to make a trip around the sun. However, it takes Uranus 84 Earth years and Pluto 248 Earth years to orbit the sun one time.

Write.

_____

_____

_____

_____

_____

_____

_____

_____

_____

_____

_____

_____

From Hot to Cold

Some planets are so hot or so cold that people cannot live on them. Some days it is 750°F on Mercury. On Venus, the temperature is nearly 900°F! The temperature on Uranus and Neptune is about -350°F. Earth's highest recorded temperature is 136°F and the lowest is -127°F.

Write.

_____

_____

_____

_____

_____

_____

_____

_____

_____

_____

_____

_____

_____

Scholastic Professional Books.

How Many Moons?

In our solar system, scientists have named over 60 moons. Saturn has 18 named moons. Jupiter has 16 moons, and Earth has only one. Some scientists believe Pluto was one of Neptune's moons that escaped from its orbit!

Write.

Speedy Mercury

Mercury is the planet that is closest to the sun. It spins slowly, but it moves around the sun very quickly. Mercury was named after the speedy Roman messenger for the gods.

Write.

Scholastic Professional Books

Beautiful Venus

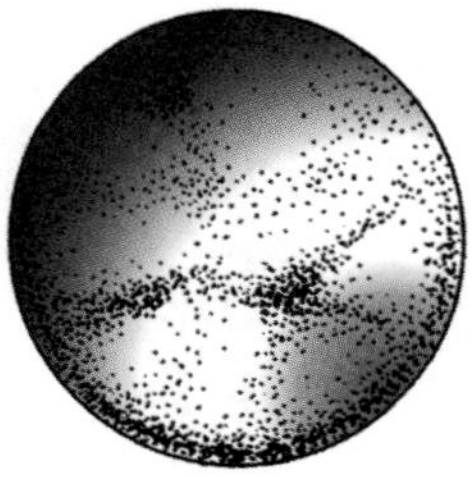

Venus is the easiest planet to see in the sky because it is the closest to Earth. It is sometimes called the Evening Star. The Romans named Venus after their goddess of love and beauty. Venus is so hot, it could melt lead. It has an orange sky.

Write.

_____

_____

_____

_____

_____

_____

_____

_____

_____

_____

_____

_____

Our Incredible Earth

Earth is the only planet known to have life. It is the right distance from the sun to give it the perfect temperature to have water in all three forms—liquid, vapor, and ice. Although 70 percent of Earth's surface is water, its name means "soil."

Write.

_____

_____

_____

_____

_____

_____

_____

_____

_____

_____

_____

_____

_____

_____

Mysterious Mars

Has there ever been life on Mars? That remains a mystery. Scientists are studying the the possibility of past, present, or future life there. Mars is often called the Red Planet because the rocks on its surface look like rust. Mars was named after the Roman god of war.

Write.

_____
_____
_____
_____
_____
_____
_____
_____
_____
_____
_____
_____
_____
_____

Sensational Saturn

Saturn is the second largest planet in our solar system. It is most famous for its seven rings made of glittering pieces of ice. Saturn was named after the Roman god of agriculture.

Write.

_____

_____

_____

_____

_____

_____

_____

_____

_____

_____

King Jupiter

Jupiter is the largest planet. It is so big that 1,300 Earths could fit inside of it! That is why the Romans named it after the king of the Roman gods. Jupiter spins faster than all the other planets.

Write.

_____
_____
_____
_____
_____
_____
_____
_____
_____
_____
_____
_____
_____

Understanding Uranus

How can anyone understand very much about a planet nearly two billion miles away? Uranus was the first planet to be discovered through a telescope. It was named after the Roman god who was Saturn's father.

Write.

_____

- -

_____

- -

_____

- -

_____

- -

_____

- -

_____

- -

_____

- -

_____

- -

_____

- -

_____

- -

_____

Not Much About Neptune

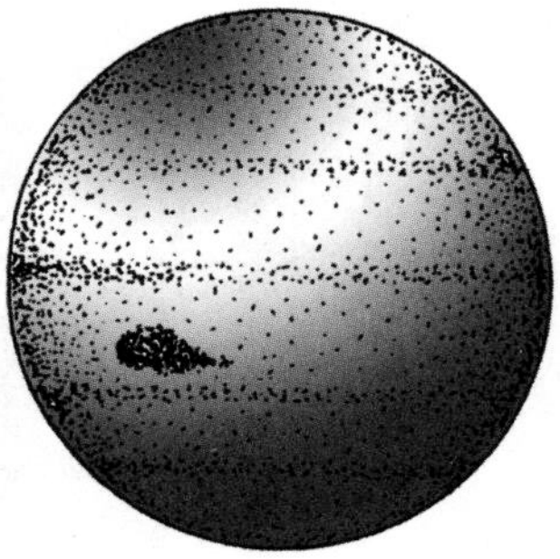

Neptune is difficult to see even if you have a telescope. It is nearly three billion miles from the sun. Neptune takes 165 Earth years to orbit the sun once. Neptune was named after the Roman god of the sea.

Write.

_____

_____

_____

_____

_____

_____

_____

_____

_____

_____

_____

_____

Where's Pluto?

Pluto, the smallest planet, is far, far away from the sun—3,666,200,000 miles! Pluto's orbit crosses Neptune's every 248 years. When that happens, Neptune is farther from the sun than Pluto.

Write.

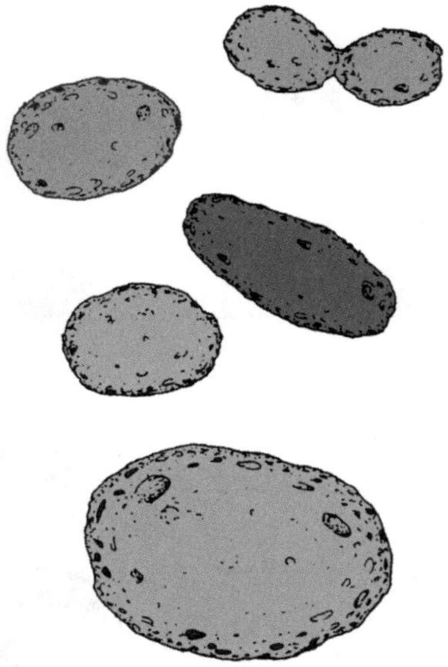

Flying Rocks

Between Mars and Jupiter are chunks of rock that circle the sun. There are thousands and thousands of these flying rocks called asteroids. Asteroids come in many shapes and sizes. Some even look like potatoes!

Write.

_____
_____
_____
_____
_____
_____
_____
_____
_____
_____
_____
_____
_____
_____
_____

Scholastic Success With

GRAMMAR

Statements and Questions

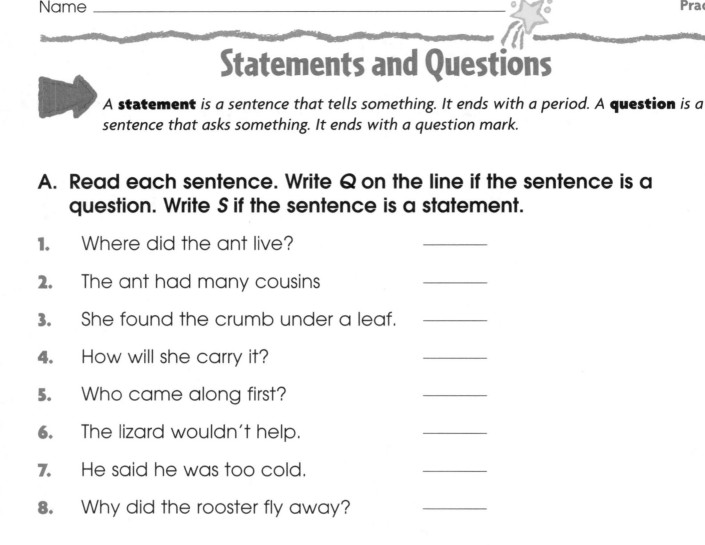

*A **statement** is a sentence that tells something. It ends with a period. A **question** is a sentence that asks something. It ends with a question mark.*

A. Read each sentence. Write Q on the line if the sentence is a question. Write S if the sentence is a statement.

1.   Where did the ant live?   ———

2.   The ant had many cousins   ———

3.   She found the crumb under a leaf.   ———

4.   How will she carry it?   ———

5.   Who came along first?   ———

6.   The lizard wouldn't help.   ———

7.   He said he was too cold.   ———

8.   Why did the rooster fly away?   ———

B. The sentences below do not make sense. Rewrite the words in the correct order.

1.   How crumb did carry the ant the? _____

_____

2.   She herself it carried.

_____

_____

Statements and Questions

*A **statement** is a sentence that tells something. It ends with a period. A **question** is a sentence that asks something. It ends with a question mark.*

A. Rewrite each sentence correctly. Begin each sentence with a capital letter. Use periods and question marks correctly.

1. can we take a taxi downtown

_____

2. where does the bus go

_____

3. the people on the bus waved to us

_____

4. we got on the elevator

_____

5. should I push the elevator button

_____

B. Write a question. Then write an answer that is a statement.

1. Question: _____

_____

2. Statement: _____

_____

Statements and Questions

Look at the underlined part of each sentence. Decide if it is correct. Fill in the bubble next to the correct answer.

1. The ant found a big crumb.
    - ○ Found the ant
    - ○ Ant the found
    - ○ correct as is

2. The ant needs help?
    - ○ help
    - ○ help.
    - ○ correct as is

3. The coyote not help would.
    - ○ help not would
    - ○ would not help
    - ○ correct as is

4. the ants live in an anthill.
    - ○ The ants
    - ○ the Ants
    - ○ correct as is

5. She has many cousins?
    - ○ cousins
    - ○ cousins.
    - ○ correct as is

6. the man didn't see the ant.
    - ○ The Man
    - ○ The man
    - ○ correct as is

7. Did he lose his hat?
    - ○ hat
    - ○ hat.
    - ○ correct as is

8. He ran the ant from.
    - ○ from the ant.
    - ○ ant from the.
    - ○ correct as is

9. I am the strongest?
    - ○ strongest.
    - ○ strongest
    - ○ correct as is

10. do you think you can?
    - ○ Do you
    - ○ Do You
    - ○ correct as is

Exclamations and Commands

*An **exclamation** is a sentence that shows strong feeling. It ends with an exclamation point. A **command** is a sentence that gives an order. It ends with a period.*

A. Read each sentence. Write *E* on the line if the sentence is an exclamation. Write *C* if the sentence is a command.

1. They chase buffaloes! _____

2. You have to go, too. _____

3. Wait at the airport. _____

4. It snows all the time! _____

5. Alligators live in the sewers! _____

6. Look at the horse. _____

7. That's a great-looking horse! _____

8. Write a letter to Seymour. _____

B. Complete each exclamation and command. The punctuation mark at the end of each line is a clue.

1. I feel _____!

2. Help your _____.

3. That's a _____!

4. I lost _____!

5. Turn the _____.

6. Come watch the _____.

7. Please let me _____.

Exclamations and Commands

 *A **sentence** tells a complete thought. It tells who or what, and it tells what happens.*

A. Draw a line between the words in Column A and Column B to form complete sentences. Then write the complete sentences on the lines below. Remember to add an exclamation mark or a period.

Column A	**Column B**
There's a	the buffaloes
Look at	your toys and games
Pack	Gila monster at the airport

1. _____

2. _____

3. _____

B. Write sentence after each complete thought. Write not a sentence after each incomplete thought. Then make each incomplete thought into a sentence.

1. I ate a salami sandwich. _____

2. I like to ride horses. _____

3. Subway driver. _____

4. There are horned toads. _____

5. Kids on our street _____

6. We are moving tomorrow. _____

Exclamations and Commands

Look at the underlined part of each sentence. Decide if it is correct. Fill in the bubble next to the correct answer.

1. <u>I'm going to Texas!</u>
   - ○ I'm going to Texas?
   - ○ I'm to Texas!
   - ○ correct as is

2. I am so <u>excited</u>
   - ○ excited!
   - ○ excited?
   - ○ correct as is

3. Please help me <u>pack!</u>
   - ○ pack?
   - ○ pack.
   - ○ correct as is

4. Her baby brother is <u>adorable</u>
   - ○ adorable?
   - ○ adorable!
   - ○ correct as is

5. I can't <u>wait!</u>
   - ○ wait.
   - ○ wait
   - ○ correct as is

6. <u>Help me find.</u>
   - ○ Help me find a game.
   - ○ Help find game.
   - ○ correct as is

7. We'll have such <u>fun!</u>
   - ○ fun
   - ○ fun?
   - ○ correct as is

8. <u>It be!</u>
   - ○ It will be great!
   - ○ It great!
   - ○ correct as is

9. Remember <u>to write to me</u>
   - ○ to write to
   - ○ to write to me.
   - ○ correct as is

10. My <u>team the game!</u>
    - ○ team won the game!
    - ○ team won game!
    - ○ correct as is

Singular and Plural Nouns

A **singular noun** names one person, place, or thing. A **plural noun** names more than one person, place, or thing. Add **-s** to form the plural of most nouns.

A. Each sentence has an underlined noun. On the line, write *S* if it is a singular noun. Write *P* if it is a plural noun.

1. She has a new <u>baby</u>.   ———

2. <u>It</u> is very cute.   ———

3. She has small <u>fingers</u>.   ———

4. She drinks from a <u>bottle</u>.   ———

5. I can tell my <u>friends</u> all about it.   ———

B. Read each sentence. Underline the singular noun. Circle the plural noun.

1. The baby has two sisters.

2. The nightgown has pockets.

3. Her hand has tiny fingers.

4. My parents have a baby.

5. The family has three girls.

C. Complete the chart. Write the singular or plural of each noun.

Singular	Plural
fence	
	trains
gate	
	cows

Singular and Plural Nouns

*A **singular noun** names one person, place, or thing. A **plural noun** names more than one person, place, or thing. Add **-s** to form the plural of most nouns. Add **-es** to form the plural of nouns that end in **ss**, **x**, **ch**, or **sh**. Some nouns change their spelling to form the plural.*

A. Finish the chart. Write singular nouns in each column.

Nouns that end in *ch, sh, ss, x*	Nouns that end in *y*	Nouns that end in *f*
bench	party	loaf

B. Complete each sentence with the plural form of the noun in ( ).

1. Mia picks _____ from the trees in her backyard. (cherry)

2. There are also many _____ with tiny berries. (bush)

3. Fresh _____ are her favorite snack. (peach)

4. She loads _____ with these different fruits. (box)

5. The kitchen _____ are filled with delicious jams. (shelf)

6. Mia shares the fruit with the third-grade _____. (class)

C. Use the words *story* and *stories* in one sentence. Use *fox* and *foxes* in another sentence.

1. _____

   _____

2. _____

   _____

Singular and Plural Nouns

Read each riddle. Decide if the underlined noun is correct. Fill in the bubble next to the correct answer.

1. We are square and made from cardboard. We are <u>boxs</u>.
   - ◯ boxes
   - ◯ box
   - ◯ correct as is

2. We help you chew your food. We are <u>tooth</u>.
   - ◯ tooths
   - ◯ teeth
   - ◯ correct as is

3. You can find us on a farm. We are <u>geese</u>.
   - ◯ goose
   - ◯ gooses
   - ◯ correct as is

4. Be sure not to drop us when you take a drink. We are <u>glassess</u>.
   - ◯ glass
   - ◯ glasses
   - ◯ correct as is

5. We are messages sent over telephone lines. We are <u>fax</u>.
   - ◯ faxs
   - ◯ faxes
   - ◯ correct as is

6. You can use us to comb your hair. We are <u>brush</u>.
   - ◯ brushes
   - ◯ brushs
   - ◯ correct as is

7. You can buy us in a food store. We are <u>grocerys</u>.
   - ◯ grocery
   - ◯ groceries
   - ◯ correct as is

8. We are places trains can stop. We are <u>stations</u>.
   - ◯ station
   - ◯ stationes
   - ◯ correct as is

9. We like to eat cheese. We are <u>mouse</u>.
   - ◯ mice
   - ◯ mices
   - ◯ correct as is

10. We are tales to read. We are <u>story</u>.
    - ◯ stories
    - ◯ storys
    - ◯ correct as is

Common and Proper Nouns

A **common noun** names any person, place, or thing. A **proper noun** names a particular person, place, or thing. A proper noun begins with a capital letter.

A. Is the underlined word a common noun or a proper noun? Write *common* or *proper*.

1. The <u>girl</u> likes to learn. _____

2. She goes to two <u>schools</u>. _____

3. She lives in <u>America</u>. _____

B. Underline the common nouns. Circle the proper nouns.

1. April has a brother and a sister.

2. Their names are Julius and May.

3. Their parents were born in Taiwan.

4. April goes to school on Saturday.

5. She is learning a language called Mandarin.

6. May read a book about the Middle Ages.

C. Underline the common nouns. Circle the proper nouns. Then write them on the chart in the correct category.

1. Last August David went to camp.

2. Many children go to a picnic on the Fourth of July.

Common Nouns	Proper Nouns
_____	_____
_____	_____
_____	_____

Common and Proper Nouns

*A **common noun** names any person, place, or thing. A **proper noun** names a particular person, place, or thing. A proper noun begins with a capital letter.*

A. Read each word in the box. Write it where it belongs on the chart.

doctor   park   football   Tangram   Pat   Atlanta

Category	Common Nouns	Proper Nouns
1. Person		
2. Place		
3. Thing		

B. Complete each sentence with a common noun or proper noun. In the box, write *C* if you wrote a common noun. Write *P* if you wrote a proper noun.

1. I threw the ball to _____. (person)

2. I have visited _____. (place)

3. My favorite food is _____. (thing)

4. My family lives in _____. (place)

5. My favorite author is _____. (person)

6. I wish I had a _____. (thing)

7. I like to read about _____. (historical event)

8. My favorite holiday is _____. (holiday)

Common and Proper Nouns

Is the underlined part of each sentence correct? Fill in the bubble next to the right answer.

1. The <u>fourth of July</u> is my favorite holiday.
    - ○ Fourth of July
    - ○ fourth of july
    - ○ correct as is

2. In Australia, winter begins in the <u>month of June</u>.
    - ○ Month of June
    - ○ month of june
    - ○ correct as is

3. I love <u>tom's apple pie</u>.
    - ○ Tom's apple pie
    - ○ tom's Apple Pie
    - ○ correct as is

4. Our <u>teacher, Dr. ruffin</u>, is from Louisiana.
    - ○ teacher, dr. Ruffin
    - ○ teacher, Dr. Ruffin
    - ○ correct as is

5. He speaks <u>Spanish and Japanese</u>.
    - ○ spanish and japanese
    - ○ Spanish and japanese
    - ○ correct as is

6. Susan's family is from <u>Kansas City, missouri</u>.
    - ○ Kansas City, Missouri
    - ○ kansas city, Missouri
    - ○ correct as is

7. Let's have a <u>new year's day</u> party!
    - ○ new year's Day
    - ○ New Year's Day
    - ○ correct as is

8. There will be no <u>school on monday</u>.
    - ○ School on Monday
    - ○ school on Monday
    - ○ correct as is

9. Dogs are the most popular <u>pets in north america</u>.
    - ○ pets in North America
    - ○ pets in North america
    - ○ correct as is

10. Do you want to go to <u>the Movies on Saturday</u>?
    - ○ the movies on Saturday
    - ○ the Movies on saturday
    - ○ correct as is

Singular and Plural Pronouns

A **singular pronoun** *takes the place of a noun that names one person, place, or thing.*
A **plural pronoun** *takes the place of a noun that names more than one person, place, or thing.*

A. Underline the pronoun in each sentence. On the line, write *S* if it is singular or *P* if it is plural.

1. He is called Spider. _____

2. I can see Spider has eight long legs. _____

3. They asked Spider a question. _____

4. We want to know what's in the pot. _____

5. It contains all the wisdom in the world. _____

B. Read each pair of sentences. Circle the pronoun in the second sentence. Then underline the word or words in the first sentence that it replaces. Write the pronoun under *Singular* or *Plural*.

	Singular	**Plural**
1. This story is funny. It is about wisdom.	_____	_____
2. The author retold the story. She is a good writer.	_____	_____
3. My friends and I read the story aloud. We enjoyed the ending.	_____	_____
4. Two boys acted out a scene. They each took a different role.	_____	_____

C. For each noun write a subject pronoun that could take its place.

1. Spider _____

3. Tortoise and Hare _____

2. the pot _____

4. Spider's mother _____

Singular and Plural Pronouns

A **subject pronoun** takes the place of a noun or nouns as the subject of a sentence. A subject pronoun can be singular or plural. **I**, **you**, **she**, **he**, **it**, **we**, and **they** are subject pronouns. An **object pronoun** takes the place of a noun or nouns in the predicate. An object pronoun can be singular or plural. **Me**, **you**, **him**, **her**, **it**, **us**, and **them** are object pronouns.

A. Underline the object pronoun in each sentence. Circle _S_ if it is singular or _P_ if it is plural.

1. Darren and Tracy were
    playing soccer with us.   S or P
2. Tracy passed the ball to him.   S or P
3. He kicked the ball back to her.   S or P
4. She stopped it in front of the net. S or P
5. Tracy kicked the ball toward me.   S or P
6. I kept them from scoring a goal.   S or P

B. Complete each sentence. Write the correct pronoun in ( ) on the line.

1. Ms. Stone gave _____ a funny assignment. (we, us)
2. She asked _____ to tell a funny story. (I, me)
3. Ray and Pete brought _____ a book of jokes. (she, her)
4. She thanked _____. (them, they)
5. Dina acted out a story with _____. (him, he)

C. Write one sentence using it as a subject pronoun. Write another sentence using it as an object pronoun.

_____

_____

Singular and Plural Pronouns

Is the underlined pronoun correct? Fill in the bubble next to the right answer.

1. My parents took the three of <u>we</u> to a garage sale.
   - ○ us
   - ○ I
   - ○ her
   - ○ correct as is

2. Mom and Dad really wanted <u>I</u> to go.
   - ○ She
   - ○ me
   - ○ They
   - ○ correct as is

3. Mom wouldn't take "no" for an answer. <u>She</u> said that I might find something good.
   - ○ Her
   - ○ Me
   - ○ Them
   - ○ correct as is

4. The drive was boring. <u>He</u> was the longest trip I'd ever taken.
   - ○ She
   - ○ It
   - ○ They
   - ○ correct as is

5. My two sisters were sleepy. I let <u>they</u> lean on me.
   - ○ them
   - ○ she
   - ○ us
   - ○ correct as is

6. Dad found some golf clubs. <u>Him</u> was so excited.
   - ○ You
   - ○ Me
   - ○ He
   - ○ correct as is

7. Mom liked a vase. Dad bought it for <u>her</u>.
   - ○ she
   - ○ they
   - ○ I
   - ○ correct as is

8. Sonya and Kara both found mysteries. <u>They</u> began to read right away.
   - ○ Her
   - ○ Them
   - ○ It
   - ○ correct as is

9. There was a dusty box in the corner. <u>Him</u> was covered in cobwebs.
   - ○ Them
   - ○ It
   - ○ Her
   - ○ correct as is

10. I pulled out an old baseball mitt. <u>Me</u> was so surprised!
    - ○ I
    - ○ Them
    - ○ Him
    - ○ correct as is

Scholastic Professional Books

Action Verbs

Action verbs *are words that tell what the subject of the sentence does.*

A. Underline the action verb in each sentence.

1. The villagers cheered loudly.

2. They added flavor to the cheese.

3. Please give them the milk.

4. He serves the cheese.

5. He emptied the buckets.

B. Circle the action verb in ( ) that paints a more vivid picture of what the subject is doing.

1. The villagers (walked, paraded) across the floor.

2. Father (whispered, talked) to the baby.

3. The puppy (ate, gobbled) down his food.

4. The girl (skipped, went) to her chair.

5. The ball (fell, bounced) down the stairs.

C. Write an action verb from the box to complete each sentence.

whispered   laughed   sighed

1. We ———————————— at the playful kittens.

2. She ———————————— deeply and fell asleep.

3. Megan ———————————— to her friend in the library.

Action Verbs

Action verbs are words that tell what the subject of the sentence does. Some action verbs help to paint a clearer picture in the reader's mind.

A. On the line, write the action verb in ( ) that paints a clearer picture.

1. A squirrel _____ an acorn. (took, snatched)

2. It _____ the acorn open. (cracked, broke)

3. The squirrel _____ the nut. (nibbled, ate)

4. Then it _____ up the tree. (went, scrambled)

B. Circle each verb. Then write the verb from the box that gives a livelier picture of the action.

| shouted | honked | ran | bounced | grabbed |

1. The bus driver blew the horn. _____

2. The girl got her books. _____

3. She said, "Good-bye," to her family. _____

4. She went to the bus. _____

5. The bus moved down the bumpy road. _____

C. Write two sentences that show action. Use the verb *dashed* in the first sentence. Use the word *tiptoed* in the second sentence. Underline the verbs.

1. _____

2. _____

Action Verbs

A. Fill in the bubble next to the action verb in each sentence.

1. Crystal's whole family arrived for dinner.
   - ○ dinner
   - ○ family
   - ○ arrived

2. Her grandmother hugged everyone.
   - ○ grandmother
   - ○ hugged
   - ○ everyone

3. Her aunt and uncle roasted a huge turkey.
   - ○ roasted
   - ○ turkey
   - ○ huge

4. Everyone ate the delicious meal.
   - ○ ate
   - ○ Everyone
   - ○ meal

5. They cheered for the cooks!
   - ○ cooks
   - ○ They
   - ○ cheered

B. Read each sentence. Fill in the bubble next to the more vivid verb.

1. The puppy ——— after the ball.
   - ○ went
   - ○ chased

2. She ——— all around the house and yard.
   - ○ dashed
   - ○ went

3. A yellow cat ——— through the wooden fence.
   - ○ looked
   - ○ peeked

4. Then the puppy ——— high into the air.
   - ○ leaped
   - ○ moved

5. She ——— the ball.
   - ○ got
   - ○ grabbed

Present- and Past-Tense Verbs

Present-tense verbs *show action that is happening now. They agree in number with who or what is doing the action.* **Past-tense verbs** *show action that took place in the past. Most past-tense verbs end in* **-ed**.

A. Read each sentence. If the underlined verb is in the present tense, write *present* on the line. If it is in the past tense, write *past*.

1. We <u>worked</u> together on a

   jigsaw puzzle. _____

2. Mom <u>helped</u> us. _____

3. She <u>enjoys</u> puzzles, too. _____

4. Tom <u>picked</u> out the border pieces. _____

5. He <u>dropped</u> a puzzle piece on the floor. _____

6. I <u>looked</u> for the flower pieces. _____

7. Dad <u>likes</u> crossword puzzles better. _____

8. My little sister <u>watches</u> us. _____

9. Mom <u>hurries</u> us before dinner. _____

10. We <u>rushed</u> to finish quickly. _____

B. Underline the verb in each sentence. Then rewrite the sentence. Change the present-tense verb to the past. Change the past-tense verb to the present.

1. The man crosses the river.

   _____

2. He rowed his boat.

   _____

Present- and Past-Tense Verbs

Present-tense verbs *must agree in number with the subject. The letters* **-s** *or* **-es** *are usually added to a present-tense verb when the subject of the sentence is a singular noun or* **he**, **she**, *or* **it**.

A. Read each sentence. On the line, write the correct form of the present-tense verb in ( ).

1. The crow _____ the pitcher with pebbles. (fill, fills)

2. The man _____ the crow. (watch, watches)

3. Then he _____ the cabbage across the river. (take, takes)

4. The man and the goat _____ the wolf behind. (leave, leaves)

5. They _____ back on the last trip. (go, goes)

B. Write the correct past-tense form of the verb in ( ).

1. J.J. _____ for the hidden picture. (look)

2. He _____ at it for a long time. (stare)

3. Ana _____ by. (walk)

4. Then she _____ solve the puzzle. (help)

C. Write three sentences. Use the verb in ( ) in your sentence.

1. (play) _____

_____

2. (plays) _____

_____

3. (played) _____

_____

Present- and Past-Tense Verbs

Is the underlined verb in each sentence correct? Fill in the bubble next to the right answer.

1. Mr. Henry <u>bakes</u> delicious apple pies.
    - ◯ bake
    - ◯ baking
    - ◯ correct as is

2. He <u>wash and peel</u> each apple carefully.
    - ◯ washes and peels
    - ◯ wash and peeled
    - ◯ correct as is

3. He <u>slices</u> each apple into eight pieces.
    - ◯ slicing
    - ◯ slice
    - ◯ correct as is

4. Mr. Henry's children <u>enjoys</u> the pies very much.
    - ◯ enjoy
    - ◯ enjoying
    - ◯ correct as is

5. Last summer, Mr. Henry <u>enter</u> a pie-baking contest.
    - ◯ enters
    - ◯ entered
    - ◯ correct as is

6. His whole family <u>travel</u> to the competition.
    - ◯ traveling
    - ◯ traveled
    - ◯ correct as is

7. They <u>arrives</u> just in time.
    - ◯ arriving
    - ◯ arrived
    - ◯ correct as is

8. The judges <u>awards</u> Mr. Henry's pie a blue ribbon.
    - ◯ awarded
    - ◯ awarding
    - ◯ correct as is

9. They <u>tasted</u> Mr. Henry's pie and said it was wonderful.
    - ◯ tastes
    - ◯ taste
    - ◯ correct as is

10. All the people <u>enjoys</u> the day!
    - ◯ enjoying
    - ◯ enjoyed
    - ◯ correct as is

Scholastic Professional Books

The Verb *BE*

*The verb **be** tells what the subject of a sentence is or was. **Am**, **is**, and **are** tell about someone or something in the present. **Was** and **were** tell about someone or something in the past.*

A. Read each sentence. Circle the word that is a form of the verb *be*.

1. Captain Fossy was Mr. Anning's good friend.
2. Mary Anning said, "The dragon is gigantic!"
3. "Its eyes are as big as saucers!" she told her mother.
4. "I am inside the cave!" she shouted to her brother.
5. The scientists were amazed by the remarkable fossil.

B. Read each sentence. If the underlined verb is in the past tense, write *past* on the line. If it is in the present tense, write *present*.

1. Mary Anning <u>was</u> a real person. _____

2. I <u>am</u> interested in fossils, too. _____

3. There <u>are</u> many dinosaurs in the museum. _____

4. The exhibits <u>were</u> closed yesterday. _____

5. This <u>is</u> a map of the first floor. _____

C. Write the form of *be* that completes each sentence.

> **am   is   are**

1. I _____ on the bus with my mother and father.

2. Buses _____ fun to ride.

3. The bus driver _____ a friendly woman.

The Verb *BE*

*Some verbs show action. Others, such as the verb **be**, show being, or what something is or was. The form of **be** must agree with the subject of the sentence.*

A. Circle each verb. If the verb shows action, write *action* on the line. If the verb shows being, write *being*.

1. The sunshine is bright and hot. _____

2. We carried our umbrellas. _____

3. The sailboats were still. _____

4. There are no rocks on the beach. _____

B. Circle the verb that best completes the sentence. Remember that the form of the verb *be* must agree with the subject.

1. I (is, am) a third grader.

2. Pat and I (is, are) partners in class.

3. Jimmy (was, were) my partner last month.

4. Mrs. Boynton (is, are) the science teacher.

5. The students (was, were) interested in the experiment.

C. Write two sentences that tell about someone or something. Use *is* in one sentence. Use *was* in the other.

1. _____

   _____

2. _____

   _____

The Verb *BE*

Is the underlined verb in each sentence correct? Fill in the bubble next to the right answer.

1. All dinosaurs <u>is</u> extinct.
   - ○ am
   - ○ are
   - ○ correct as is

2. A brontosaurus <u>is</u> a kind of dinosaur.
   - ○ am
   - ○ are
   - ○ correct as is

3. Many people <u>are</u> puzzled about what happened to dinosaurs.
   - ○ am
   - ○ was
   - ○ correct as is

4. Dinosaurs <u>was</u> plant-eaters or meat-eaters.
   - ○ is
   - ○ were
   - ○ correct as is

5. I <u>are</u> interested in Tyrannosaurus rex.
   - ○ am
   - ○ were
   - ○ correct as is

6. It <u>were</u> a fierce meat-eater.
   - ○ are
   - ○ was
   - ○ correct as is

7. Dinosaurs <u>was</u> like some reptiles that live today.
   - ○ is
   - ○ were
   - ○ correct as is

8. Their teeth, bones, and skin <u>was</u> like those of crocodiles.
   - ○ were
   - ○ is
   - ○ correct as is

9. Large dinosaurs <u>were</u> the largest land animals that ever lived.
   - ○ am
   - ○ was
   - ○ correct as is

10. I <u>are</u> amazed by their extraordinary size!
    - ○ am
    - ○ were
    - ○ correct as is

Main Verbs and Helping Verbs

*A **main verb** is the most important verb in a sentence. It shows the action. A **helping** **verb** works with the main verb. Forms of **be** and **have** are helping verbs. The helping verb **will** shows future tense.*

A. Read each sentence. Write *M* if a main verb is underlined. Write *H* if a helping verb is underlined. Circle the main and helping verbs that show future tense.

1. We will <u>learn</u> about new buildings.   _____

2. The backhoe <u>is</u> digging the foundation.   _____

3. It <u>had</u> filled several dump trucks.   _____

4. The dump trucks are <u>removing</u> the dirt.   _____

5. Workers <u>are</u> building the outer wall.   _____

6. A cement truck is <u>pouring</u> the concrete.   _____

7. It <u>will</u> need several days to dry.   _____

8. At noon the workers will <u>eat</u> their lunch.   _____

B. Choose the correct main and helping verb from the box to complete each sentence. Write it on the line. Circle the main and helping verbs that show future tense.

had climbed	have lifted	will watch	are reading	is going

1. We _____ a movie about skyscrapers.

2. A building _____ up.

3. The workers _____ the plans.

4. Cranes _____ the heavy beams.

5. A worker _____ a tall ladder.

Main Verbs and Helping Verbs

A **main verb** is the most important verb in a sentence. It shows the action. A **helping verb** works with the main verb. Forms of **be** and **have** are helping verbs.

A. Read each sentence. Circle the helping verb. Draw a line under the main verb.

1. Jamal had built his first model rocket last year.
2. He has painted it red, white, and blue.
3. Now Jamal is building another rocket.
4. It will fly many feet into the air.
5. A parachute will bring the rocket back to Jamal.
6. I am buying a model rocket, too.

B. Complete each sentence with the correct main verb or helping verb in ( ). Write the word on the line.

1. Kim _____ making a clay vase. (is, has)

2. The clay _____ arrived yesterday. (was, had)

3. I am _____ to watch her work. (go, going)

4. She is _____ a potter's wheel. (used, using)

5. The sculpture _____ go above the fireplace. (will, is)

6. People _____ admired Kim's beautiful vases. (are, have)

C. Write two sentences about something you will do later in the week. Use the future tense helping verb. Be sure to use a main verb and helping verb in each sentence.

1. _____

2. _____

Main Verbs and Helping Verbs

A. Read each sentence. Fill in the bubble next to the main verb.

1. Ed is reading a book in the park.
   - ◯ Ed
   - ◯ is
   - ◯ reading

2. The children are playing baseball nearby.
   - ◯ are
   - ◯ playing
   - ◯ baseball

3. I have walked to the park, too.
   - ◯ walked
   - ◯ have
   - ◯ park

4. Tomorrow, my sister will come along.
   - ◯ Tomorrow
   - ◯ come
   - ◯ will

5. She will share her lunch with me.
   - ◯ share
   - ◯ will
   - ◯ lunch

B. Read each sentence. Fill in the bubble next to the helping verb.

1. Jill has visited her grandparents many times this year.
   - ◯ Jill
   - ◯ has
   - ◯ visited

2. She is sending them an E-mail now.
   - ◯ E-mail
   - ◯ is
   - ◯ sending

3. In June, they will drive to Washington, D.C.
   - ◯ they
   - ◯ driving
   - ◯ will

4. Jill and her brother will go with them.
   - ◯ will
   - ◯ go
   - ◯ them

5. They have waited for this trip for a long time.
   - ◯ waited
   - ◯ this
   - ◯ have

Scholastic Professional Books

Linking Verbs

*A **linking verb** tells what someone or something is, was, or will be. The linking verb most often used is a form of the verb* be, *such as* **am**, **is**, **are**, **was**, **were**, *and* **will be**.

A. Find the linking verb in each sentence. Write it on the line.

1. This book is a biography about Thomas Edison. _____

2. I am interested in books about inventors. _____

3. Thomas Edison was a hard worker. _____

4. His inventions were wonderful. _____

5. They are still important for us today. _____

6. You will be amazed by this book. _____

B. Read each sentence and underline the linking verb. Then circle the word that tells if it is past or present.

1. I am a fan of Thomas Edison.   Past or Present

2. Thomas Edison was a famous inventor.   Past or Present

3. Many of his inventions are well-known.   Past or Present

4. His parents were friendly.   Past or Present

5. Jared is Edison's great-great-grandson.   Past or Present

C. Finish each sentence correctly. Write *are*, *am*, or *was* on the line.

1. I _____ excited.

2. This book _____ great!

3. Inventors _____ interesting people.

Linking Verbs

*A **linking verb** tells what someone or something is, was, or will be. **Am**, **is**, and **was** are used when the subject of the sentence is singular. **Are** and **were** are used when the subject is plural. **Are** and **were** are also used with **you**.*

A. Underline the linking verb in each sentence. Circle *S* if the subject is singular. Circle *P* if the subject is plural.

1. I was very bored.   S or P

2. Now I am so happy.   S or P

3. Stacey and Leda are my new neighbors.   S or P

4. They were surprised by my visit.   S or P

5. Stacey is very funny.   S or P

B. Complete each sentence with the correct linking verb in ( ). Write the word on the line.

1. Roberto Clemente _____ a great baseball player. (was, were)

2. All baseball fans _____ amazed by his talents. (were, was)

3. I _____ one of his biggest fans. (is, am)

4. He _____ a true hero to me. (are, is)

5. Sammy Sosa and Henry Aaron _____ my other favorite players. (is, are)

C. Think of a favorite animal. Write two sentences to describe it. Use one of these linking verbs in each sentence: *am, is, are, was, were, will be.*

_____

_____

Linking Verbs

A. Read each sentence. Fill in the bubble next to the linking verb.

1. My new computer is fast.
- ⬭ new
- ⬭ is
- ⬭ fast

2. I am excited about it.
- ⬭ am
- ⬭ I
- ⬭ excited

3. The two mouse pads are colorful.
- ⬭ two
- ⬭ pads
- ⬭ are

4. The speakers were heavy.
- ⬭ were
- ⬭ heavy
- ⬭ speakers

5. All of the software was free.
- ⬭ software
- ⬭ was
- ⬭ free

B. Read each sentence. Fill in the bubble next to the correct linking verb.

1. My mom _____ a rafting teacher.
- ⬭ is
- ⬭ are
- ⬭ were

2. The trip last week _____ so much fun.
- ⬭ will be
- ⬭ were
- ⬭ was

3. The rafts _____ very soft and bouncy.
- ⬭ are
- ⬭ is
- ⬭ was

4. Yesterday, the docks _____ crowded.
- ⬭ will be
- ⬭ was
- ⬭ were

5. I _____ a raft instructor in the future.
- ⬭ will be
- ⬭ am
- ⬭ is

Subjects and Predicates

*The **complete subject** tells whom or what the sentence is about. The **complete predicate** tells who or what the subject is or does. The **simple subject** is the main word in the complete subject. The **simple predicate** is the verb in the complete predicate.*

A. Draw a line between the complete subject and the complete predicate.

1. All of the families traveled to California.

2. Baby Betsy, Billy, Joe, and Ted stayed in the cabin.

3. My father told us stories.

4. I baked a pie.

B. Draw a circle around the simple subject in each sentence. Then write it on the line.

1. Betsy learned how to walk. _____

2. The miners ate it up. _____

3. The new baby looks like me. _____

4. My feet are tired. _____

5. The man started a laundry. _____

C. Draw a circle around the simple predicate in each sentence. Then write it on the line.

1. We made a pie together. _____

2. First we rolled the crust. _____

3. Then we added the berries. _____

4. It bakes for one hour. _____

5. Everybody loves our pie! _____

Scholastic Professional Books

Subjects and Predicates

The **simple subject** is the main word in the complete subject. The **simple predicate** is the main word in the complete predicate.

A. Read each sentence. Draw a line between the complete subject and the complete predicate. Then write the simple subject and the simple predicate.

		Simple Subject	Simple Predicate
1.	Mrs. Perez's class took a trip to the museum.	_____	_____
2.	Many large paintings hung on the walls.	_____	_____
3.	Maria saw a painting of an animal alphabet.	_____	_____
4.	All the children looked at the painting.	_____	_____
5.	Paul pointed to a cat on a leash.	_____	_____
6.	His friend liked the dancing zebra.	_____	_____
7.	Everyone laughed at the purple cow.	_____	_____
8.	Many people visited the museum that day.	_____	_____
9.	The bus took us to school.	_____	_____

B. Finish the sentences. Add a complete subject to sentence 1. Add a complete predicate to sentence 2.

1. _____ was funny.

2. My class _____.

Subjects and Predicates

A. Is the underlined part of the sentence the complete subject or a complete predicate? Fill in the bubble next to the correct answer.

1. <u>My little brother</u> carried his backpack.
   - ○ complete subject
   - ○ complete predicate

2. I <u>found my old fishing rod</u>.
   - ○ complete subject
   - ○ complete predicate

3. <u>My dad</u> put air in our bicycle tires.
   - ○ complete subject
   - ○ complete predicate

4. Our whole family <u>rode to the big lake</u>.
   - ○ complete subject
   - ○ complete predicate

5. <u>Many pink flowers</u> bloomed on the trees.
   - ○ complete subject
   - ○ complete predicate

B. Fill in the bubble that tells if the underlined word is the simple subject or the simple predicate.

1. A man <u>rowed</u> a boat on the lake.
   - ○ simple subject
   - ○ simple predicate

2. My <u>brother</u> played ball in the field.
   - ○ simple subject
   - ○ simple predicate

3. Some other <u>children</u> joined in the game.
   - ○ simple subject
   - ○ simple predicate

4. Our large <u>basket</u> sat unopened on the picnic table.
   - ○ simple subject
   - ○ simple predicate

5. We <u>ate</u> cheese sandwiches and fruit.
   - ○ simple subject
   - ○ simple predicate

Adjectives

Adjectives describe nouns. They can tell what color, size, and shape something is. They can also tell how something sounds, feels, or tastes.

A. Look at each underlined noun. Circle the adjective or adjectives that describe it. Then write the adjectives on the lines.

1. My big <u>brother</u> likes to eat sweet <u>fruits</u>.   _____ _____

2. He eats them on many hot <u>days</u>.   _____ _____

3. He cuts the red <u>apple</u> into four <u>pieces</u>.   _____ _____

4. The ripe <u>bananas</u> and juicy <u>peaches</u> are his favorites.   _____ _____

5. Mom bought him a large, round <u>watermelon</u>.   _____ _____

6. He made a delicious, colorful <u>salad</u> for all of us!   _____ _____

B. Write two adjectives to describe each noun. Use words that describe color, size, shape, sound, or how something tastes or feels.

1. the _____, _____ balloon

2. a _____, _____ apple

3. a _____, _____ day

C. Write a sentence about a pet. Use two adjectives to describe the pet.

_____

_____

Adjectives

*An **adjective** is a word that describes a person, place, or thing.*

A. Read each sentence. Write the adjective that describes the underlined noun on the line.

1. We live near a sparkling <u>brook.</u> _____

2. It has clear <u>water</u>. _____

3. Large <u>fish</u> swim in the brook. _____

4. Busy <u>squirrels</u> play near the brook. _____

5. You can enjoy breathing in the fresh <u>air</u> near the brook. _____

B. Complete each sentence by adding an adjective.

1. I love _____ apples.

2. I see a _____ ball.

3. I smell _____ flowers.

4. I hear _____ music.

5. I like the _____ taste of pickles.

Write three sentences that tell about the foods you like the best. Use adjectives in your description.

Scholastic Professional Books

Adjectives

A. Read each sentence. Fill in the bubble next to the word that is an adjective.

1. Several relatives from Mexico visited us.
   - ○ Several
   - ○ relatives
   - ○ visited

2. The trip took six hours.
   - ○ trip
   - ○ six
   - ○ hours

3. They took many pictures of my family.
   - ○ took
   - ○ many
   - ○ pictures

4. My uncle wore a blue hat.
   - ○ uncle
   - ○ blue
   - ○ hat

5. My aunt wore a colorful serape.
   - ○ aunt
   - ○ wore
   - ○ colorful

B. Fill in the bubble next to the adjective that best completes the sentence.

1. We ate the ——— food.
   - ○ loud
   - ○ fuzzy
   - ○ delicious

2. There were ——— people in the restaurant.
   - ○ one
   - ○ many
   - ○ green

3. My dad ordered ——— tortillas.
   - ○ sharp
   - ○ loud
   - ○ some

4. My cousin José ate ——— tamales!
   - ○ noisy
   - ○ five
   - ○ curly

5. Everyone had a ——— time!
   - ○ cold
   - ○ wonderful
   - ○ purple

Articles and Other Adjectives

The words a, an, *and* the *are special adjectives called* **articles**. **A** *is used before words that begin with a consonant.* **An** *is used before words that begin with a vowel.* **The** *is used before either.*

A. Circle the articles in each sentence.

1. The elk, moose, and bears grazed in the forest.

2. There was an abundant supply of grass and plants.

3. A bolt of lightning struck a tree and started a fire.

4. Fires have always been an important part of forest ecology.

5. The heat of the summer left the forest very dry.

6. The fires spread over a thousand acres.

7. The helicopters and an airplane spread chemicals on the fire.

8. Firefighters made an attempt to stop the flames.

B. Circle the article in ( ) that completes each sentence correctly. Then write it on the line.

1. Last summer I visited _____ National Park. (a, an)

2. We took a bus through _____ forests. (an, the)

3. The bus carried us up _____ narrow roads. (a, the)

4. I saw _____ elk grazing on some grass. (a, an)

5. We stayed in _____ old log cabin. (a, an)

6. Deer came up to _____ cabin window. (an, the)

7. We made _____ new friend. (a, an)

8. I wrote my friend _____ letter. (a, an)

Articles and Other Adjectives

*The article **A** is used before words that begin with a consonant. **An** is used before words that begin with a vowel. **The** is used before either.*

A. Circle the article that correctly completes the sentence.

1. I saw (a, an) octopus at the aquarium.

2. A trainer was feeding fish to (a, an) dolphin.

3. We took (a, an) elevator to the main floor.

4. We had (a, an) up-to-date listing of exhibits.

5. There was (a, an) exhibit about the ocean floor.

6. It was (a, an) day to remember!

B. Write a noun on each line to complete the sentences.

1. We read a _____ about a _____.

2. The _____ in a funny story had an _____ for a pet.

3. We went to the _____ to get an _____.

4. Angela saw a _____ on the _____.

5. A _____ was curled up on the _____.

C. Complete the sentence with three singular nouns. Use the article *a* or *an*.

Molly drew a picture of _____

_____

Articles and Other Adjectives

A. Fill in the bubble next to the article that correctly completes the sentence.

1. I want to be ___ firefighter in our class play.
- ○ the
- ○ an

2. My friend plans to play one of ___ astronauts.
- ○ an
- ○ the

3. Sue read an exciting story about ___ acrobat.
- ○ an
- ○ a

4. We wrote letters to ___ authors of the book.
- ○ a
- ○ the

5. ___ illustrations were done in bright colors.
- ○ The
- ○ An

B. Fill in the bubble next to the word that best completes the sentence.

1. A few days ago, we went on an ___ ride!
- ○ train
- ○ elephant
- ○ boat

2. John visited an ___ outside the city.
- ○ airport
- ○ zoo
- ○ museum

3. Bill and Michelle shared an ___.
- ○ seat
- ○ umbrella
- ○ peach

4. At the edge of the water, Keesha saw a ___.
- ○ oyster
- ○ eel
- ○ crab

5. Rachel drew pictures of a ___.
- ○ octopus
- ○ lobster
- ○ egg

Possessive Nouns

A **possessive noun** shows ownership. Add **'s** to make a singular noun show ownership. Add an apostrophe (') after the **s** of a plural noun to show ownership.

A. Underline the possessive noun in each sentence.

1. The king's palace is beautiful.

2. The palace's garden has many flowers.

3. The flowers' sweet smell fills the air.

4. The trees' branches shade the garden paths.

5. The gardener's tools are well-oiled and sharp.

6. People listen to the birds' songs.

7. The singers' voices are very beautiful.

8. The diamond reflects the sun's rays.

9. The diamond's light fills the palace.

10. Visitors' eyes open wide when they see all the colors.

B. Write each singular possessive noun from Part A.

1. _____   2. _____   3. _____

4. _____   5. _____

C. Write each plural possessive noun from Part A.

1. _____   2. _____   3. _____

4. _____   5. _____

Possessive Nouns

A **possessive noun** shows ownership. Add **'s** to make a singular noun show ownership. Add an apostrophe (') after the **s** of a plural noun to show ownership.

A. Underline the possessive noun in each sentence. Write _S_ on the line if the possessive noun is singular. Write _P_ if the possessive noun is plural.

1.   Anna's family took a walk in the woods.   _____

2.   They saw two birds' nests high up in a tree.   _____

3.   A yellow butterfly landed on Brad's backpack.   _____

4.   Anna liked the pattern of the butterfly's wings.   _____

5.   A turtle's shell had many spots.   _____

6.   Anna took pictures of two chipmunks' homes.   _____

7.   The animals' tails had dark stripes.   _____

B. Complete each sentence with the singular possessive form of the noun in ( ).

1.   Jim was going to play basketball at _____ house. (Carol)

2.   One of _____ new sneakers was missing. (Jim)

3.   He looked under his _____ desk. (sister)

4.   He crawled under his _____ bed to look. (brother)

5.   It was outside in his _____ flower garden. (dad)

6.   The _____ lace had been chewed. (sneaker)

7.   Jim saw his _____ footprints in the dirt. (dog)

Possessive Nouns

A. Choose the singular possessive noun to complete each sentence.

1. Joan _____ backpack was stuffed with library books.
   ○ Kramer
   ○ Kramers'
   ○ Kramer's

2. She should have borrowed her _____ large book bag.
   ○ mothers'
   ○ mother's
   ○ mothers

3. Her little _____ book was due back by five o'clock.
   ○ brother's
   ○ brothers'
   ○ brothers

4. A sign on a _____ desk warned of fines for late books.
   ○ librarians'
   ○ librarians
   ○ librarian's

5. _____ heart raced as she got there just in time.
   ○ Joan's
   ○ Joan
   ○ Joans'

B. Choose the plural possessive noun to complete each sentence.

1. All the _____ telescopes were loaded onto the space shuttle
   ○ astronomers'
   ○ astronomers
   ○ astronomer's

2. At take-off both _____ trails were long and straight.
   ○ engine's
   ○ engines'
   ○ engines

3. The _____ loud cheers filled the air.
   ○ spectators
   ○ spectator's
   ○ spectators'

4. Everyone applauded for the many _____ good work.
   ○ scientists'
   ○ scientist's
   ○ scientists

5. The four _____ pictures appeared on the news.
   ○ astronauts
   ○ astronaut's
   ○ astronauts'

Subject and Object Pronouns

A **pronoun** *takes the place of a noun or nouns in a sentence. The words* **I**, **you**, **she**, **he**, **it**, **we**, *and* **they** *are subject pronouns. Use one of these pronouns to take the place of a subject in a sentence.*

A. Underline the subject pronoun in each sentence.

1. We are going to the dentist.

2. It won't take long.

3. I went in first.

4. She asked the assistant for help.

5. He gave the dentist some pink toothpaste.

6. They said the toothpaste would taste like strawberries.

7. You will like the taste, too.

B. Decide which pronoun in the box can replace the underlined subject. Write the pronoun on the line. Remember to capitalize.

she	he	it	we	they

1. Dr. De Soto is a popular dentist. _____

2. Mrs. De Soto is his assistant. _____

3. The fox and the rabbit are waiting to be seen. _____

4. The fox has a bad toothache. _____

5. The chair is ready for the next patient. _____

6. Dr. and Mrs. De Soto do not trust the fox. _____

7. Roger and I enjoy reading this story. _____

Subject and Object Pronouns

*A **pronoun** takes the place of a noun or nouns in a sentence. The words **me**, **you**, **him**, **her**, **it**, **us**, and **them** are object pronouns. Use these object pronouns in the predicates of sentences.*

A. Underline the object pronoun in each sentence.

1. Aunt Cindy gave us a football.

2. Our dog Rex found it.

3. He thinks the ball is for him.

4. I said, "Rex, that's not for you!"

5. Aunt Cindy gave me another ball for Rex.

6. Now Rex always wants to play with her.

7. I like to watch them.

B. Decide which object pronoun below can replace the underlined word or words. Write the object pronoun on the line.

1. I went to the movies with <u>Rachel and Kevin</u>.   _____

2. Kevin asked <u>Rachel</u> for some popcorn.   _____

3. Rachel was happy to share <u>the popcorn</u>.   _____

4. I accidentally bumped <u>Kevin</u>.   _____

5. The popcorn spilled all over <u>Rachel, Kevin, and me</u>.   _____

C. Write two sentences. In one sentence use a subject pronoun. In the other sentence use an object pronoun.

1. _____

2. _____

Subject and Object Pronouns

Decide which pronoun can replace the underlined words.
Fill in the bubble next to the correct answer.

1. Uncle Sean is taking <u>Melina and me</u> ice skating at the pond.
   - ○ they
   - ○ us
   - ○ her

2. <u>The pond</u> freezes by late December.
   - ○ He
   - ○ You
   - ○ It

3. <u>Melina</u> knows how to skate.
   - ○ She
   - ○ Her
   - ○ I

4. Uncle Sean shows <u>Melina</u> how to skate backwards.
   - ○ her
   - ○ she
   - ○ them

5. I spot <u>skaters</u> nearby.
   - ○ us
   - ○ we
   - ○ them

6. <u>Pablo and Kim</u> are my friends.
   - ○ Us
   - ○ They
   - ○ Them

7. <u>Uncle Sean</u> skates over to say hello.
   - ○ It
   - ○ He
   - ○ Us

8. <u>Pablo, Kim, and I</u> listen to Uncle Sean's jokes.
   - ○ We
   - ○ Them
   - ○ Us

9. Everyone likes <u>Uncle Sean</u>.
   - ○ me
   - ○ he
   - ○ him

10. They will join <u>Uncle Sean, Melina, and me</u> for hot apple cider.
   - ○ it
   - ○ we
   - ○ us

Possessive Pronouns

A **possessive pronoun** shows ownership or belonging. It takes the place of a noun that shows ownership. **My**, **your**, **his**, **her**, **its**, **our**, and **their** are possessive pronouns.

A. Circle the subject pronoun in each sentence. Then underline the possessive pronoun. Use these answers to fill in the chart.

1. I am planning a trip with my family.

2. Will you wear your sunglasses?

3. He will bring his camera.

4. She will take her dog along.

5. It will eat all its food.

6. We will enjoy our vacation.

7. They will show their pictures.

Subject Pronouns	Possessive Pronouns
I	my

B. Underline the possessive pronoun in each sentence.

1. The desert is their home.

2. Her umbrella blocks out the sun.

3. That javelina likes to play his guitar.

4. His address is 1 Tumbleweed Avenue.

5. Coyote said, "My stomach is growling."

6. "I'll blow your house down," Coyote shouted.

7. Its walls are made of tumbleweeds.

8. "Our house is strong," the third Javelina said.

Possessive Pronouns

*A **possessive pronoun** shows ownership or belonging. It takes the place of a noun that shows ownership. **My**, **your**, **his**, **her**, **its**, **our**, and **their** are possessive pronouns.*

A. Complete each sentence. Write the correct pronoun in ( ) on the line.

1. Nicole likes to pick apples at _____ farm. (we, our)

2. Autumn is _____ favorite season. (her, she)

3. Dad says, "Please use _____ special basket." (I, my)

4. It was _____ birthday present from Grandpa. (he, his)

5. Dad said that _____ handle was carved by a famous artist.
   (their, its)

6. I tell Dad, "We will not forget to take _____ basket." (your, you)

7. Later, my mom and dad enjoyed _____ apple pie. (their, they)

B. Read each sentence. Write the possessive pronoun that can replace the underlined word or words.

1. The art project was due soon, but <u>Zach's</u> computer

   was broken. _____

2. My brother was using <u>my family's</u> computer.   _____

3. Zach borrowed <u>Angela's</u> computer instead.   _____

4. He loaded a picture into <u>the computer's</u> scanner.   _____

5. <u>Zach's</u> idea was to stretch the picture into a funny shape. _____

6. <u>Tim's and Ming's</u> projects were exactly the same!   _____

C. Write a sentence using the possessive pronouns *my* and *her*.

_____

Possessive Pronouns

A. Read each sentence. Fill in the bubble next to the possessive pronoun.

1. She is fixing her tree fort.
   - ○ She
   - ○ is
   - ○ her

2. Its roof started leaking after a storm.
   - ○ Its
   - ○ a
   - ○ after

3. Now we can eat our lunch without getting wet.
   - ○ we
   - ○ our
   - ○ without

4. I will share my favorite snack with a friend.
   - ○ I
   - ○ my
   - ○ will

5. He will bring his CD player.
   - ○ his
   - ○ He
   - ○ will

B. Choose the possessive pronoun that can replace the underlined word or words.

1. Erika's tire-patch kit is very helpful.
   - ○ My
   - ○ Our
   - ○ Her

2. She will use it to fix Brad's flat tire.
   - ○ he
   - ○ his
   - ○ their

3. The tire's inner tube has a slow leak.
   - ○ Its
   - ○ Our
   - ○ Their

4. Joel's and Diane's bike chains need to be oiled.
   - ○ Our
   - ○ Their
   - ○ Her

5. Now everyone can bike to my family's picnic.
   - ○ its
   - ○ our
   - ○ your

Compound Subjects and Predicates

A **compound subject** is two or more nouns connected by and. A **compound predicate** is two or more verbs connected by **and**.

A. Underline the nouns that form each compound subject. Then circle the word that connects the nouns.

1. Laura and Ramona are popular story characters.

2. In one story, Pa, Ma, and Laura traveled far.

3. The dog and horses trotted along.

4. Ma and Pa drove the wagon all day.

5. Grass and trees grow on the prairie.

B. Underline the verbs that form each compound predicate. Then circle the word that connects the verbs.

1. The wagon swayed and creaked.

2. Laura hummed and sang.

3. The road twisted and turned.

4. Pet and Patty neighed and snorted.

5. The deer stopped and stared.

C. Complete sentence 1 with two nouns joined by and. Complete sentence 2 with two verbs joined by and.

1. The _____ sang all day.

2. The dog _____ all the way home.

Compound Subjects and Predicates

*A **compound subject** is two or more nouns connected by and. A **compound predicate** is two or more verbs connected by **and**.*

A. Underline the compound subject or the compound predicate in each sentence. Write *CS* above each compound subject and *CP* above each compound predicate.

1. Mike and Jody moved away.

2. They often call and e-mail us.

3. Mike jogs and swims every day.

4. Phil and Jan will visit them.

5. Juan and Yoshi moved here from other countries.

6. They speak and read English very well.

7. Lori, Sam, and Beth wrote a play about moving.

8. They practiced and presented it to the class.

9. We clapped and smiled at the end.

10. The parents and the principal liked the play.

B. Complete one sentence with the compound subject. Complete the other sentence with the compound predicate.

My dad and sister   **barked and jumped**

1. Buster _____ when we got home.

2. _____ played word games for an hour.

Compound Subjects and Predicates

A. Look at the underlined part of each sentence. Fill in the bubble that tells if it is a compound subject or a compound predicate.

1. <u>My brother and I</u> went to the grocery store in town.
   ○ compound subject
   ○ compound predicate

2. We <u>talked and laughed</u> all the way there.
   ○ compound subject
   ○ compound predicate

3. <u>My sister and Mom</u> met us at the store.
   ○ compound subject
   ○ compound predicate

4. We <u>cooked and ate</u> some delicious blueberry pancakes.
   ○ compound subject
   ○ compound predicate

5. <u>The bus and train</u> arrived late in the station.
   ○ compound subject
   ○ compound predicate

B. Complete each sentence. Fill in the bubble next to the compound subject or compound predicate.

1. ——— planned the class trip.
   ○ Paul, Luz, and Annie
   ○ The family
   ○ The children

2. The ——— painted pictures of bears.
   ○ I
   ○ teacher and students
   ○ We all

3. Jane ——— her poem.
   ○ read
   ○ wrote and proofread
   ○ practiced

4. Dad ——— the letter.
   ○ copied
   ○ e-mailed
   ○ stamped and mailed

5. My little brother ———.
   ○ slept
   ○ ran, skipped, and jumped
   ○ woke up

Scholastic Professional Books

Contractions

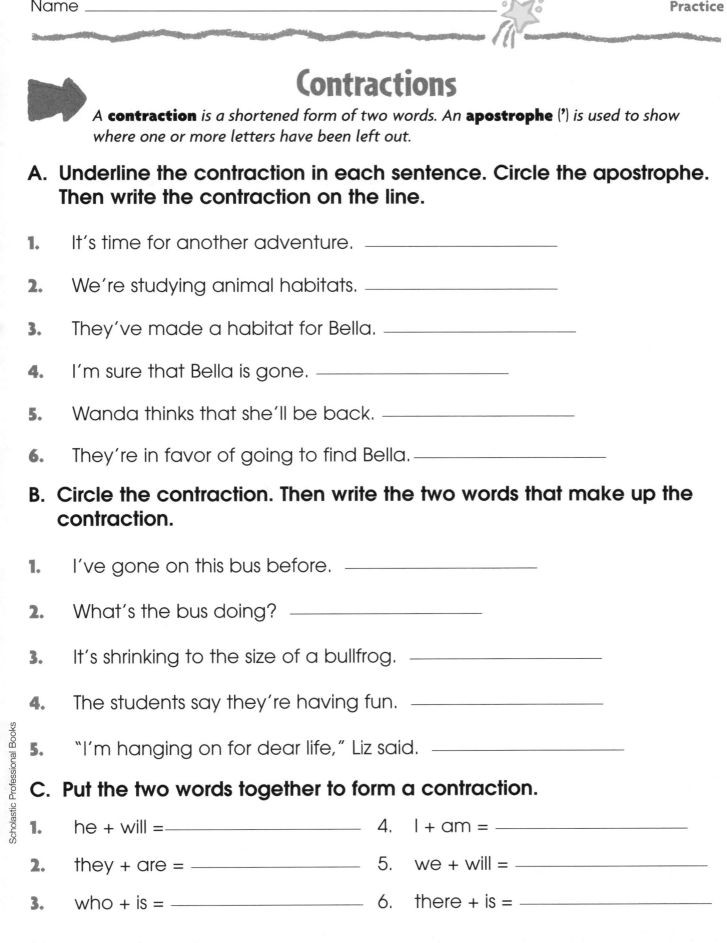

A **contraction** is a shortened form of two words. An **apostrophe** (') is used to show where one or more letters have been left out.

A. Underline the contraction in each sentence. Circle the apostrophe. Then write the contraction on the line.

1. It's time for another adventure. _____

2. We're studying animal habitats. _____

3. They've made a habitat for Bella. _____

4. I'm sure that Bella is gone. _____

5. Wanda thinks that she'll be back. _____

6. They're in favor of going to find Bella. _____

B. Circle the contraction. Then write the two words that make up the contraction.

1. I've gone on this bus before. _____

2. What's the bus doing? _____

3. It's shrinking to the size of a bullfrog. _____

4. The students say they're having fun. _____

5. "I'm hanging on for dear life," Liz said. _____

C. Put the two words together to form a contraction.

1. he + will = _____   4. I + am = _____

2. they + are = _____   5. we + will = _____

3. who + is = _____   6. there + is = _____

Contractions

A **contraction** is a shortened form of two words. An **apostrophe** (') is used to show where one or more letters have been left out.

Complete each sentence with a contraction made from the two words in parentheses. Write the contraction on the line.

1.   _____ in the package? (What is)

2.   My mom says _____ for me. (it is)

3.   _____ so excited! (I am)

4.   _____ birthdays great? (Are not)

5.   I _____ wait to open my gifts. (cannot)

6.   I hope my mom _____ mind if I tear the wrapping

     paper. (does not)

7.   "Be careful. _____ very delicate," she says. (They are)

8.   I _____ want to wait another second. (did not)

9.   In fact, _____ never been very patient. (I have)

10. I _____ mean to keep you wondering. (do not)

11. In the box, _____ a tiny cat family made of china.

     (there is)

Imagine not using any contractions when you talk. How long do you think you could keep it up? Write what you think.

Contractions

A. **Fill in the bubble next to the two words that make up the underlined contraction.**

1. <u>We're</u> going to see a nature movie.
   - ⭘ We have
   - ⭘ We is
   - ⭘ We are

2. "<u>You'll</u> learn about living things," our teacher said.
   - ⭘ You are
   - ⭘ You will
   - ⭘ I will

3. <u>We've</u> been studying animal habitats in science.
   - ⭘ We have
   - ⭘ We are
   - ⭘ You are

4. <u>I'm</u> writing a report on how animals communicate.
   - ⭘ I have
   - ⭘ I am
   - ⭘ I will

5. <u>It's</u> about how animals use their senses.
   - ⭘ It is
   - ⭘ Is not
   - ⭘ He is

B. **Fill in the bubble next to the contraction for the underlined words.**

1. The teacher asked, "<u>Who is</u> writing about birds?"
   - ⭘ Won't
   - ⭘ Who's
   - ⭘ What's

2. <u>There is</u> a new bird exhibit at the museum.
   - ⭘ There's
   - ⭘ They've
   - ⭘ Where's

3. I hope <u>she will</u> be there Saturday morning.
   - ⭘ she's
   - ⭘ I'll
   - ⭘ she'll

4. The museum <u>does not</u> open until 10 A.M.
   - ⭘ doesn't
   - ⭘ didn't
   - ⭘ isn't

5. <u>Do not</u> forget your notebook and pencil.
   - ⭘ Doesn't
   - ⭘ Don't
   - ⭘ Shouldn't

Using Punctuation

Quotation marks *show the exact words of a speaker.* **Commas** *appear between the day and year in a date, between the city and state in a location, and between the lines of an address.*

A. Add quotation marks to show the speaker's exact words.

1.   I have a strange case, said Mr. Brown.

2.   What's strange about it? asked Encyclopedia.

3.   Seventeen years ago Mr. Hunt found an elephant, began Mr. Brown.

4.   Where did he find it? asked Mrs. Brown.

5.   The elephant just appeared in his window, answered Mr. Brown.

6.   He must have fainted! exclaimed Encyclopedia.

7.   No, Mr. Hunt bought him, said Mr. Brown.

B. Add commas wherever they are needed.

1.   I go to the library in Huntsville Alabama.

2.   It is located at 12 Oak Street Huntsville Alabama 36554.

3.   The last time I was there was January 8 2001.

4.   The books I checked out were due January 22 2001.

5.   My cousin Jeb goes to the branch library at 75 Peachtree Lane Farley Alabama 35802.

6.   Is it true that Donald Sobol once spoke at the library in Redstone Park Alabama?

7.   He spoke there on September 29 2000.

8.   He will soon read at 47 Draper Road Newportville Pennsylvania.

Using Punctuation

Quotation marks *show the exact words of a speaker.* **Commas** *appear between the day and year in a date, between the city and state in a location, between the lines of an address, and after all but the last item in a series.* **Underlining** *shows book titles.*

A. Read each sentence. Add any missing commas.

1. Mrs. Wu's bank is located at 92 Maple Avenue Inwood Texas 75209.

2. She opened an account there on September 8 2001.

3. She also uses the branch office in Lakewood Texas.

4. That branch is open weekdays Saturdays and some evenings.

5. The main office is closed Saturdays Sundays and all holidays.

6. Mrs. Wu saw Ms. Ames Mr. Pacheco and Mrs. Jefferson at the bank on Saturday.

7. They carried checks bills and deposits.

8. Mr. Pacheco has had an account at that bank since May 2 1974.

B. Read the sentences below. Add any missing quotation marks, commas, or underlining.

1. My favorite author is Jerry Spinelli said Rick.

2. Spinelli was born on February 1 1941.

3. His home town is Norristown Pennsylvania.

4. What are your favorite books by him? asked Teresa.

5. I like Maniac Magee Dump Days and Fourth Grade Rats   replied Rick.

Write a sentence that tells your own mailing address. Then name three things you enjoy receiving in the mail, such as letters from friends, magazines, or catalogs.

Using Punctuation

A. Each sentence is missing one type of punctuation: quotation marks, commas, or underlining. Fill in the bubble next to the type of punctuation that needs to be added to the sentence to make it correct.

1. We read a book called At the Zoo.
  ○ quotation mark
  ○ commas
  ○ underlining

2. It had pictures of a lion monkeys and bears.
  ○ quotation mark
  ○ commas
  ○ underlining

3. "Can we go to the wild animal show? asked Brent.
  ○ quotation mark
  ○ comma
  ○ underlining

4. The show will be in town on June 8 2002.
  ○ quotation mark
  ○ comma
  ○ underlining

B. Look at the underlined part of each sentence. Fill in the bubble that shows the correct answer.

1. I have a new baby sister! shouted Liz.
  ○ "I have a new baby sister"!
  ○ "I have a new baby sister!"
  ○ correct as is

2. She was born on April 3 2002.
  ○ April 3, 2002
  ○ April, 3 2002
  ○ correct as is

3. She was born at 1800 River Road, Centerville, North Carolina.
  ○ 1800 River Road Centerville, North Carolina
  ○ 1800 River Road Centerville North Carolina
  ○ correct as is

4. She has tiny fingers tiny toes and a big scream
  ○ tiny fingers, tiny toes and a big scream.
  ○ tiny fingers, tiny toes, and a big scream
  ○ correct as is

Irregular Verbs

Irregular verbs *do not form the past tense by adding* **-ed**. *They change their form.*

A. In each sentence, underline the past tense of the verb in ( ). Then write the past-tense verb on the line.

1. Jessi told Jackie to be ready early. (tell) _____

2. He was nervous about his science fair project. (is) _____

3. Jackie's friends came to the table. (come) _____

4. They saw the volcano there. (see) _____

5. Jackie knew his speech by heart. (know) _____

6. The sign on the exhibit fell over. (fall) _____

7. The teacher lit the match for Jackie. (light) _____

8. Jackie threw his hands into the air. (throw) _____

B. Complete each sentence. Write the correct verb on the line.

fell   threw   saw   knew

1. Jackie _____ all about volcanoes.

2. He once _____ a real volcano.

3. It _____ ashes and fire into the air.

4. The ashes _____ all over the ground.

C. Complete each sentence. Use the past form of *know* in one and the past form of *tell* in the other. Sample answers are given.

1. When I was five, I _____

2. My brother _____

Irregular Verbs

Irregular verbs *do not form the past tense by adding* **-ed**. *They change their form.*

A. Complete each sentence. Write the past form of the verb in ( ).

1. Erin _____ dry lima beans at the store. (buy)

2. Her family _____ lima beans for dinner. (eat)

3. Erin _____ six lima bean plants for the science fair. (grow)

4. She _____ her project on Saturday. (begin)

5. Erin _____ three plants water and light. (give)

6. The other plants _____ all day in a dark closet. (sit)

B. Circle the past-tense form of the verb in ( ) to complete each sentence.

1. The judges (come, came) to Erin's table.

2. She (won, win) a blue ribbon.

3. Erin's family (went, go) to the fair.

4. One lima bean plant (is, was) 6 inches tall.

5. Two plants (fall, fell) over in the pot.

6. Erin (said, say), "I learned a lot."

C. Write a sentence about growing something. Use a past-tense irregular verb in your sentence.

_____

_____

Scholastic Success With

WRITING

Dinnertime

A **sentence** is a group of words that expresses a complete thought.
A **fragment** is an incomplete thought.

Write *S* for sentence or *F* for fragment.

_____ 1. Insects eat many different things.

_____ 2. Some of these things.

_____ 3. The praying mantis eats other insects.

_____ 4. Water bugs eat tadpoles and small frogs.

_____ 5. Flower nectar makes good.

_____ 6. Build nests to store their food.

_____ 7. The cockroach will eat almost anything.

_____ 8. Termites.

_____ 9. A butterfly caterpillar.

_____ 10. Bite animals and people.

_____ 11. Some insects will even eat paper.

_____ 12. Insects have different mouth parts to help

them eat.

 On another piece of paper, write about three things you did during the day using only sentence fragments. Have someone read it. Did they understand it? Why or why not?

Scholastic Professional Books

Name _____

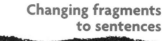
A Real Meal

A **sentence** is a group of words that expresses a complete thought.

Change each fragment from page 224 to a sentence by adding words from the Bug Box. Remember to use a capital letter at the beginning and a period at the end of each sentence.

1. _____

2. _____

3. _____

4. _____

5. _____

6. _____

are wood eaters.

Mosquitoes

are wood, plants, and nectar.

eats leaves.

food for bees.

Wasps

BUG BOX

 On another piece of paper, write a fragment about your favorite dinner. Then change it into a sentence.

Name _____

Rock Your World

*A telling sentence is called a **statement**.*
A statement begins with a capital letter and ends with a period.

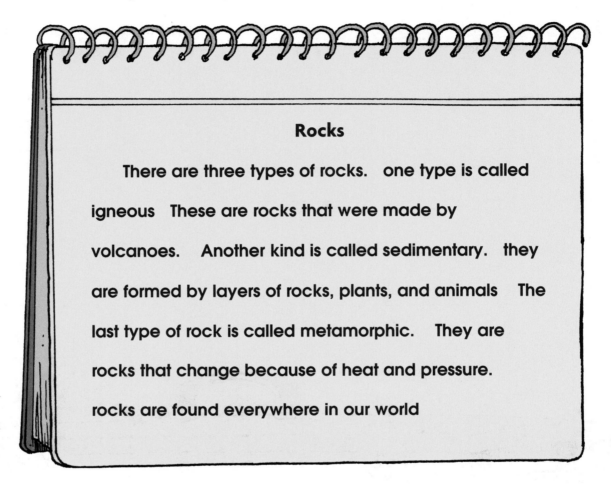

Rocks

There are three types of rocks.   one type is called igneous   These are rocks that were made by volcanoes.   Another kind is called sedimentary.   they are formed by layers of rocks, plants, and animals   The last type of rock is called metamorphic.   They are rocks that change because of heat and pressure. rocks are found everywhere in our world

Find the three statements that are missing a capital letter and a period. Rewrite the three statements correctly.

1. _____

2. _____

3. _____

Rock and Roll

A statement is used to answer a question.

Use a complete sentence to write the answer
to each question.

1. How many types of rocks are on our planet? (three)

There are three types of rocks on our planet.

2. How hot is the melted rock inside the earth? (more than 2000°F)

_____

3. Where are most igneous rocks formed? (inside the earth)

_____

4. What type of rock is marble? (metamorphic)

_____

5. In what type of rock are fossils found? (sedimentary)

_____

Scholastic Professional Books

Name _____

Wacky World

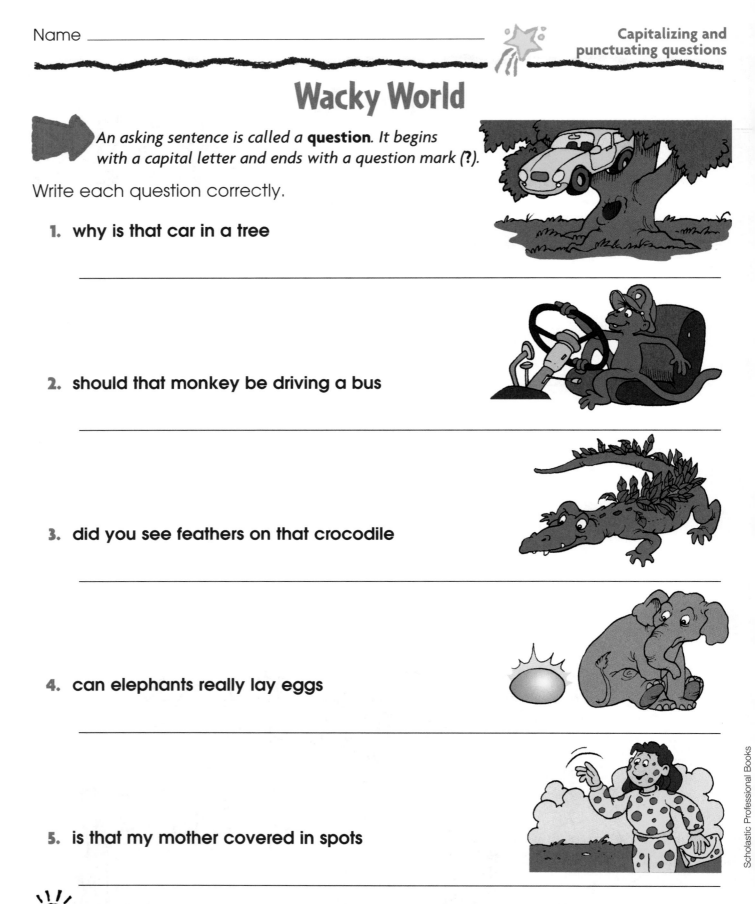

*An asking sentence is called a **question**. It begins
with a capital letter and ends with a question mark (**?**).*

Write each question correctly.

1. why is that car in a tree

_____

2. should that monkey be driving a bus

_____

3. did you see feathers on that crocodile

_____

4. can elephants really lay eggs

_____

5. is that my mother covered in spots

_____

**On another piece of paper, draw your own picture of a wacky world. Write two questions
about your picture.**

Scholastic Professional Books

The Real World

 A question begins with a capital letter and ends with a question mark (?). It often begins with one of the words listed below.

Who	*When*
Will	*Can*
What	*Why*
Would	*Did*
Where	*How*
Should	*Is*

Imagine that you are interviewing your favorite famous person (for example, an actor, a president, or a rock star). Write five questions you would ask this person. Use a different beginning word for each question.

I am interviewing _____.

1. _____

2. _____

3. _____

4. _____

5. _____

💡 **On another piece of paper, write an answer to each question.**

The Dry Desert

A sentence that shows strong feeling or excitement is called an **exclamation**. It ends with an exclamation point (**!**).

Finish each sentence with a period, a question mark, or an exclamation point.

1. It is hard for plants and animals to get water in the desert

2. Can a cactus live without enough water

3. Some deserts are hot, and others are cool

4. A lizard is running toward us

5. Does a camel really store water in its hump

6. Some deserts are cold and covered with ice

7. How often does it rain in the desert

8. The largest desert is the Sahara

9. Are there any deserts in the United States

10. There is a long snake slithering across the sand

11. People who live in the desert travel to find water

12. I see water up ahead

 Read these two sentences aloud: I hear a noise. I hear a noise!
How does your voice change when you read an exclamation?

Scholastic Professional Books

The Sunny Sahara

Every sentence begins with a capital letter.
A statement ends with a period.
A question ends with a question mark.
An exclamation ends with an exclamation point.

Write each sentence correctly.

1. the Sahara Desert is in Africa

_____

2. do people live in the Sahara Desert

_____

3. the Sahara Desert is about the same size as the United States

_____

4. how high is the temperature in the Sahara Desert

_____

5. once the temperature reached 138°F

_____

On another piece of paper, write a sentence with two mistakes. Ask a friend to circle the mistakes.

Scholastic Professional Books

A Snowy Scene

Complete:

Every sentence begins with a _____.

A statement ends with a _____.

A question ends with a _____.

An exclamation ends with an _____.

Write two statements, questions, and exclamations about the picture.

Statements:

1. _____

2. _____

Questions:

1. _____

2. _____

Exclamations:

1. _____

2. _____

On another piece of paper, turn this statement into a question and an exclamation: It snowed ten inches last night.

A Snowy Story

*After you write a sentence, go back and look for mistakes. This is called **proofreading** your work.*

Use these proofreading marks to correct 11 mistakes in the story.

mars = **Make a capital letter.**

⊙ = **Add a period.**

(?) = **Add a question mark.**

(!) = **Add an exclamation point.**

Snow Day

the kids at Elm School had been waiting for a

snowstorm? they knew school would be

canceled if the storm brought a lot of snow last

week their wish came true it snowed 12 inches

school was canceled, and the kids spent the day

sledding, building snowmen, and drinking hot

chocolate. it was a great snow day

Find two sentences that had two mistakes and write them correctly.

1. _____

2. _____

On another piece of paper, write a sentence with two mistakes. Ask a friend to find the mistakes.

Sentences That Slither

A sentence tells about someone or something.
This is called the **subject**.

Write the letter to show the subject of each sentence.

A. The short blind snake

B. Tree snakes

C. The flowerpot snake

D. Bird snakes

E. A pit viper snake

F. All snakes

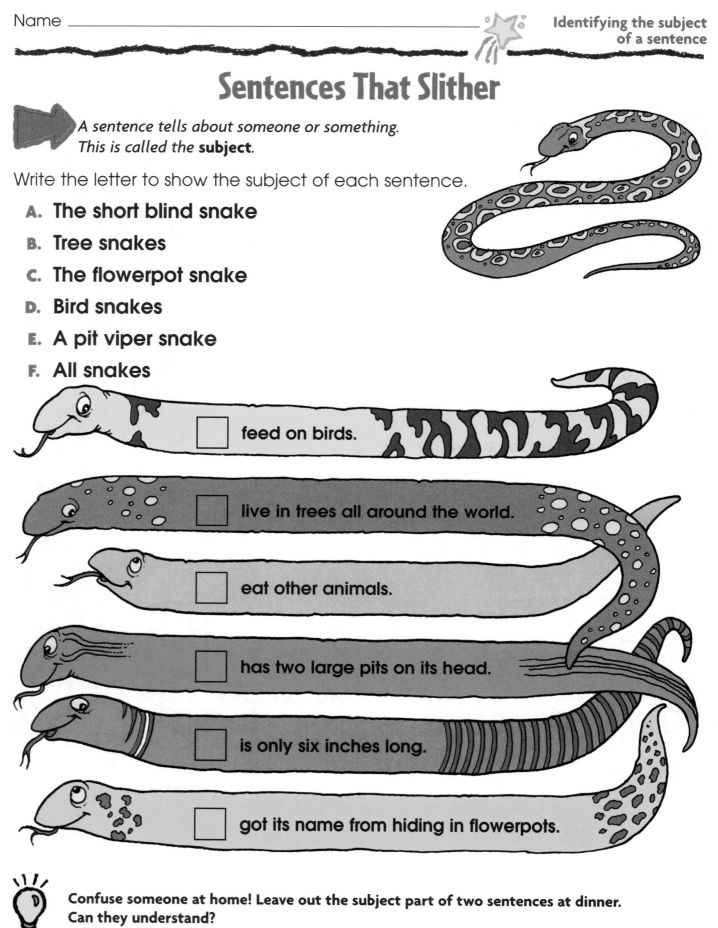

□ feed on birds.

□ live in trees all around the world.

□ eat other animals.

□ has two large pits on its head.

□ is only six inches long.

□ got its name from hiding in flowerpots.

Confuse someone at home! Leave out the subject part of two sentences at dinner.
Can they understand?

Scholastic Professional Books

A Reptile Fact Sheet

*A sentence tells what the subject does or is. This part of the sentence is called the **verb**.*

Use the list of subjects as the beginning for eight sentences. Then add a verb to tell what the subject is doing.

Snakes

Lizards

Crocodiles

Turtles

Dinosaurs

Iguanas

Alligators

Pythons

1. _____

2. _____

3. _____

4. _____

5. _____

6. _____

7. _____

8. _____

On another piece of paper, write three sentences about your favorite things to do after school. Circle the verb in each sentence.

Stretching Sentences

A sentence is more interesting when it includes more than just a subject and a verb. It may tell where or when the sentence is happening. It may also tell why something is happening.

Write a sentence describing each set of pictures. Include a part that tells where, why, or how something is happening.

1. _____

2. _____

3. _____

4. _____

 Find a cartoon in the newspaper. Use the pictures to write a sentence on another piece of paper that includes a subject, a verb, and a part that tells where, when, or why.

Scholastic Professional Books

Stretch It!

A sentence includes a subject and a verb. A sentence is more interesting when it also includes a part that tells where, when, or why.

Add more information to each sentence by telling where, when, or why. Write the complete new sentence.

1. Mom is taking us shopping. *Where?*

_____

2. The stores are closing. *When?*

_____

3. We need to find a gift for Dad. *Why?*

_____

4. I will buy new jeans. *Where?*

_____

5. We may eat lunch. *When?*

_____

Find two sentences in your favorite book that include a subject, verb, and a part that tells where, when, or why. Write the sentences on another piece of paper.

Ketchup and Mustard

Sometimes two sentences can be combined to make one sentence.

Sentences that share the same subject seem to go together like ketchup and mustard. Rewrite the sentences by combining their endings with the word *and*.

1. I ordered a hamburger.
   I ordered a milkshake.

   I ordered a hamburger and a milkshake.

2. I like salt on my French fries.
   I like ketchup on my French fries.

   _____

3. My mom makes great pork chops.
   My mom makes great applesauce.

   _____

4. My dad eats two huge helpings of meat loaf!
   My dad eats two huge helpings of potatoes!

   _____

5. My brother helps set the table.
   My brother helps clean the dishes.

   _____

6. We have cookies for dessert.
   We have ice cream for dessert.

   _____

Scholastic Professional Books

Let's Eat Out!

 Two sentences can be combined to make one sentence by using the words **although**, **after**, **because**, **until**, *and* **while**.

Choose a word from the menu to combine the two sentences into one sentence.

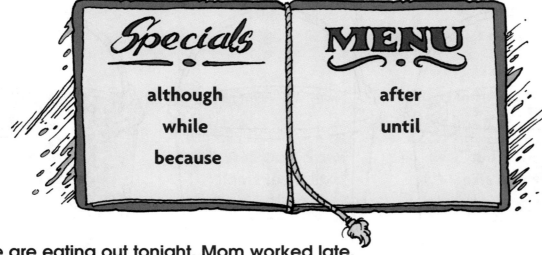

Specials

although

while

because

MENU

after

until

1. We are eating out tonight. Mom worked late.

_____

2. We are going to Joe's Fish Shack. I do not like fish.

_____

3. Dad said I can play outside. It's time to leave.

_____

4. We can play video games. We are waiting for our food.

_____

5. We may stop by Ida's Ice Cream Shop. We leave the restaurant.

_____

 Read the back of a cereal box. Find two sentences that could be combined.

Buckets of Fun

A **describing word** *helps you imagine how something looks, feels, smells, sounds, or tastes.*

Write a list of describing words on each bucket to fit the bucket's category.

words that
describe size

words that describe
taste or smell

words that
describe sounds

words that describe
how something feels

words that describe
weather

words that describe
feelings

Make a "mystery bag" by putting a secret object inside. Tell someone at home about the object inside using describing words!

At the Beach

A **describing word** *makes a sentence more interesting.*

Read the describing words found in the beach balls. Add the describing words to make each sentence more interesting. Write each new sentence.

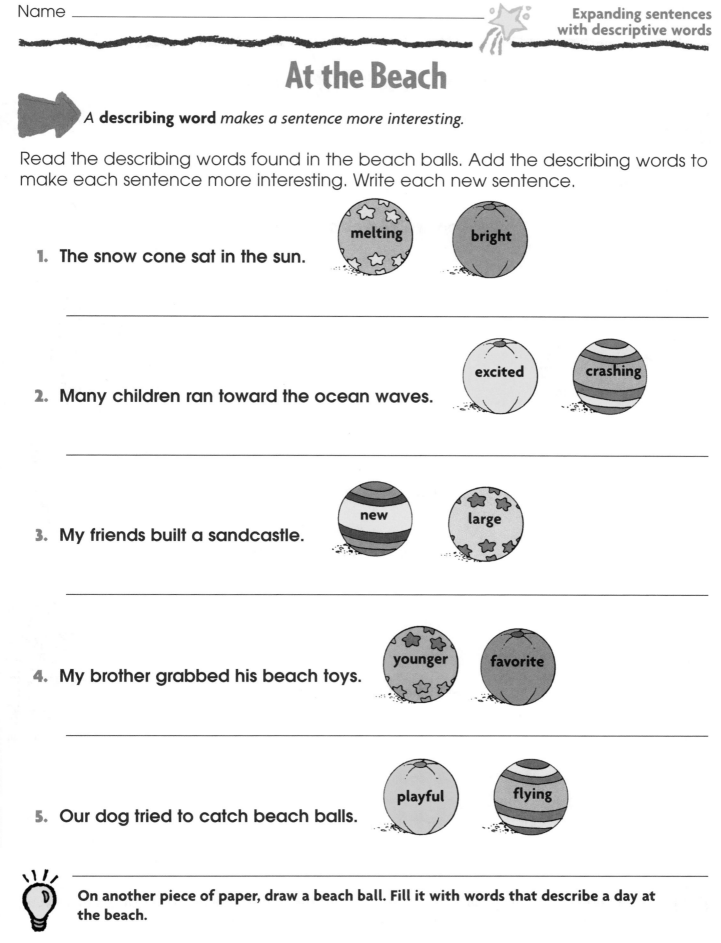

1. The snow cone sat in the sun.

   melting   bright

   _____

2. Many children ran toward the ocean waves.

   excited   crashing

   _____

3. My friends built a sandcastle.

   new   large

   _____

4. My brother grabbed his beach toys.

   younger   favorite

   _____

5. Our dog tried to catch beach balls.

   playful   flying

   _____

On another piece of paper, draw a beach ball. Fill it with words that describe a day at the beach.

The Great Outdoors

A **describing word** *can tell more about a subject or a verb.*

Add describing words to make each sentence more interesting.

1. The _____ hikers walked back to camp _____.

2. The _____ bird sang _____.

3. The _____ tree grew _____.

4. _____ children played _____.

5. My _____ sister swam _____.

6. The _____ crickets chirped _____.

7. The _____ flowers bloomed _____.

8. The _____ swing set creaked _____.

9. The _____ ice cream melted _____.

10. The _____ trees shook _____ in the storm.

Where do you like to spend time outside? On another piece of paper, write the name of your favorite outdoor place. Then write three words that describe it.

Outdoor Excitement

A **describing word** can be added to a sentence.

☐ = **Add a describing word.**   **She wore a** red **dress.**

Read the sentences about each picture. Then use proofreading marks to add a describing word to each sentence.

1. **The girl picked flowers.**

2. **The girl swatted the bees.**

3. **A bee stung the girl.**

1. **The boy played a game.**

2. **The boy won a trophy.**

3. **The boy held his trophy.**

Add two describing words to this sentence: The campers heard a sound in the night.

Crazy Cartoons

A story is more interesting when the characters talk with one another.

Use the speech bubbles to show what each character is saying.

Cut a comic strip from the newspaper. Glue it to another piece of paper and make large speech bubbles. Rewrite the cartoon with your own words.

What Did She Say?

Quotation marks (" ") *are used to show a character is talking in a story. They surround only the character's words.*

Fill in the speech bubbles to match the paragraph below each picture.

1. Daisy put on her rain boots, coat, and hat. "I think it's fun to splash in the puddles," she said.

2. As the rain continued, the puddles turned to streams. "Rain, rain, don't go away!" Daisy sang.

3. "Wow! I should have worn my bathing suit!" Daisy shouted as the water rose higher.

4. Then Daisy had an idea. She turned her umbrella upside down and climbed in. "It's a perfect day to go sailing," she said.

Ask someone at home for an old photograph of yourself and someone else. Glue it to another piece of paper and make speech bubbles to show what you may have been saying when the picture was taken.

Look Who's Talking!

Quotation marks surround a character's exact words. In a statement, use a comma to separate the character's exact words from the rest of the sentence. In a question and an exclamation, use the correct ending punctuation after the character's exact words.

Statement: **"I have to go now,"** said my friend.
Question: **"Where are you?"** asked my mom.
Exclamation: **"Wow!"** the boy exclaimed.

Write a sentence to match each speech bubble. Use the examples above to help you.

Somebody turned out the lights!

_____

_____

What makes you think I've been eating cookies?

_____

_____

My parents finally let me get my ears pierced.

_____

_____

On another piece of paper, write a conversation you had with a friend during the day. Use quotation marks to show what you and your friend each said.

Scholastic Professional Books

Chitchat

Quotation marks can be added to a story using these proofreading marks.

mars = **Make a capital letter.**   ⟨?⟩ = **Add a question mark.**   ⟨!⟩ = **Add an exclamation point.**

⟨•⟩ = **Add a period.**   ⟨,⟩ = **Add a comma.**   ⟨"⟩ ⟨"⟩ = **Add quotation marks.**

Find 16 mistakes in the story. Use proofreading marks to correct them.

Lucky Day

Drew woke up early on Saturday. No school today, he said He found

his mom working in the garden What are you doing ” he asked.

“I am planting these flowers, she answered.

Drew looked down He couldn't believe it. A four-leaf clover” he shouted

“This should help us win our big game today he said.

Drew's entire day was perfect. his sister shared her toys, the ice-cream

truck brought his favorite flavor, and his team won the big game “What a

day! he whispered to himself as he fell asleep that night.

On another piece of paper, write about your luckiest day. Include at least two sets of
quotation marks.

Under the Big Top

Sentences can be written in order of beginning (B), middle (M), and ending (E) to make a paragraph.

Write a middle and ending sentence to complete each paragraph.

B The circus started with a roll of drums and flashing lights.

M Next, _____

E Last, _____

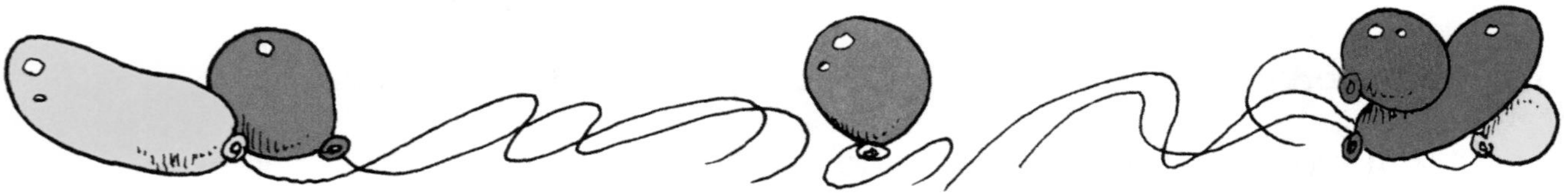

B The tightrope walker stepped into the spotlight.

M Next, _____

E Last, _____

B The lion tamer came on stage.

M Next, _____

E Last, _____

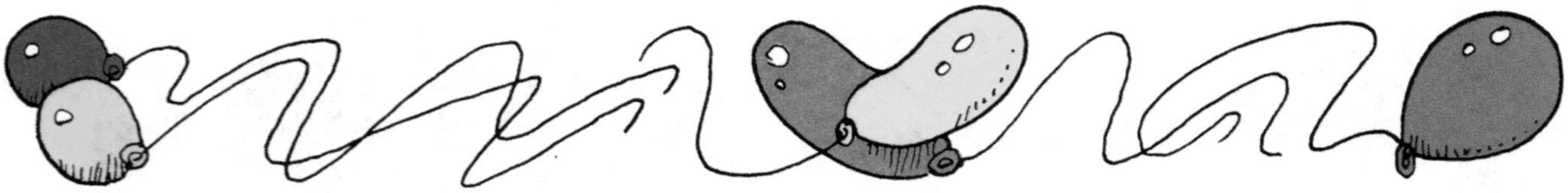

B The dancing ponies appeared in the center ring.

M Next, _____

E Last, _____

A Circus Train

 Sometimes a paragraph tells a story.

Write three sentences about each set of pictures to make a short story paragraph.

_____

_____

_____

_____

_____

_____

 **Read your paragraphs to a friend.**

Terrific Topics

A **paragraph** *is a group of sentences that tells about one idea, called the* **topic**.

Imagine that you are planning to write a paragraph about each topic below. Write three ideas for each topic.

gardening	fish	homework
1. flowers	1.	1.
2. vegetables	2.	2.
3. pesky insects	3.	3.
summer sports	**friends**	**favorite books**
1.	1.	1.
2.	2.	2.
3.	3.	3.
favorite movies	**American history**	**healthy foods**
1.	1.	1.
2.	2.	2.
3.	3.	3.

Scholastic Professional Books

It Just Doesn't Belong!

➤ *The sentence that tells the topic of a paragraph is called the* **topic sentence**.

Draw a line through the sentence that does not belong with the topic.

Topic: Dogs make great family pets.

Dogs have great hearing, which helps them protect a family from danger.

Most dogs welcome their owners with wagging tails.

My favorite kind of dog is a boxer.

Many dogs are willing to play with children in a safe manner.

Topic: The history of the American flag is quite interesting.

The first American flag had no stars at all.

Not much is known about the history of Chinese flags.

Historians cannot prove that Betsy Ross really made the first American flag.

The American flag has changed 27 times.

Topic: Hurricanes are called by different names depending on where they occur.

Hurricanes have strong, powerful winds.

In the Philippines, hurricanes are called baguios.

Hurricanes are called typhoons in the Far East.

Australian people use the name willy-willies to describe hurricanes.

Read a paragraph from a favorite chapter book. Read the topic sentence to someone at home.

Missing Topics

A topic sentence is sometimes called the **main idea**.

Read the groups of sentences. Then write a topic sentence that tells the main idea of the paragraph.

_____

_____

One reason is that guinea pigs do not usually bite. Second, guinea pigs don't make as much noise as other rodents might during the night. Last, they are large enough that they can be found if they ever get lost in a house.

_____

_____

First, spread peanut butter on two pieces of bread. Next, cut a banana into slices and lay them on top of the peanut butter. Then close the two pieces of bread into a sandwich. Last, eat up!

_____

_____

Frogs usually have longer legs and wetter skin than toads do. Many frogs live near a water source of some kind while toads prefer a damp, muddy environment. Frog eggs and toad eggs are different in shape.

 On another piece of paper, make a list of three subjects you know a lot about. Write a possible topic sentence for each of the subjects.

Scholastic Professional Books

Try These Topics

Writing a topic sentence takes thought because your entire paragraph must follow the main idea.

Write a topic sentence for each subject.

1. My Chores

_____

2. The Best Book Ever

_____

3. My Favorite After-School Activity

_____

4. Appropriate TV Shows for Kids

_____

5. Types of Coins

_____

6. Our Greatest Presidents

_____

Name _____

That Drives Me Crazy!

The sentences that follow the topic sentence tell more about the topic. They are called **supporting sentences**.

Read the paragraph below. Cross out the three sentences that do not support the topic.

My Pet Peeves

I am a pretty agreeable person, but there are a few things around my house that drive me crazy. One such thing is when my younger brothers go into my bedroom and destroy my building creations. My three-year-old brothers both have blonde hair. I also get upset when my sister sings at the dinner table. Her favorite sport is gymnastics. My greatest pet peeve is when my older brother taps his pencil on the kitchen table while I am studying spelling words. I wish I had a fish tank in my room. My brothers and sister are really great, but there are moments when they make me crazy!

Rewrite the paragraph above skipping the sentences that you crossed out. The new paragraph should have one topic sentence followed by the supporting sentences.

_____

_____

_____

_____

_____

_____

Do You Agree?

The supporting sentences in a paragraph tell more about the topic.

Write three supporting sentences to complete each paragraph.

Shorter Weeks

I think the school week should be shortened to four days for three

reasons. The first reason is _____

_____

_____ Another reason is _____

_____

_____ The last reason is _____

_____

_____ I think four-day

weeks just make more sense!

Looking Back:

Now proofread your paragraph for:

    capital letters and periods

    complete sentences

    describing words

    sentences that support the topic

On another piece of paper, write a paragraph that begins with this topic sentence: I think I should be able to stay up later for three reasons.

A Great Trick

The supporting sentences should be in an order that makes sense.

Read the topic sentence, then number the supporting
ideas first (1) to last (4).

Last week I played a great trick on my mom.

_____ won a huge rubber snake

_____ went to a carnival

_____ called my mom outside

_____ put snake in my mom's flower garden

Now use the topic sentence and ideas in the correct order to write a paragraph
telling the story. Be sure to use complete sentences.

_____

_____

_____

_____

_____

_____

_____

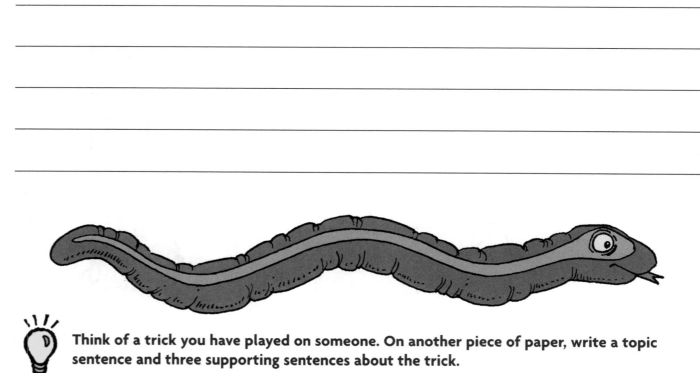

**Think of a trick you have played on someone. On another piece of paper, write a topic
sentence and three supporting sentences about the trick.**

Scholastic Professional Books

Good to Know

A good paragraph has at least three supporting sentences.

Finish the paragraphs below by writing three sentences that support each topic sentence.

Airplanes are useful in many ways. First, _____

_____

Second, _____

_____

Third, _____

_____

Life as a child today is quite different from the way it was when my

parents were young. First, _____

_____

Second, _____

_____

Third, _____

_____

Clip a topic sentence from a magazine or newspaper article. Glue it to another piece of paper and write three supporting sentences.

Closing Time!

*The last sentence in a paragraph is called the **closing sentence**. It retells the topic sentence in a new way.*

Find a closing sentence to match each topic sentence. Write the closing sentence.

Closing Sentences

Some gardeners in Florida and Texas can enjoy their flowers all year long.

Of all the seasons, autumn is the best.

Life would never be the same without computers.

There are many subjects in school, but math is the most difficult.

Though dangerous, the job of an astronaut is
---

1. Fall is my favorite season in the year.

_____

2. Astronauts have one of the most exciting and dangerous jobs.

_____

3. Math is the toughest part of our school curriculum.

_____

4. Many types of flowers grow year-round in the southern states.

_____

5. Computer technology has changed many aspects of our lives.

_____

That's All Folks!

The **closing sentence** *retells the topic sentence or main idea of a paragraph.*

Write a closing sentence for each paragraph.

    All cyclists should wear helmets while riding their bikes. Many injuries occur to the head in biking accidents. Helmets could help prevent the injuries. Helmets also make cyclists more easily noticed by car drivers. _____

_____

_____

    There are many things to do on a rainy day. If you like to write, you could send a letter to a friend or make a book. If you prefer craft projects, you could make a bookmark or a collage. If you really enjoy games, you could play cards or build a puzzle. _____

_____

    The wheel must be one of the world's most important inventions. First, we would have no means of transportation if it were not for wheels. Second, we would not be able to enjoy many of our favorite pastimes, like in-line skating and riding a bike. Last, it would be very difficult to move heavy objects around without wheels. _____

_____

A Paragraph Plan

Follow these steps in planning a paragraph.
  1. Choose a topic (main idea).
  2. Brainstorm ideas about the topic. (You will need at least three.)
  3. Write a topic sentence.
  4. Write a closing sentence by retelling the topic sentence.

Follow this plan to write a paragraph about Ben Franklin.

1. Ben Franklin

2. a) inventor of bifocal eyeglasses and Franklin stove
   b) scientist who proved that lightning is electricity
   c) involved in writing the Declaration of Independence

3. Ben Franklin was a man of many talents.

4. Ben Franklin displayed his talents in many ways.

_____

_____

_____

_____

_____

_____

_____

_____

_____

Read your paragraph to yourself. Then add a describing word to each supporting sentence.

Scholastic Professional Books

My Very Own Paragraph

 Use a paragraph plan before you begin writing.

It is time to plan and write your own paragraph. You may want to use your own topic or one of the following topics: My Favorite Vacation, Collecting Coins, Our Pet Snake.

1. Choose a topic. _____

2. Brainstorm three supporting ideas.

   a) _____

   b) _____

   c) _____

3. Write a topic sentence. _____

4. Write a closing sentence. _____

Use the plan to write your own paragraph.

_____

_____

_____

_____

_____

_____

_____

Scholastic Professional Books

Do I Have a Story for You!

*A paragraph that tells a story is called a **narrative paragraph**. Its supporting sentences tell what happen at the beginning, middle, and end. A **story map** helps you plan the story's setting, characters, problem, and solution.*

Write a sentence about each part of the map. Then complete the plan for a narrative paragraph using the story map.

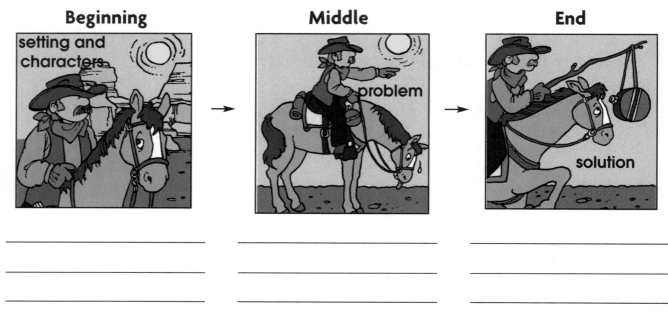

Beginning	**Middle**	**End**
setting and characters	problem	solution

1. Write a topic sentence. _____

   _____

2. Write a supporting sentence for the beginning, middle, and end.

   B) _____

   M) _____

   E) _____

3. Write a closing sentence. _____

   _____

On another piece of paper, use the plan to write a narrative paragraph.

Map It Out

Use a story map to help plan a narrative paragraph before you begin writing.

Draw pictures to complete the map. Then use it to write a narrative paragraph.

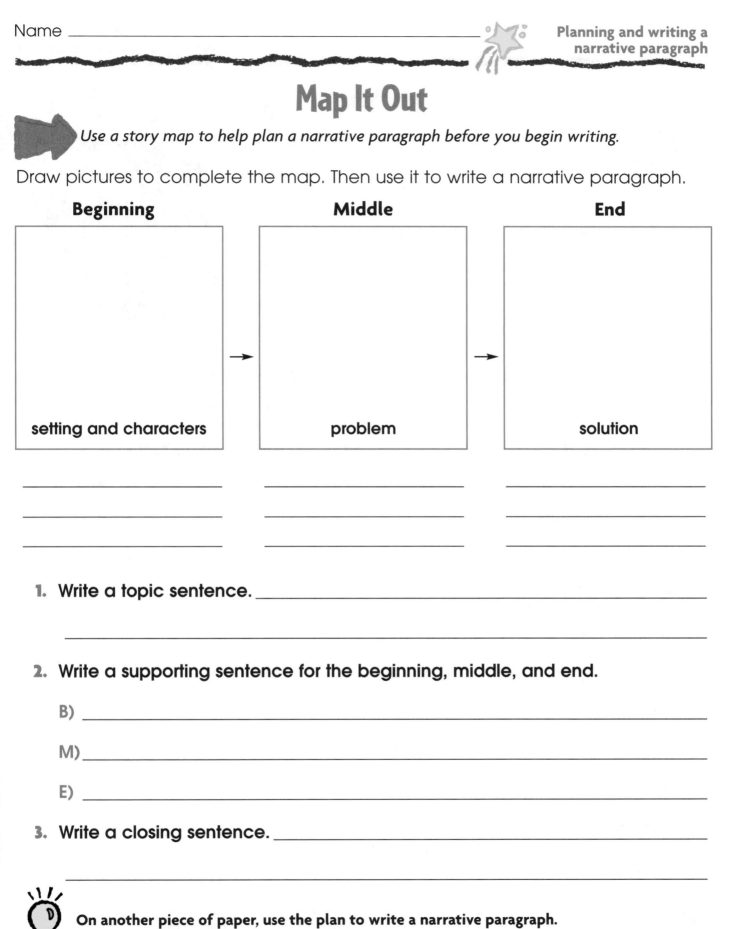

Beginning	**Middle**	**End**
setting and characters	problem	solution

_____   _____   _____

_____   _____   _____

_____   _____   _____

1. Write a topic sentence. _____

_____

2. Write a supporting sentence for the beginning, middle, and end.

B) _____

M) _____

E) _____

3. Write a closing sentence. _____

_____

On another piece of paper, use the plan to write a narrative paragraph.

I'm Sure You'll Agree!

A **persuasive paragraph** gives your opinion and tries to convince the reader to agree. Its supporting ideas are reasons that back up your opinion.

Reason 1

Topic sentence

→ Our family should have a dog for three reasons.

First, pets teach responsibility. If we get a dog, I will

feed him and take him for walks after school. The

second reason for having a pet is that he would ← Reason 2

make a good companion for me when everyone else is busy. I won't

drive Dad crazy always asking him to play catch with me. The third ← Reason 3

reason we need a dog is for safety. He would warn us of danger and

keep our house safe. For all of these reasons, I'm sure you'll agree that

we should jump in the car and head toward the adoption agency right

away. I don't know how we have made it this long without a dog! ← closing
sentence

Plan and write a persuasive paragraph asking your parents for something (such as a family trip, expensive new shoes, or an in-ground pool).

1. Choose a topic. _____

2. Write a topic sentence. _____

3. Brainstorm three supporting reasons.

Reason 1 _____

Reason 2 _____

Reason 3 _____

On another piece of paper, use your plan to write a persuasive paragraph.

Scholastic Professional Books

That's a Fact!

➤ *An **expository paragraph** provides facts or explains ideas. The supporting sentences give more details about the topic.*

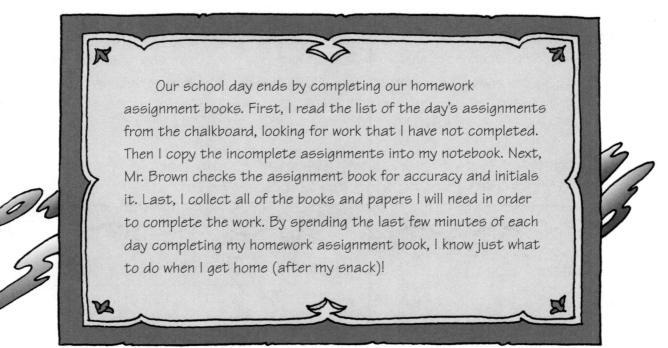

Our school day ends by completing our homework assignment books. First, I read the list of the day's assignments from the chalkboard, looking for work that I have not completed. Then I copy the incomplete assignments into my notebook. Next, Mr. Brown checks the assignment book for accuracy and initials it. Last, I collect all of the books and papers I will need in order to complete the work. By spending the last few minutes of each day completing my homework assignment book, I know just what to do when I get home (after my snack)!

Plan an expository paragraph explaining one part of your school day.

Write the topic sentence. _____

_____

List the four supporting ideas.

1) _____

2) _____

3) _____

4) _____

Write the closing sentence. _____

_____

💡 **On another piece of paper, use your plan to write an expository paragraph.**

Paragraph Pen Pals

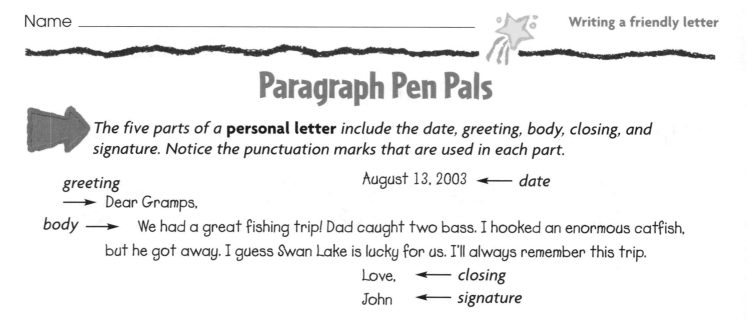

*The five parts of a **personal letter** include the date, greeting, body, closing, and signature. Notice the punctuation marks that are used in each part.*

August 13, 2003 ◄—— *date*

greeting
——► Dear Gramps,

body ——►   We had a great fishing trip! Dad caught two bass. I hooked an enormous catfish, but he got away. I guess Swan Lake is lucky for us. I'll always remember this trip.

Love, ◄—— *closing*

John ◄—— *signature*

Write a letter to an out-of-town family member. For the body of your letter, write an expository paragraph using the plan on page 265.

_____ (today's date)

_____

_____

_____

_____

_____

_____

_____

_____ ,

_____ (your name)

Scholastic Success With

MAPS

Map Basics

A map is a drawing of a place from above. A map can show all of Earth or just a small part of it. The map on this page shows a community.

Mill Town

Park Drive

Sable River

River Road

Doe Avenue

Market Street

Long Drive

Grand Street

Summer Street

Map Key

River   Library

Bridge   Fire house

Hospital   Store

Park   Playground

School

N
W   E
S

A map has symbols on it. A **symbol** is a drawing that stands for something real. A symbol can also be a color or a pattern. To learn what a map's symbols stand for, check the **map key**. The map key tells what each symbol means.

Scholastic Professional Books

Use the map and map key to answer these questions.

1. What is the name of this community? _____

2. What does the symbol 🏥 stand for? _____

3. What is the symbol for a park? _____

4. What body of water runs through the park? _____

5. How do you get across the river? _____

6. On what street are most of the stores? _____

7. Name three buildings you would see if
   you walked along Market Street. _____

   _____

   _____

8. On what street is the hospital? _____

9. Mill Town needs a new
   playground.
   Create your own symbol in the
   space at right and then draw it
   on the map and in the key.

Understanding Directions

This picture shows a **globe**.
A globe is a model of Earth.
A globe is the same shape as
Earth but much smaller.

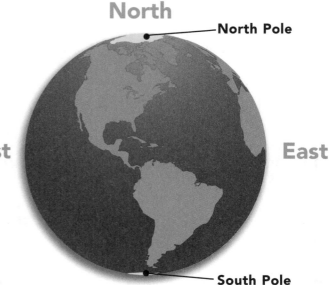

Read the labels on the globe.
The North and South poles help
you tell directions. North is toward
the North Pole. South is toward the
South Pole. When you face north,
east is to your right. West is to your left.

A compass rose is a symbol that
shows the four main directions on a map.
On a compass rose the letters **N, S, E,**
and **W** stand for the four directions.

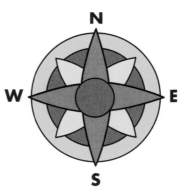

Complete these sentences.

1. The most northern place on the globe is the _____.

2. The _____ is the most southern place on a globe.

3. On a compass rose, the letter W stands for _____.

4. The direction East is sometimes written as _____ on a
    compass rose.

Scholastic Professional Books

Name _____

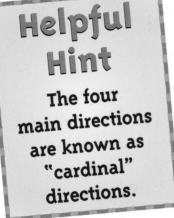

Helpful Hint

The four main directions are known as "cardinal" directions.

This map shows Lakeview. Use the compass rose to help answer these questions.

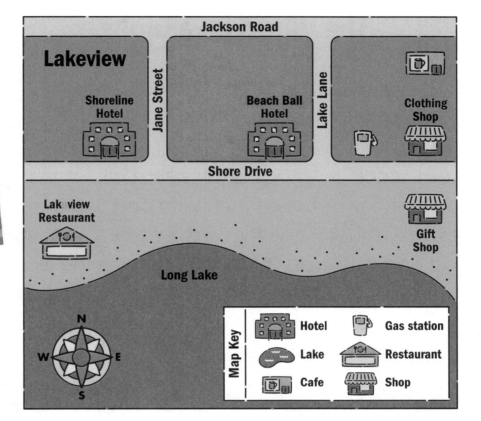

1. Is the lake on the north or south side of Lakeview?

   _____

2. In which direction are the hotels from the lake?

   _____

3. In which direction is the gift shop from the restaurant?

   _____

4. Can you go north on Jackson Road? _____

5. What building is east of the gas station? _____

Word Search

Find and circle the four main directions.

R	E	A	S	T
H	T	R	O	N
L	S	Q	U	Z
O	E	N	T	Y
P	W	Y	H	L

The World on a Globe

A globe shows all of Earth. You can see Earth's continents and oceans on a globe.

Helpful Hint
"Hemi" means half. A "hemisphere" is half of a sphere.

The **equator** is an imaginary line that circles the globe halfway between the North and South poles. The equator divides Earth into two halves called **hemispheres**. The northern half is the Northern Hemisphere. What do you think the southern half is called? Earth can also be divided into Western and Eastern Hemispheres. Study the hemispheres on the globes.

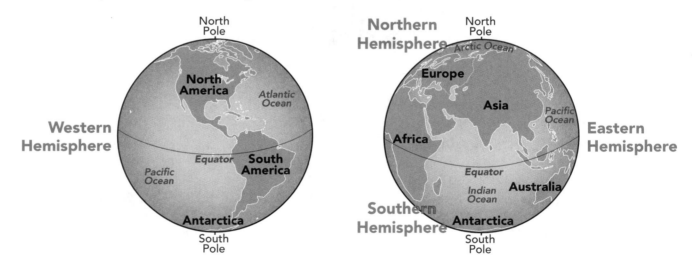

1. Does the equator run through North America? _____

2. What are the seven continents? _____

3. What are the four oceans? _____

4. In what hemispheres is most of South America? _____

Scholastic Professional Books

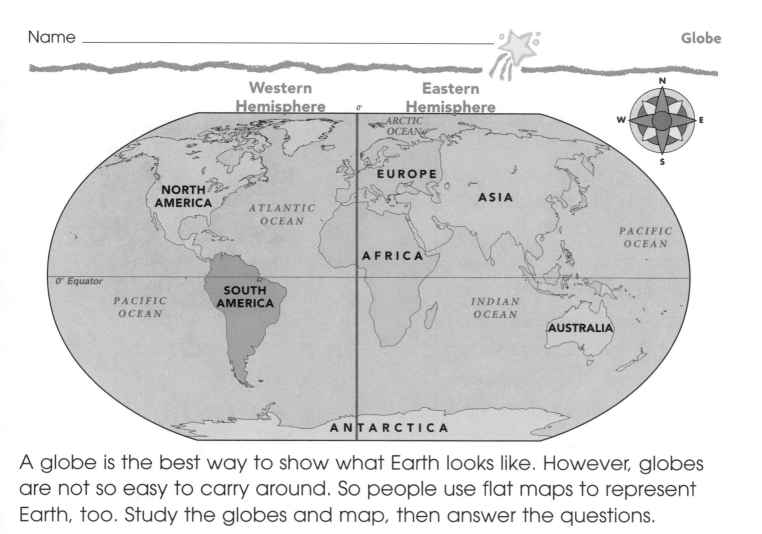

A globe is the best way to show what Earth looks like. However, globes are not so easy to carry around. So people use flat maps to represent Earth, too. Study the globes and map, then answer the questions.

1. Is Asia in the Eastern or Western Hemisphere? _____

2. What ocean is entirely north of the equator? _____

3. On the map, is east to the right or to the left? _____

4. The North Pole is at the _____ of the globe.

5. The area south of the equator is called the Southern _____ .

Code Word   **Fill in the blanks with the first letter of the answers for questions 1-5 to figure out the secret code word.**

_____   _____   _____   _____   _____
1.   2.   3.   4.   5.

Intermediate Directions

You know that a compass rose has four main directions.

A compass rose can show **intermediate directions**, too. Intermediate directions are between the main directions. For example, the direction between north and west is northwest. Letters sometimes stand for the intermediate directions on a compass rose. For example, NE stands for northeast.

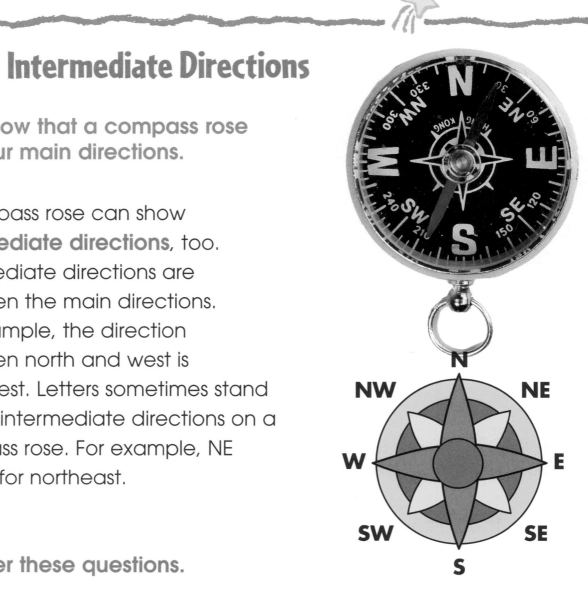

Answer these questions.

1. What direction is between south and east? _____

2. What direction is between north and east? _____

3. What direction is opposite of northwest? _____

4. What do the letters NW stand for on a compass rose? _____

5. What letters stand for southwest? _____

This map shows an **intersection**.
An intersection is where two roads cross.
Find the bank on the map. It is east of Water Street and north of Central Avenue. So the bank is on the northeast corner of the intersection.

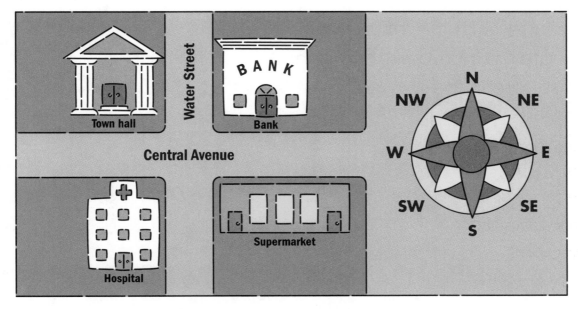

Color each compass rose to show the correct direction.

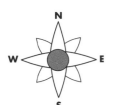

1. In what direction is the town hall from the hospital?

2. On which corner is the supermarket?

3. On which corner is the hospital?

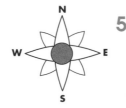

4. You ran out of money at the supermarket. In which direction do you go to get more?

5. In which direction would you go from the supermarket to the town hall?

Using a Map Grid

Some maps have a **grid** on them.

A grid is a pattern of lines that cross to form squares.
Each square on a grid has a letter and a number.
Find the letter A at the left side of the map.
Then locate the number 1 along the top of the map.
The first square in the top row is A1. Now find A2.

Helpful Hint

A grid makes it easier to pinpoint places on a map.

Use the map to answer these questions.

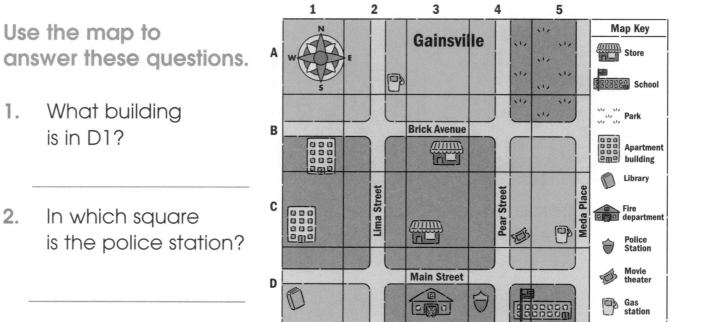

1. What building is in D1?

_____

2. In which square is the police station?

_____

3. Name all the squares that Lima Street runs through.

_____

4. In which squares is the school located? _____

5. Can you buy gas in C5? _____

Sometimes a map has letters and numbers along the side and top, but no grid lines. Then you must imagine where the lines go. For example, look in B1 and C1 to find the apartment buildings in Gainsville.

Use the map to answer these questions.

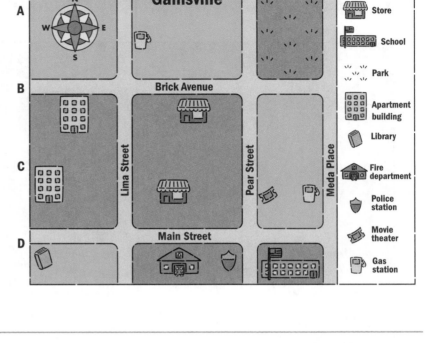

1. What building is in D3? _____

2. Find the park in A4. In what other square is the park? _____

3. What squares does Meda Place run through? _____

4. What is in C3? _____

5. Find C4. What can you do there? _____

My Tour of Gainsville

Pretend you are giving a new friend a tour of Gainsville. You visit the squares in this order: C1, D1, C3, A4, C4. Write a list describing the places you will visit.

1. _____

2. _____

3. _____

4. _____

5. _____

Understanding Distance

A map can show where places are in relation to one another.

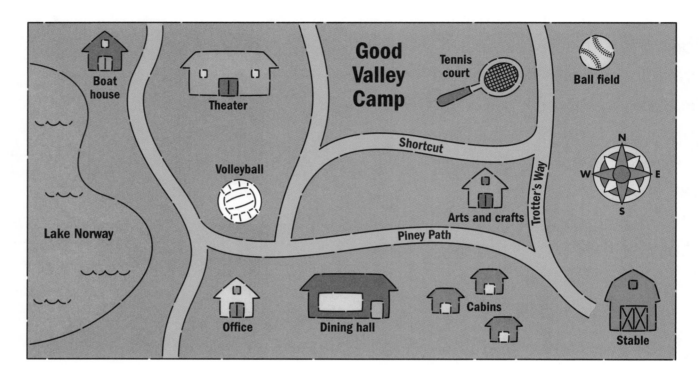

Use the map to answer these questions.

1. What is the nearest building to the lake? _____

2. What building is farthest from the theater? _____

3. What is the nearest building to
    the west of the dining hall? _____

4. What is the nearest building to
    the north of the cabins? _____

5. Is the volleyball court nearer
    the ball field or the tennis court? _____

A map can show **distance**, or how far it is from one place to another. This map has lines between the towns. The number on each line tells how many miles it is from one town to another. For example, it is 20 miles from Dover to Clark City.

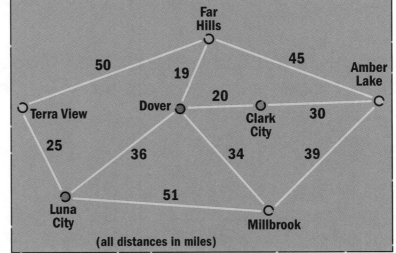

(all distances in miles)

1. How far is it from Terra View to Luna City? _____

2. How many miles is Amber Lake from Far Hills? _____

3. Will it take longer to drive from Millbrook to Luna City or from Millbrook to Dover? _____

4. What is the shortest way from Clark City to Terra View? _____

   How many miles would it be? _____

5. What is the closest town to Dover? _____

Distance is one thing that you need to know when you plan a trip. Other things make a difference, too. For example, it takes longer to drive over a mountain than it does to cross a plain. Draw a picture of something else that could make a car trip take longer.

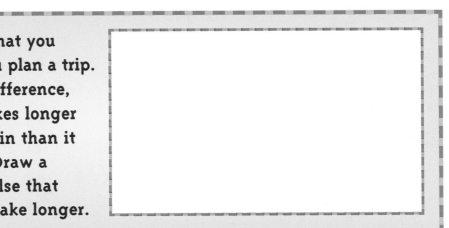

Learning About Scale

A map is not the same size as the place it shows. It is much smaller. Places on a map are inches or less apart. To show distance on a map, mapmakers use a **scale**.

A scale is a kind of ruler that helps you measure distance on a map. Look at the scale on this map. It shows that one inch equals ten feet. That means one inch on the map stands for ten feet of the real place.

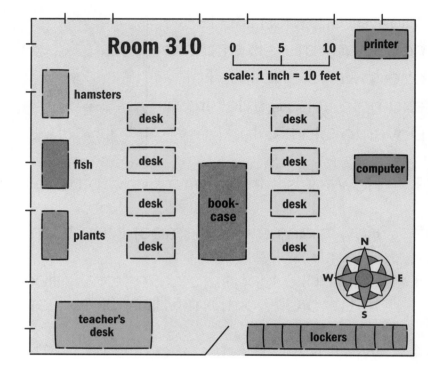

Use a ruler to measure the distances on the map.

1.   How many feet is the classroom from the east side to the west side? _____

2.   How far is the bookcase from the door? _____

3.   How far is the teacher's desk from the lockers? _____

4.   How far are the fish from the computer? _____

Always check the map scale to find the distance it represents. Use a ruler to help you answer these questions.

1. How long is Fair Road? _____

2. How wide is the parking lot? _____

3. About how many feet is it from
   the games entrance to the crafts entrance? _____

4. How far is it from the pet show
   entrance to the gate of the go carts? _____

5. If a pony goes once around the
   pony path, how far does it go? _____

Using a Map Scale

A map scale often looks like this:

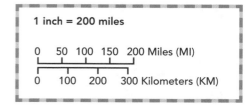

The MI on the scale stands for miles, and the KM stands for kilometers. Kilometers are a way of measuring distance in the Metric System.

Helpful Hint

When measuring distance on a map, always line up the end of the ruler with the "zero" on the map scale.

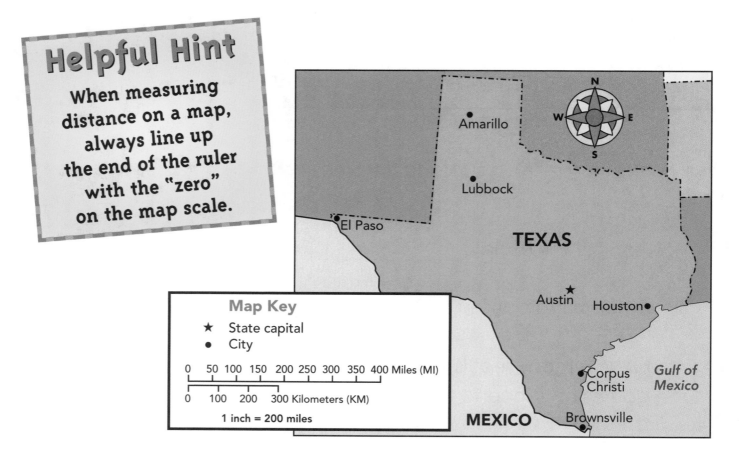

Use the map scale to answer these questions.

1. From Houston to Austin it is about _____ miles.

2. Corpus Christi is about _____ miles from Houston.

3. Lubbock is about _____ miles from El Paso.

4. Is a kilometer longer or shorter than a mile?_____

5. It is a little less than 450 miles from Austin to _____ .

Helpful Hint

If you don't have a ruler, lay the edge of a piece of paper along the map scale. Mark the paper, then use it to measure distances on the map.

6. Are Brownsville and Corpus Christi more or less than 150 miles apart? _____

7. Corpus Christi and Austin are about 300_____ apart.

8. From the capital of Texas to El Paso it is about_____ miles.

9. From its most northern part to its most southern part, Texas is about_____ miles long.

10. The widest part of Texas is about 1,200_____ across.

Word Search

Find and circle four Texas cities.

N	O	R	A	O	Z	X	L	Y
A	S	L	U	B	B	O	C	K
M	A	V	S	K	Y	E	G	J
S	P	T	T	L	P	S	U	W
O	L	L	I	R	A	M	A	O
T	E	Q	N	H	O	X	F	B

Comparing Maps

Maps can show places of different sizes.

Look at the maps on these pages. One map shows a state. One map shows a country, and the third map shows a continent.

Helpful Hint

Even on maps with different scales, the distance between two places is always the same.

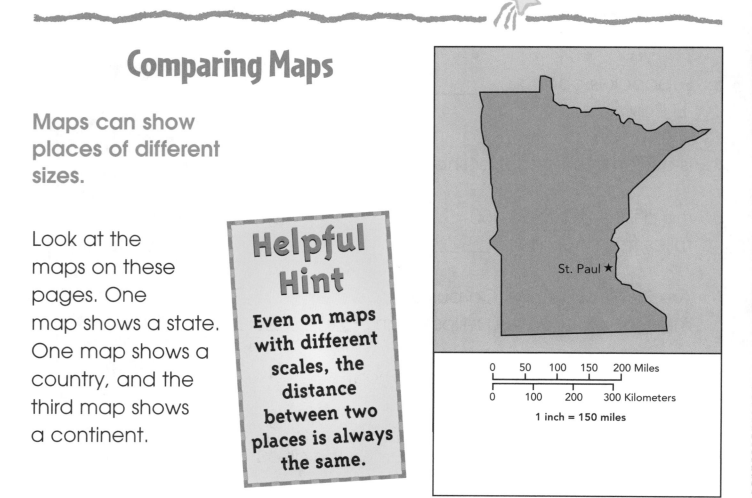

St. Paul ★

0   50   100   150   200 Miles

0   100   200   300 Kilometers

1 inch = 150 miles

Use the maps to answer these questions.

1. What state does Map 1 show? _____

2. What does one inch stand for on the scale for Map 1? _____

3. The abbreviation for this state is MN. Find it on Map 2. Does Map 1 or Map 2 cover a larger area? _____

4. What does one inch stand for on Map 2? _____

5. About how many miles is it from the coast of California (CA) to the coast of Virginia (VA)? _____

Scholastic Professional Books

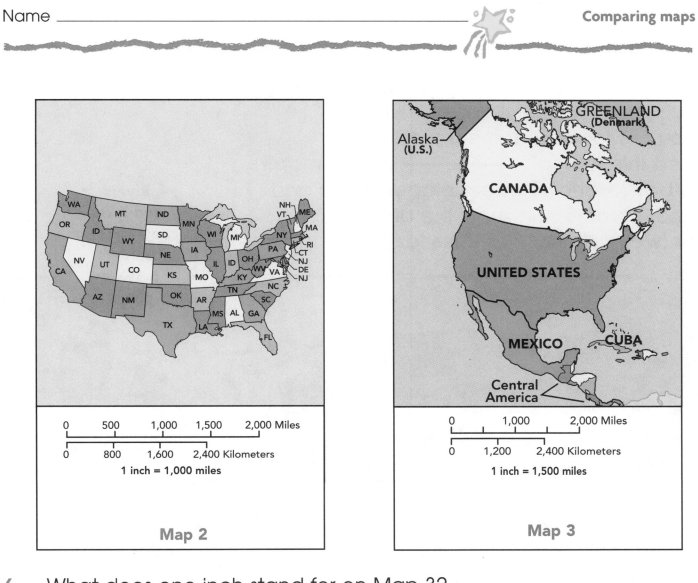

Map 2

0   500   1,000   1,500   2,000 Miles

0   800   1,600   2,400 Kilometers

1 inch = 1,000 miles

Map 3

0   1,000   2,000 Miles

0   1,200   2,400 Kilometers

1 inch = 1,500 miles

6. What does one inch stand for on Map 3? _____

7. What does Map 3 show? _____

8. Which of the maps shows the largest area? _____

9. Which of the maps shows the smallest area? _____

10 . On Map 3, draw a box that shows the area shown on Map 2.
     Then draw another box on the map to show the area on Map 1.

The United States

You are looking at the United States.
Find this symbol ————— on the map.
A **border** shows where places begin and
end. Borders can show the dividing lines
between states, countries, and other places.

Rivers
and lakes
can also form
borders
between
places.

Read the map, then answer these questions.

1. Find Alabama. What state shares
    a border with it on the west? _____

2. Find Colorado. What states share
    a border with it on the east? _____

Scholastic Professional Books

3. What lake forms part of the northwest border of Pennsylvania?

   _____

Helpful Hint

Two states do not touch any other states. Both of these states are far from the rest of the country. These states are shown in small boxes called inset maps.

4. What river forms the western border of Tennessee?

   _____

5. Which states are shown in the inset maps? _____

6. What is the capital of Alaska? _____

7. Hawaii is in the Pacific Ocean. In which direction is it from California? _____

"Speedy Map Planner"

Imagine that you are taking a trip from the Atlantic Ocean to the Pacific Ocean. Plan a route that passes through the fewest number of states possible. Can you do it in less than eight states? Write the states on the chart.

1. _____   5. _____

2. _____   6. _____

3. _____   7. _____

4. _____   8. _____

North America

The United States is on the continent of North America.

Two countries, Canada and Mexico, share borders with the United States. North America also includes Greenland, the countries of Central America, and many islands.

Helpful Hint

One state, Hawaii, is not part of North America.

Use the map to answer these questions about North America.

1. In which direction is Mexico from the United States? _____

2. Name two other countries that share a border with Mexico. _____

3. What country shares a border on the north with the United States? _____

4. What state is on the northwest part of North America? _____

5. What oceans border the east and west coasts of North America? _____

6. What ocean is north of this continent? _____

7. What is the capital of Canada? _____

8. What river forms part of the border between the U.S. and Mexico? _____

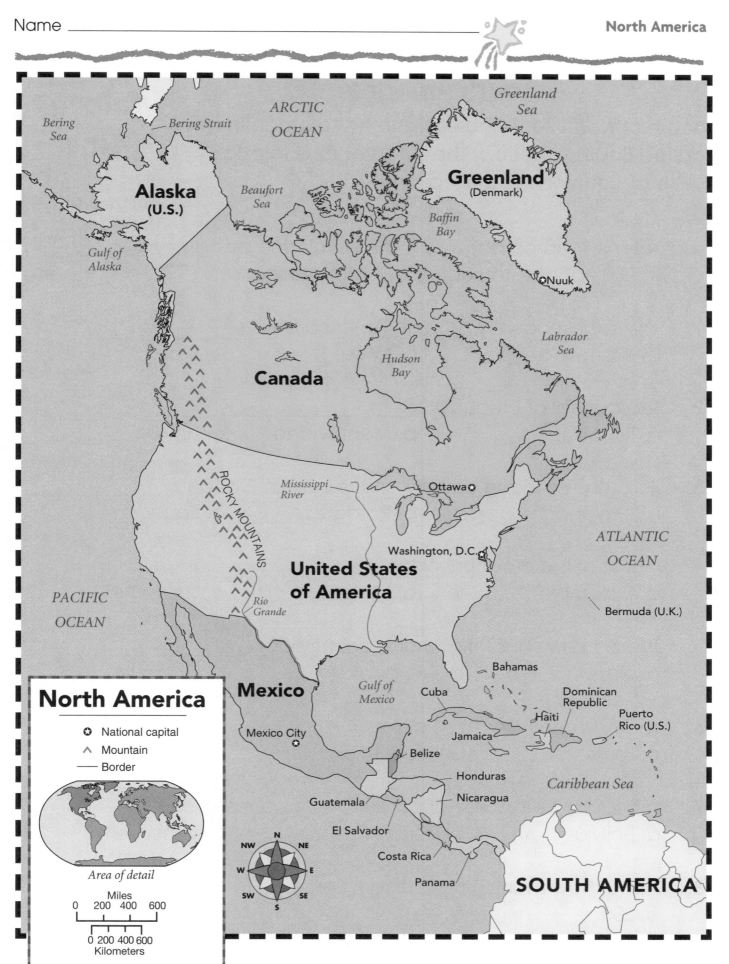

North America

ARCTIC OCEAN

Greenland Sea

Bering Sea

Bering Strait

Alaska (U.S.)

Beaufort Sea

Greenland (Denmark)

Baffin Bay

Gulf of Alaska

Nuuk

Labrador Sea

Canada

Hudson Bay

ROCKY MOUNTAINS

Mississippi River

Ottawa ✪

ATLANTIC OCEAN

Washington, D.C.

United States of America

PACIFIC OCEAN

Rio Grande

Bermuda (U.K.)

North America

✪ National capital
∧ Mountain
— Border

Area of detail

Mexico

Gulf of Mexico

Bahamas

Cuba

Dominican Republic

Haiti

Puerto Rico (U.S.)

Mexico City

Jamaica

Belize

Caribbean Sea

Honduras

Guatemala

Nicaragua

El Salvador

N
NW   NE
W   E
SW   SE
S

Costa Rica

Panama

SOUTH AMERICA

Miles
0   200 400 600

0 200 400 600
Kilometers

Scholastic Professional Books

South America

South of North America lies another big continent called South America. The equator runs through several countries of this continent.

Helpful Hint

Most of South America is in the Southern Hemisphere.

Look at the map on page 291. Then circle the best answer for each statement about South America.

1. The largest country in South America is _____.
   a. Argentina   b. Chile   c. Brazil

2. The capital of Uruguay is _____.
   a. Santiago   b. Montevideo   c. Lima

3. A South American country on the Pacific Ocean is _____.
   a. Guyana   b. Paraguay   c. Ecuador

4. Caracas is the capital city of _____.
   a. Colombia   b. Venezuela   c. Suriname

5. The equator runs through the country of _____.
   a. Chile   b. Guyana   c. Colombia

6. The Amazon River flows across _____.
   a. Brazil   b. Argentina   c. Paraguay

7. A country that does not border on an ocean or sea is _____.
   a. Bolivia   b. Peru   c. Venezuela

8. About how many miles is it from Santiago to Montevideo? _____.
   a. 200   b. 400   c. 900

Caribbean Sea

Dominica

Trinidad and Tobago

ATLANTIC OCEAN

⊙ Caracas

Venezuela

Guyana

★ Georgetown

Orinoco River

⊙ Paramaribo

Bogota ⊙

Suriname ⊙ Cayenne

Colombia

French Guiana

★ Quito

Ecuador

Equator

Galapagos Islands
(Ecuador)

Amazon River

Peru

Brazil

⊙ Lima

Bolivia

⊙ Brasília

**PACIFIC
OCEAN**

⊙ La Paz

ANDES MOUNTAINS

⊙ Sucre

Paraná River

Paraguay

★ Asunción

South America

⊙ National capital

∧ Mountain

— Border

Area of detail

Uruguay

Santiago ⊙

★ Montevideo

Buenos Aires ⊙

Argentina

Miles

| 0 | 200 | 400 | 600 |

Chile

N
NW   NE
W   E
SW   SE
S

| 0 | 200 | 400 | 600 |

Falkland
Islands (U.K.)

Landforms

Maps are usually drawn on paper, so the land looks flat. But you know that Earth's land is not always flat. In fact, the land takes many shapes called **landforms**. The pictures show some important landforms.

A **plain** is open, flat land.

A **mountain** is very high land with steep slopes.

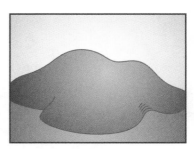

A **hill** is land that is higher than a plain but not as high or steep as a mountain.

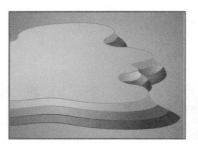

A **plateau** is high, flat land.

A **valley** is low land between mountains or hills. Rivers often run through a valley.

A **canyon** is a narrow valley with high, steep sides. Rivers sometimes flow through canyons, too.

Use the pictures to answer these questions.

1. Which landforms are high land? _____

2. Which landforms are low places? _____

3. How are a canyon and a valley alike? _____

   How are they different? _____

Name _____

More than half of Earth is covered with water.

You have learned about some of these bodies of water such as oceans, rivers, and lakes. The picture shows some other bodies of water and some other landforms.

Use the maps to help answer the questions.

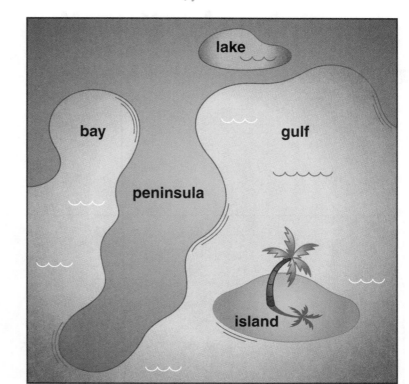

A **gulf** is part of an ocean or sea. A gulf is partly surrounded by land.

A **bay** is like a gulf but smaller.

An **island** is land that is completely surrounded by water.

A **peninsula** is an "almost island." It is land that is surrounded by water on all but one side.

1. Why might a bay be a good place to keep a boat?_____

2. How is a bay like a gulf? _____

3. Find Florida on the map on page 286.
   What landform is Florida? _____

4. How is a peninsula different from an island? _____

5. In what way are a lake and an island similar?_____

Name _____

Using a Landform Map

This is a landform map of Arkansas.

Helpful Hint

A landform map is sometimes called a relief map.

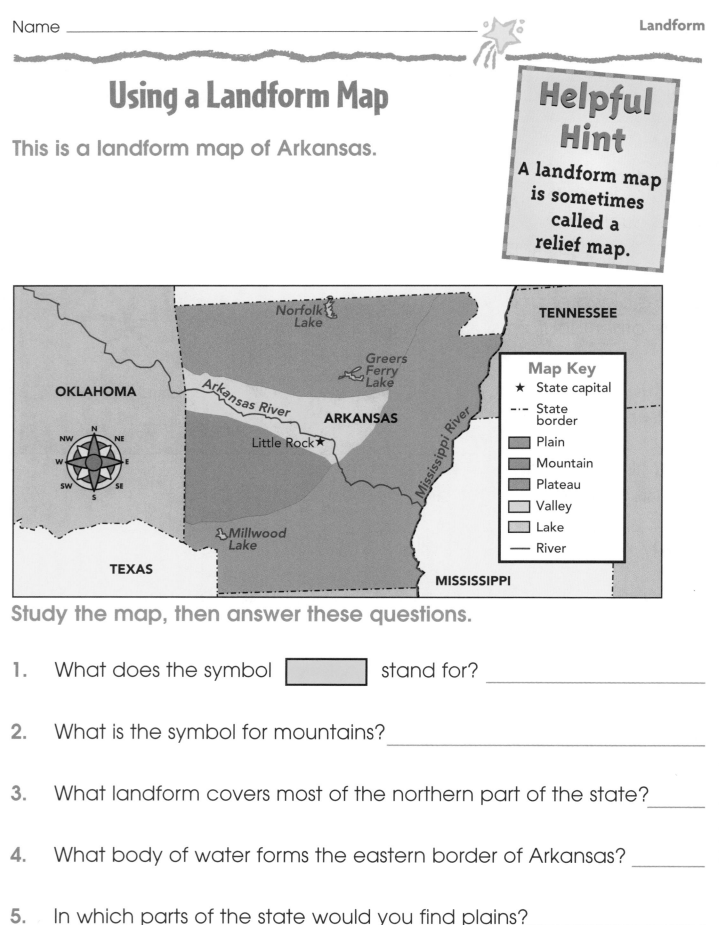

Study the map, then answer these questions.

1. What does the symbol [   ] stand for? _____

2. What is the symbol for mountains? _____

3. What landform covers most of the northern part of the state? _____

4. What body of water forms the eastern border of Arkansas? _____

5. In which parts of the state would you find plains? _____

Scholastic Professional Books

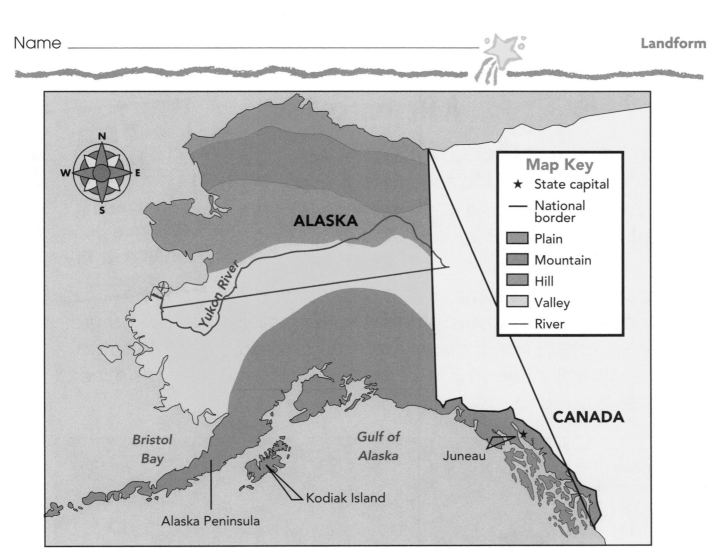

This map shows the landforms of Alaska.
Study the map, then answer these questions.

1. In which part of Alaska are there plains? _____

2. Name a large island off the
    southern part of the state. _____

3. What is the land that extends from the
    southwest part of the state called? _____

4. On what kind of land is Alaska's capital? _____

5. What river runs across the state? _____

A Resource Map

Do you know what coal is? It's a kind of rock that is burned to make heat and energy. Coal is just one of Pennsylvania's **natural resources.**

Helpful Hint

A mineral is a resource that is found in the ground.

A natural resource is something found in nature that people use. Air, water, plants, soil, and minerals are all natural resources. A map can show where natural resources are located. The map on this page shows where some of Pennsylvania's mineral resources are found.

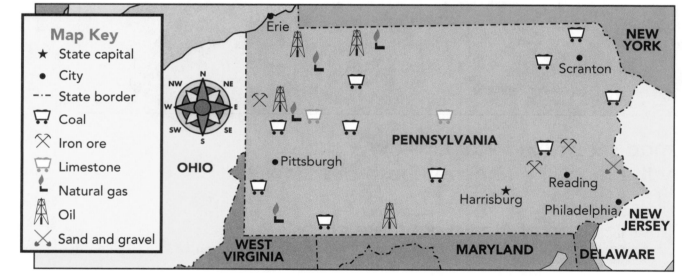

Answer these questions.

1. How are natural resources helpful to people? _____

   _____

2. What are some ways people use sand and gravel? _____

3. Why is a flame a good symbol for natural gas? _____

Much of Pennsylvania's coal
is burned to make electricity.

**Write TRUE or FALSE on the line.
Use the map on page 296 to
help you.**

_____ 1.   Most of Pennsylvania's oil is in the northwest
             part of the state.

_____ 2.   Sand and gravel are found in the east.

_____ 3.   Most of the state's iron ore is in the north.

_____ 4.   Pennsylvania has no natural gas.

_____ 5.   Pennsylvania has more coal than oil.

_____ 6.   The symbol ⚒ stands for oil.

An Amazing Journey

**Use this
Pennsylvania
maze to get
from
Philadelphia
to the oil
field in the
northwest.**

FINISH

START

A Rainfall Map

Water is the most important natural resource. Plants, animals, and people all need water. Water falls to Earth as rain, snow, sleet, and hail.

This map is called a rainfall map. It shows how much water falls in the different parts of Maine during one year.

Helpful Hint

Another word for rainfall is precipitation.

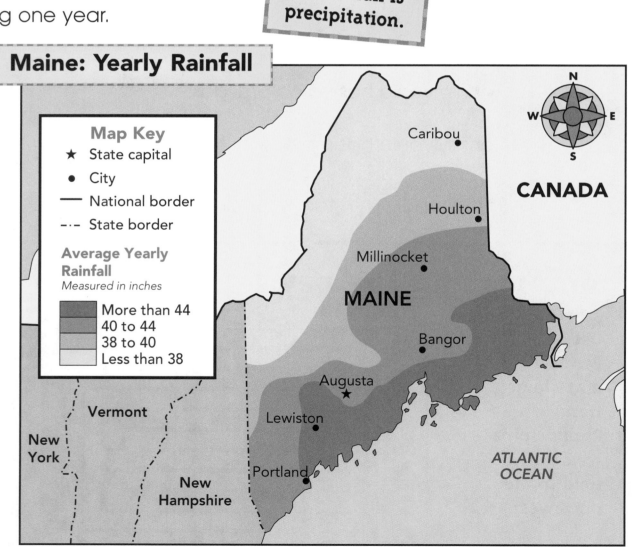

Maine: Yearly Rainfall

Map Key
★ State capital
● City
— National border
-·- State border

Average Yearly Rainfall
Measured in inches

More than 44
40 to 44
38 to 40
Less than 38

Caribou

CANADA

Houlton

Millinocket

MAINE

Bangor

Augusta ★

Vermont

Lewiston

New York

New Hampshire

Portland

ATLANTIC OCEAN

Scholastic Professional Books

Name _____

People use water to drink and to bathe. Water is also important for growing crops, washing things, and running machines.

Use the map to answer these questions.

1. This symbol [ ] stands for _____ inches.

2. The least amount of rain in Maine falls in the _____ parts of the state.

3. Bangor gets about _____ inches of rain a year.

4. A city in Maine that gets 38 to 40 inches of rain a year is _____.

5. The city on this map that gets the most rain is _____.

6. The rainfall in Houlton is _____ than in Caribou.

7. You can guess that the part of Canada near the northwest part of Maine gets _____ inches of rain a year.

Connect the words to the correct symbols.

| 1. rain | 2. snow | 3. sleet | 4. hail |

A History Map

You can learn about the past from a map. The map on this page shows the Oregon Trail. This was a route that pioneers followed when they traveled west in the 1840s. A route is a way to go from one place to another.

In the 1840s people did not have airplanes or cars. They traveled in covered wagons pulled by oxen. Some pioneers rode on horses or walked alongside the wagons. Most pioneers met in Independence, Missouri, and formed groups. The groups traveled together in wagon trains.

Use the map to answer these questions.

1. In what direction did the trail go
   from Independence to Portland? _____

2. What river flows by Independence? _____

3. After Independence, what was the
   first town along the trail?
   _____

4. What mountains did the Oregon Trail cross? _____

5. Find Three Island Crossing. On what river is it? _____

6. Why do you think the Oregon Trail
   does not follow a straight line? _____

7. The wagon trains left Independence in May for
   the five-month trip. Why do you think it was
   important to start then? _____

Helpful Hint

In 1840 most of the land west of the Mississippi River was not yet divided into states.

Word Scramble

Below are the names of four present-day states that the Oregon trail passed through. Can you figure out what they are?

NOROGE   AIHDO   ARBNAKSE   ANSSKA

_____   _____   _____   _____

A Tourist Map

A tourist is someone who travels for fun.

If you have ever been a tourist, you know that it is handy to have a map of the place you are visiting. A **tourist map** shows a place of interest and highlights the special things to see and do there.

Saguaro West is in the Sonoran Desert. This land was set aside as a park because of the special plants and animals that live there.

This map shows a large park in Arizona called Saguaro West.

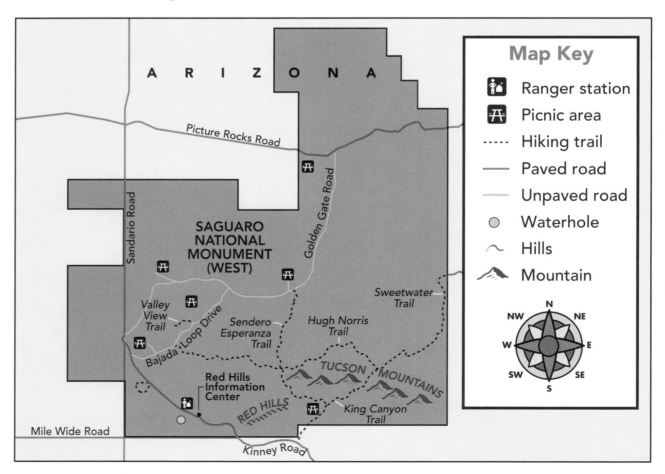

Scholastic Professional Books

Study the map, then answer these questions.

Helpful Hint

Saguaro is the name of a large cactus.

1. What does the symbol 🛆 mean? _____

2. In what part of the park is the Ranger Station? _____

3. From the Ranger Station, how would you drive to the northernmost picnic area? _____

   _____

4. What kind of plants would you expect to see in this park? _____

   _____

5. What does this symbol ⚪ mean? _____

   Why might animals come there? _____

6. What road cuts through the park on the west side going from north to south? _____

A City Map

Welcome to New York City! Part of this city is on the island of Manhattan. The map shows some of the main streets in Manhattan. Use the map to answer the questions.

1.   What river runs along the west side of Manhattan?

_____

Along the east side?

_____

2.   The direction the streets run is

from _____ to _____ .

3.   The avenues run from

_____ to _____ .

4.   One of the oldest streets is Wall Street. In which part of Manhattan is it?

_____

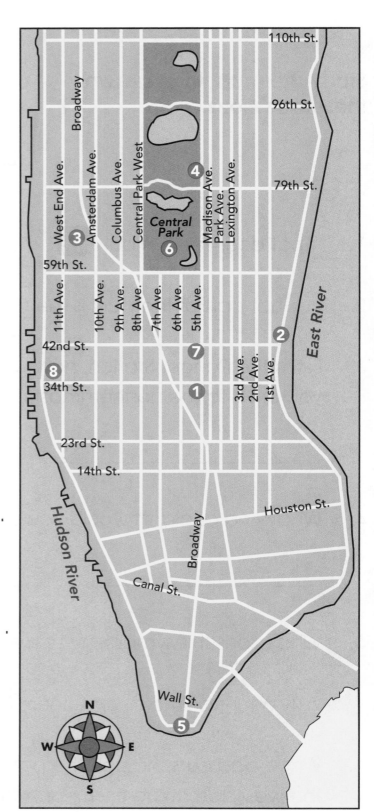

Helpful Hint

As you move north in Manhattan, the numbers of the streets get higher.

1. Empire State Building
2. United Nations
3. Lincoln Center
4. Metropolitan Museum of Art
5. Battery Park
6. Central Park
7. New York Public Library
8. Javits Center

Many of New York's streets form a grid pattern.

This grid makes it easier to find places in the city. For example, the Empire State Building is on the corner of Fifth Avenue and 34th Street. Use the map to answer the questions.

5. What street runs along the
   southern part of Central Park? _____

   What avenues run along the east
   and west sides of the park? _____

6. Find the New York Public Library.
   On what corner is it found? _____

7. On which side of the city is the United Nations? _____

8. Find the Empire State Building. In which direction
   would you walk to get to the Javits Center? _____

9. Why do you think the streets of New York City are numbered?

   _____

A Transit Map

How do you get to school? How do people in your family get to work?

In many communities people use public transportation. They take buses or trains to get from one part of the community to another. A **transit map** shows the route a bus or train takes.

Helpful Hint

San Francisco is located on a peninsula between San Francisco Bay and the Pacific Ocean.

The transit map on this page shows BART trains in San Francisco, California. BART stands for Bay Area Rapid Transit. The map shows the routes that BART trains take to connect San Francisco to communities around it.

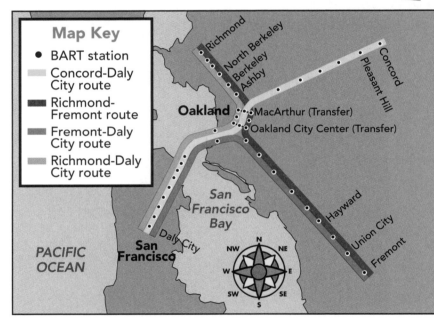

Use the map to answer these questions.

1. What does this symbol ▬▬▬▬ stand for on this map? _____

2. What color is the Richmond-Fremont Route? _____

3. On what line is the Pleasant Hill stop? _____

The BART lines come together and form a kind of X.
Find the Oakland City Center stop. Do you see the word "transfer" after it? At a transfer stop, passengers can change from one line to another.

4. Can you travel on the same train to
   get from Concord to Daly City? _____

5. What are the stops at the end of each BART line? _____

   _____

6. What is special about the MacArthur stop? _____

7. What BART line does not go into San Francisco? _____

8. In which direction do the BART lines
   go from Daly City to Oakland? _____

9. What body of water do three of the BART lines cross? _____

   _____

10. Without BART, how do you think people
    could get from Oakland to San Francisco? _____

Design a Symbol

BART is looking for a new symbol to show transfer stations on its map. Use this space to draw your own symbol.

Map Review 1

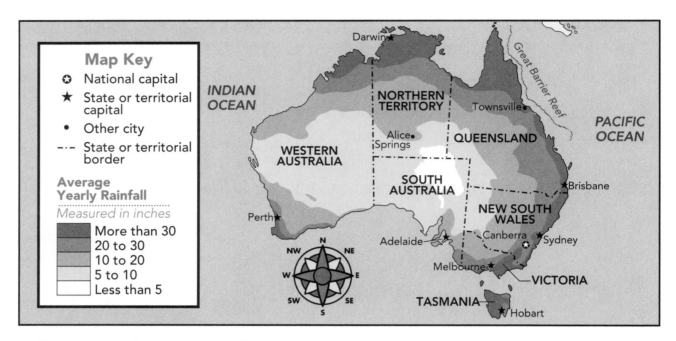

Use the map to answer the questions.

1. What does the symbol ▭ stand for? _____

2. Does Australia get more rain along the coasts or inland?

   _____

3. About how much rain a year does Alice Springs get?

   _____

4. Part of Australia is desert. About how much rain do you think this part of the country gets?

   _____

5. What is the national capital of Australia? _____

6. What oceans surround Australia? _____

7. On which part of the continent is New South Wales?

   _____

8. Check the words that are true for Australia:

   _____ continent
   _____ country
   _____ island

Scholastic Professional Books

Map Review 2

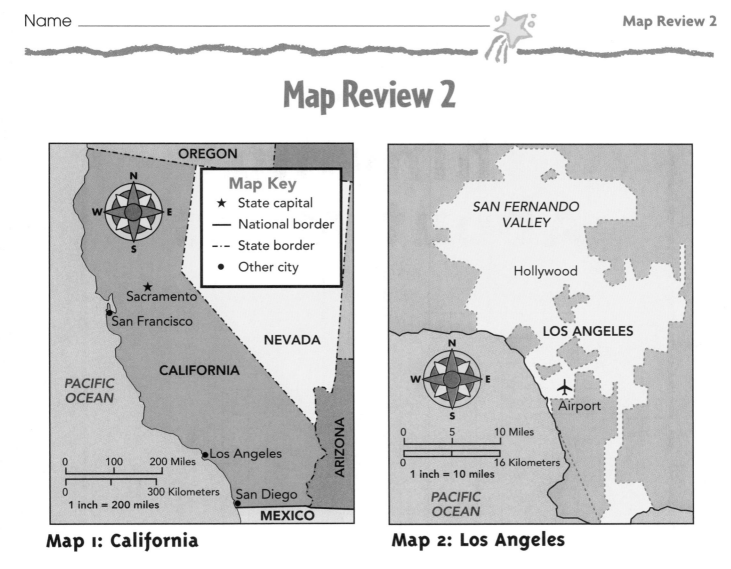

Map 1: California

Map 2: Los Angeles

Use the maps to answer these questions.

1. Which map shows a larger place? _____

2. How many miles does one inch stand for on the map of California? _____

3. How many miles does one inch stand for on the map of Los Angeles? _____

4. What is the capital of California? _____

5. About how many miles is it from Sacramento to San Diego?

   _____

6. What body of water is to the west of California? _____

7. What states border California on the east? _____

   _____

8. What does this symbol ———— stand for? _____

Thinking About Maps

Across

2. a narrow valley with steep sides

4. "Southeast" is an _____ direction.

8. lines that cross to form squares on a map

9. water that is completely surrounded by land

10. The United States is located in the northern _____.

11. This symbol shows directions.

Down

1. a dividing line between states or countries

2. South America is a _____.

3. _____ helps you measure distance on a map.

5. Coal is a natural _____.

6. how far one place is from another

7. Hills and plateaus are kinds of _____.

Scholastic Professional Books

Glossary

bay
A bay is part of an ocean or sea that is partly surrounded by land. A bay is smaller than a gulf.

border
A border shows where places begin and end. It is a dividing line between places.

canyon
A canyon is a narrow valley with high, steep sides.

compass rose
A compass rose is a symbol that shows the four main directions on a map.

distance
Distance is how far it is from one place to another.

equator
The equator is an imaginary line that circles the globe halfway between the North and South poles.

globe
A globe is a model of Earth.

grid
A grid is a pattern of lines that cross to form squares.

gulf
A gulf is part of an ocean or sea that is partly surrounded by land.

hemisphere
A hemisphere is a half of Earth. Earth can be divided into Northern and Southern hemispheres or Eastern and Western hemispheres.

inset map
An inset map is a small map in a box that is shown with a larger map.

intermediate directions
Intermediate directions are between the main directions. The direction between south and east is southeast.

intersection
An intersection is where two roads cross or intersect.

island
An island is land that is completely surrounded by water.

landform
A landform is the shape of land such as a mountain. A landform map is sometimes called a relief map.

map key
A map key is a list of symbols used on a map. A map key is also called a legend.

natural resource
A natural resource is something found in nature that people use.

peninsula
A peninsula is land that is surrounded by water on all but one side.

plateau
A plateau is high, flat land. It is sometimes called a tableland.

rainfall
Rainfall is water that falls to Earth in the form of rain, snow, sleet, and hail. Rainfall is also called precipitation.

route
A route is a way to go from one place to another.

scale
A scale is a kind of ruler that helps you measure distance on a map.

symbol
A symbol is a drawing that stands for something real. A symbol can also be a color or a pattern.

tourist map
A tourist map shows interesting places and highlights things to see and do.

transit map
A transit map shows the route that a bus or train takes.

valley
A valley is low land that runs between mountains or hills.

Scholastic Professional Books

ADDITION & SUBTRACTION

On the *Mayflower*

Add or subtract. Write the Pilgrims' names in alphabetical order by sequencing the answers from greatest to smallest.

~~Resolve~~	14 − 7 = 7 ✗
~~Susan~~	13 − 9 = 4 ✗
~~Jasper~~	6 + 7 = 13 ✗
~~Priscilla~~	8 + 2 = 10 ✗
~~Edward~~	9 + 6 = 15 ✗
~~Solomon~~	11 − 6 = 5 ✗
~~Prudence~~	18 − 9 = 9 ✗
~~Constance~~	8 + 8 = 16 ✗
~~Remember~~	17 − 9 = 8 ✗
~~Oceanus~~	7 + 5 = 12 ✗
~~Thomas~~	15 − 12 = 3 ✗
~~Samuel~~	14 − 8 = 6 ✗
~~Charity~~	6 + 12 = 18 ✗
~~Peregrine~~	16 − 5 = 11 ✗
~~Humility~~	9 + 5 = 14 ✗

Charity

Constance

Edward

Humility

Jasper

oceanus

peregrine

Priscila

prudence

~~Remember~~

Resolve

Samule

Solomon

Susan

Thomas

 Which name would your name follow in the alphabetical list of names? Write a number sentence to show where your name would follow.

Great States

Add or subtract. Connect the matching answers
to find each state's shape.

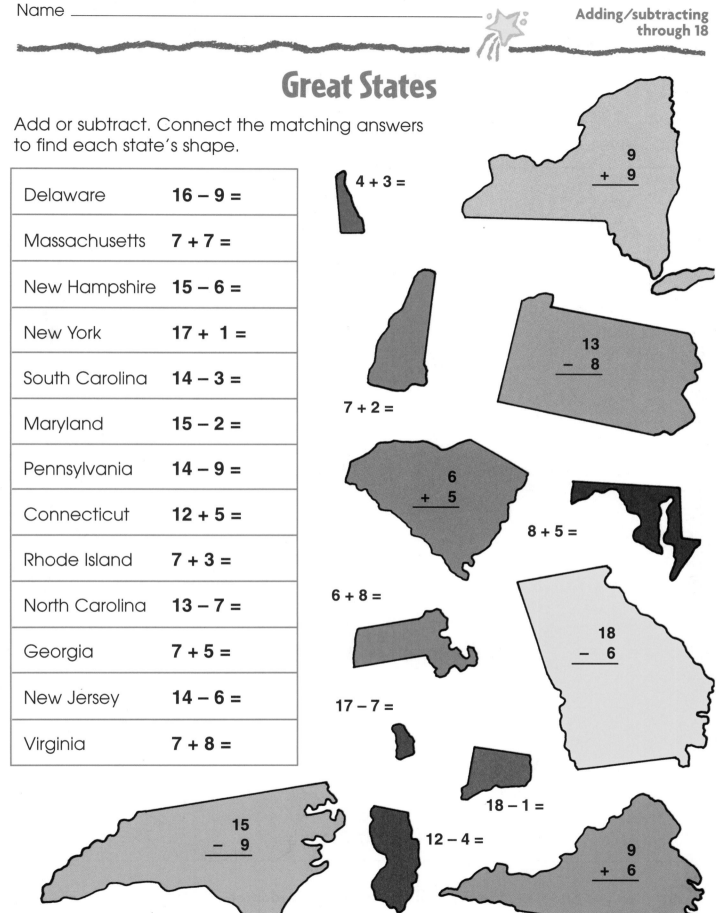

Delaware	**16 – 9 =**
Massachusetts	**7 + 7 =**
New Hampshire	**15 – 6 =**
New York	**17 + 1 =**
South Carolina	**14 – 3 =**
Maryland	**15 – 2 =**
Pennsylvania	**14 – 9 =**
Connecticut	**12 + 5 =**
Rhode Island	**7 + 3 =**
North Carolina	**13 – 7 =**
Georgia	**7 + 5 =**
New Jersey	**14 – 6 =**
Virginia	**7 + 8 =**

4 + 3 =

$\begin{array}{r} 9 \\ + 9 \\ \hline \end{array}$

$\begin{array}{r} 13 \\ - 8 \\ \hline \end{array}$

7 + 2 =

$\begin{array}{r} 6 \\ + 5 \\ \hline \end{array}$

8 + 5 =

6 + 8 =

$\begin{array}{r} 18 \\ - 6 \\ \hline \end{array}$

17 – 7 =

18 – 1 =

12 – 4 =

$\begin{array}{r} 15 \\ - 9 \\ \hline \end{array}$

$\begin{array}{r} 9 \\ + 6 \\ \hline \end{array}$

United We Stand

Add or subtract. Color answers greater than 50 green to show the United States.
Color answers less than 50 blue.

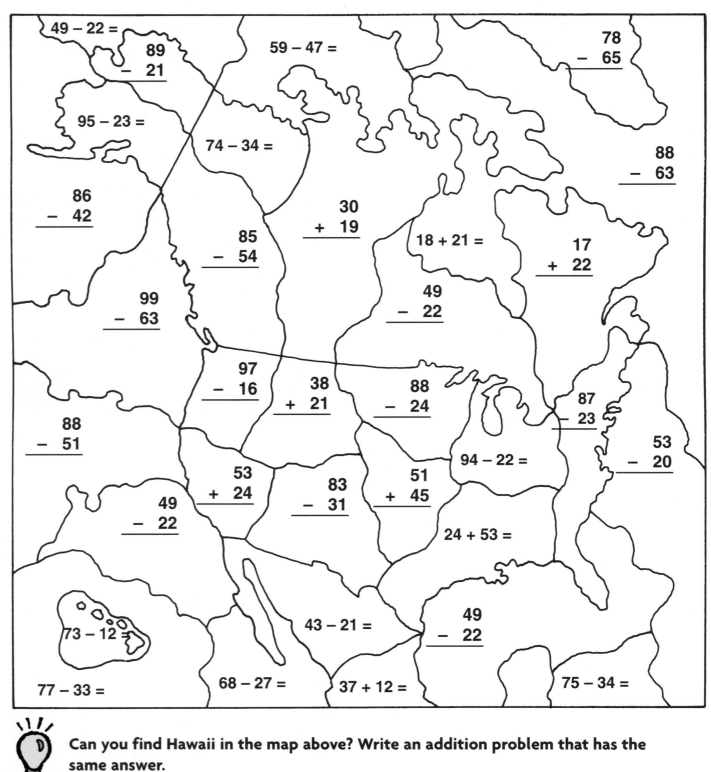

49 – 22 =

$$\begin{array}{r} 89 \\ - 21 \\ \hline \end{array}$$

59 – 47 =

$$\begin{array}{r} 78 \\ - 65 \\ \hline \end{array}$$

95 – 23 =

74 – 34 =

$$\begin{array}{r} 88 \\ - 63 \\ \hline \end{array}$$

$$\begin{array}{r} 86 \\ - 42 \\ \hline \end{array}$$

$$\begin{array}{r} 85 \\ - 54 \\ \hline \end{array}$$

$$\begin{array}{r} 30 \\ + 19 \\ \hline \end{array}$$

18 + 21 =

$$\begin{array}{r} 17 \\ + 22 \\ \hline \end{array}$$

$$\begin{array}{r} 99 \\ - 63 \\ \hline \end{array}$$

$$\begin{array}{r} 49 \\ - 22 \\ \hline \end{array}$$

$$\begin{array}{r} 97 \\ - 16 \\ \hline \end{array}$$

$$\begin{array}{r} 38 \\ + 21 \\ \hline \end{array}$$

$$\begin{array}{r} 88 \\ - 24 \\ \hline \end{array}$$

$$\begin{array}{r} 87 \\ - 23 \\ \hline \end{array}$$

$$\begin{array}{r} 88 \\ - 51 \\ \hline \end{array}$$

94 – 22 =

$$\begin{array}{r} 53 \\ - 20 \\ \hline \end{array}$$

$$\begin{array}{r} 53 \\ + 24 \\ \hline \end{array}$$

$$\begin{array}{r} 83 \\ - 31 \\ \hline \end{array}$$

$$\begin{array}{r} 51 \\ + 45 \\ \hline \end{array}$$

$$\begin{array}{r} 49 \\ - 22 \\ \hline \end{array}$$

24 + 53 =

73 – 12 =

43 – 21 =

$$\begin{array}{r} 49 \\ - 22 \\ \hline \end{array}$$

77 – 33 =

68 – 27 =

37 + 12 =

75 – 34 =

Can you find Hawaii in the map above? Write an addition problem that has the
same answer.

Scholastic Professional Books

Name _____

Stars and Stripes Forever

Circle groups of 10. Write the number of tens and ones. Write the number in the star.

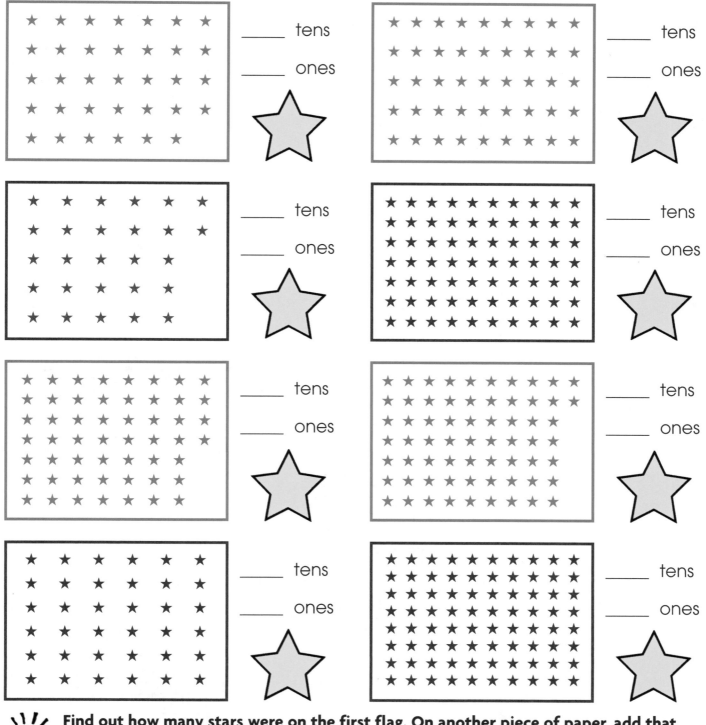

_____ tens

_____ ones

_____ tens

_____ ones

_____ tens

_____ ones

_____ tens

_____ ones

_____ tens

_____ ones

_____ tens

_____ ones

_____ tens

_____ ones

_____ tens

_____ ones

Find out how many stars were on the first flag. On another piece of paper, add that number to the number of stars on the United States flag today. How many groups of tens and ones are there?

The U.S. Capital

Add. Match each building to the correct sum.

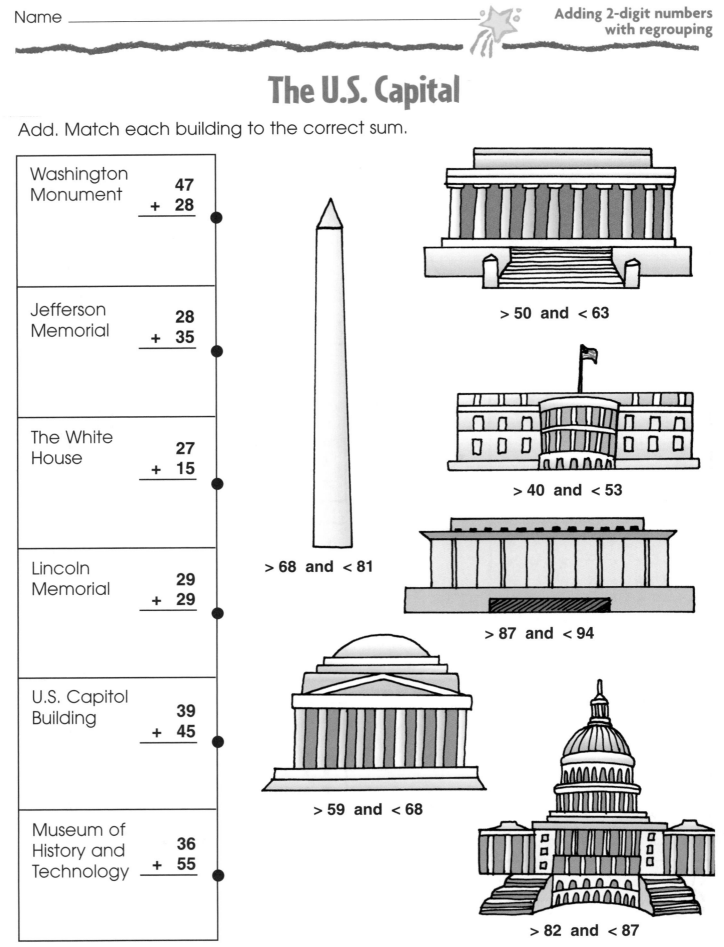

Washington Monument	47 + 28
Jefferson Memorial	28 + 35
The White House	27 + 15
Lincoln Memorial	29 + 29
U.S. Capitol Building	39 + 45
Museum of History and Technology	36 + 55

> 50 and < 63

> 40 and < 53

> 87 and < 94

> 68 and < 81

> 59 and < 68

> 82 and < 87

Name _____

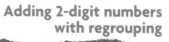

Mr. President

Add. Write the letters in the circles to identify each president.

I was a leader in the Civil War.

39 + 13	38 + 15	56 + 26	26 + 35	29 + 67	27 + 25	43 + 39

◯ ◯ ◯ ◯ ◯ ◯ ◯

I helped write the Declaration of Independence.

19 + 18	28 + 55	24 + 18	19 + 23	17 + 66	59 + 19	49 + 15	78 + 18	48 + 34

◯ ◯ ◯ ◯ ◯ ◯ ◯ ◯ ◯

I was a leader in the American Revolutionary War.

59 + 39	48 + 24	27 + 37	19 + 46	27 + 26	38 + 44	27 + 18	18 + 29	38 + 58	27 + 55

◯ ◯ ◯ ◯ ◯ ◯ ◯ ◯ ◯ ◯

Code

61 C	98 W	55 Y	83 E	45 G	82 N	78 R	65 H	52 L
96 O	42 F	86 K	47 T	72 A	37 J	64 S	53 I	36 D

 On another piece of paper, make a code and write problems for the name of our current president.

Travel the Nation

Look at the number on each form of transportation. Write the number of tens and ones. Regroup. Write the new number.

__3__ tens
__7__ ones

Trade 1 ten for 10 ones.

__2__ tens
_17_ ones

_____ tens
_____ ones

Trade 1 ten for 10 ones.

_____ tens
_____ ones

_____ tens
_____ ones

Trade 1 ten for 10 ones.

_____ tens
_____ ones

_____ tens
_____ ones

Trade 1 ten for 10 ones.

_____ tens
_____ ones

_____ tens
_____ ones

Trade 1 ten for 10 ones.

_____ tens
_____ ones

_____ tens
_____ ones

Trade 1 ten for 10 ones.

_____ tens
_____ ones

Scholastic Professional Books

Name _____

Great Vacations

Subtract. Draw a line from each difference to the vacation spot on the map.

Mount Rushmore	Niagara Falls	Gateway Arch	Four Corners Monument	Statue of Liberty
72 − 27	57 − 29	58 − 39	93 − 19	94 − 29

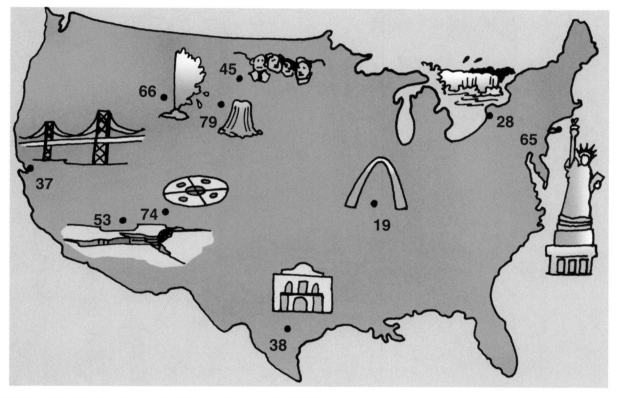

Grand Canyon	Devil's Tower	Golden Gate Bridge	The Alamo	Old Faithful
82 − 29	93 − 14	64 − 27	66 − 28	94 − 28

On the map above, mark and write the name of a vacation spot in the United States you would like to visit. Write a subtraction problem for it.

America's Favorite Pastime

Add or subtract. Use the chart to color the picture.

white	blue	brown	red	yellow
0–20	21–40	41–60	61–80	81–100

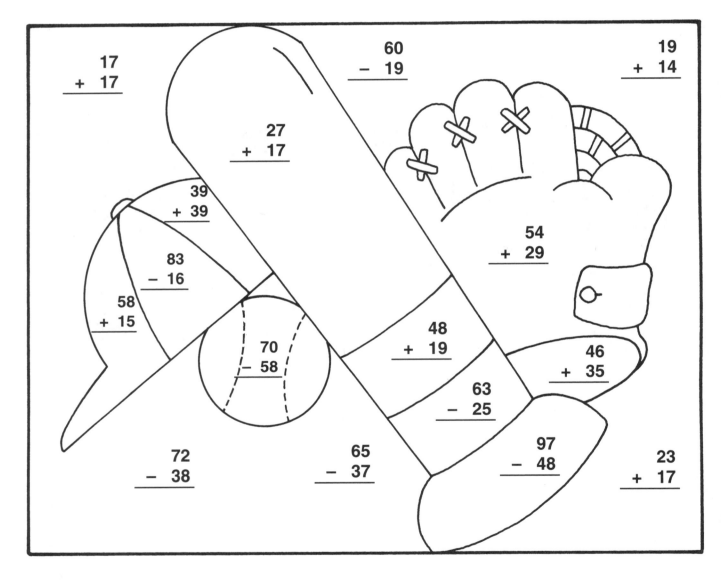

17
+ 17

60
− 19

19
+ 14

27
+ 17

39
+ 39

54
+ 29

83
− 16

58
+ 15

70
− 58

48
+ 19

46
+ 35

63
− 25

72
− 38

65
− 37

97
− 48

23
+ 17

Finish the pattern.

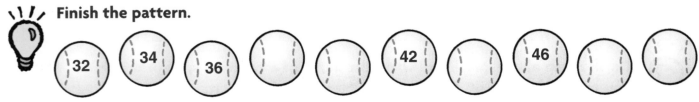

32   34   36   ___   ___   42   ___   46   ___   ___

Scholastic Professional Books

Name _____

High-Scoring Game

	1	2	3	4	5	6	7	8	9
Cardinals	16	57	91	39	68	25	83	44	72
Blue Jays	87	11	45	94	29	73	32	58	66

Find the total number of runs in each inning.

Add.

	1	2	3	4	5	6	7	8	9
	16 + 87								

Find the difference in runs in each inning.

Subtract.

	1	2	3	4	5	6	7	8	9
	87 – 16								

Solve.

A. How many runs did the Cardinals score altogether in the first and sixth inning?

_____ runs

B. How many runs did the Blue Jays score altogether in the seventh and eighth inning?

_____ runs

C. How many more runs did the Cardinals score in the third inning than the second inning?

_____ runs

D. How many more runs did the Blue Jays score in the first inning than the fifth inning?

_____ runs

More Fun Sports

Add or subtract.

91 − 67	48 + 43	92 − 45	70 − 17	63 − 47	38 + 54	29 + 36	80 − 42
skating	football	hockey	volleyball	basketball	soccer	tennis	track

Complete the puzzle with the sport that goes with each answer.

Down

1. 47
2. 53
3. 24
5. 38

Across

3. 92
4. 16
5. 65
6. 91

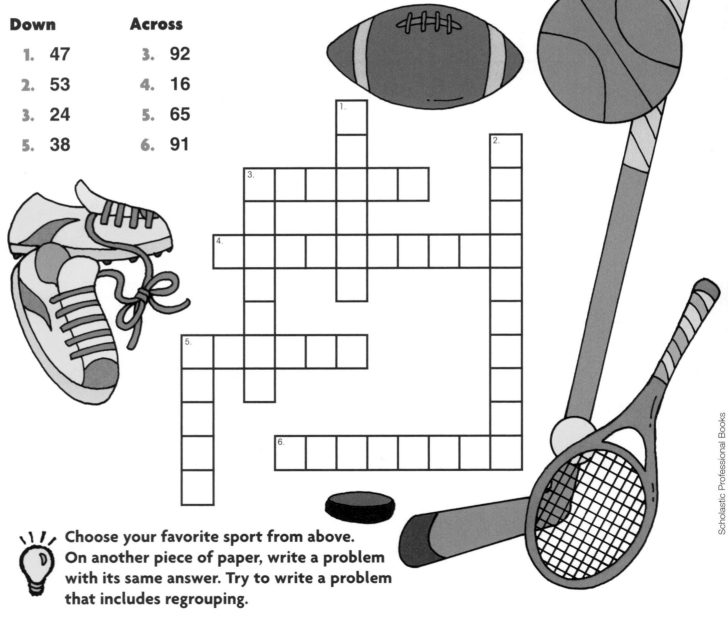

Choose your favorite sport from above. On another piece of paper, write a problem with its same answer. Try to write a problem that includes regrouping.

Name _____

Skating Shapes

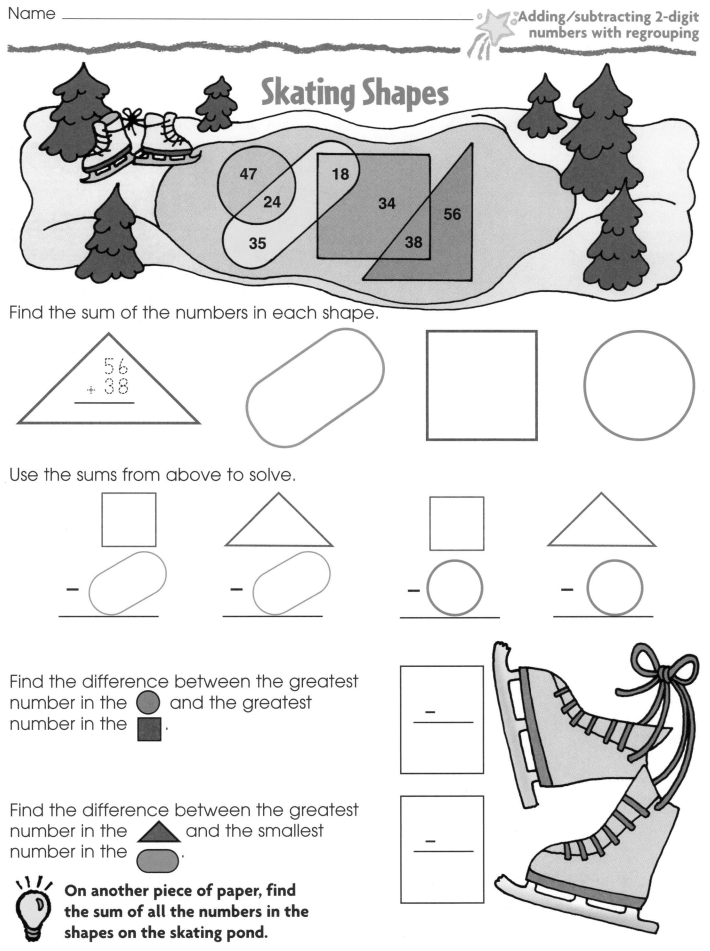

Find the sum of the numbers in each shape.

$$\begin{array}{r} 56 \\ +\ 38 \\ \hline \end{array}$$

Use the sums from above to solve.

☐
— ⬭
_____

△
— ⬭
_____

☐
— ◯
_____

△
— ◯
_____

Find the difference between the greatest number in the ◯ and the greatest number in the ⬛.

☐
—
_____

Find the difference between the greatest number in the ▲ and the smallest number in the ⬭.

☐
—
_____

💡 **On another piece of paper, find the sum of all the numbers in the shapes on the skating pond.**

Great Math Inventions

Add or subtract. Then write the problem's letter above its matching answer below.

S.　29
　+ 46

I.　48
　− 24

A.　27
　+ 38

R.　56
　− 18

R.　37
　+ 47

W.　81
　− 24

H.　23
　+ 35

I.　90
　− 26

U.　52
　− 19

O.　37
　+ 35

L.　70
　− 19

M.　82
　− 48

B.　23
　+ 48

L.　52
　+ 28

G.　91
　− 22

U.　73
　− 25

___ ___ ___ ___ ___ ___ ___　　___ ___ ___ ___ ___ ___ ___ ___ ___
57　24　80　51　64　65　34　　71　48　84　38　72　33　69　58　75

invented and patented the adding machine in St. Louis, Missouri, in 1888.

Name _____

It All Adds Up!

Add. Fill in the missing numbers.

3 2 4 + 6 3 ☐ ☐ ☐ 6	2 4 ☐ + ☐ 5 1 7 ☐ 2	☐ 5 5 + 3 ☐ 1 4 8 ☐	2 ☐ 3 + ☐ 1 3 5 2 ☐
4 1 ☐ + 3 ☐ 2 ☐ 3 7	☐ 4 3 + 1 4 ☐ 2 ☐ 9	2 ☐ ☐ + 2 1 6 ☐ 1 8	☐ 3 1 + 4 ☐ ☐ 8 5 3
1 ☐ 2 + ☐ 3 3 3 7 ☐	☐ 4 1 + 1 3 ☐ 6 ☐ 5	3 3 ☐ + ☐ ☐ 3 6 6 8	☐ 1 2 + 2 ☐ 2 9 4 ☐
2 2 ☐ + 3 1 4 ☐ ☐ 4	5 ☐ 4 + ☐ 3 4 8 4 ☐	2 2 4 + 1 ☐ 3 ☐ 6 ☐	☐ 1 6 + 1 3 ☐ 5 ☐ 8

💡 **Joe and Ellie were going to the movies. Joe brought $5.☐0, and Ellie brought $☐.35. If they had $9.75 altogether, how much money did they each have? Show your work.**

Name _____

It's Electrifying!

Regroup tens into hundreds. Draw a line to connect.

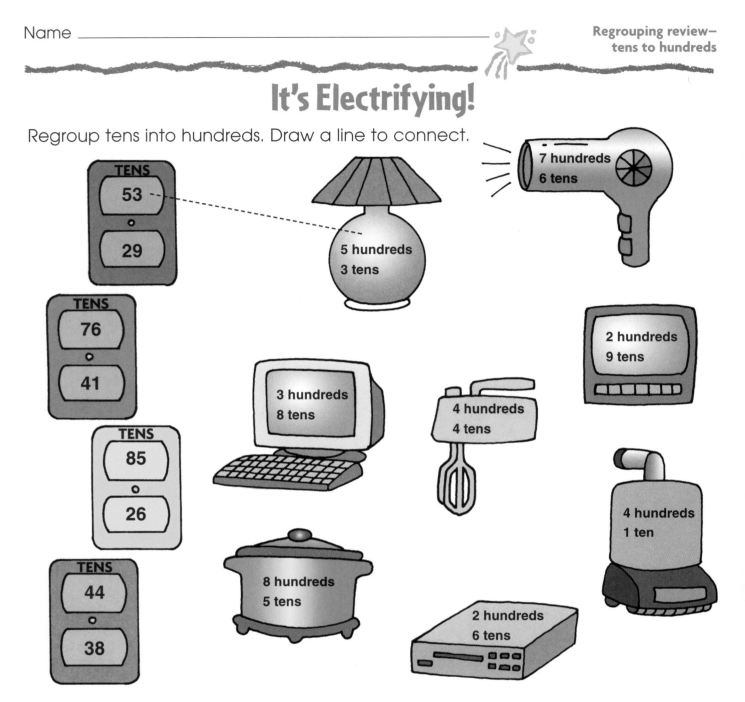

Fill in each missing number.

hundreds	tens	ones	number
200	40	7	2 4 7
400	70	6	__ __ __
300		2	__ 9 __
100	90		__ __ 3
500		1	__ 6 __

Let the Light Shine

Regroup hundreds to tens.

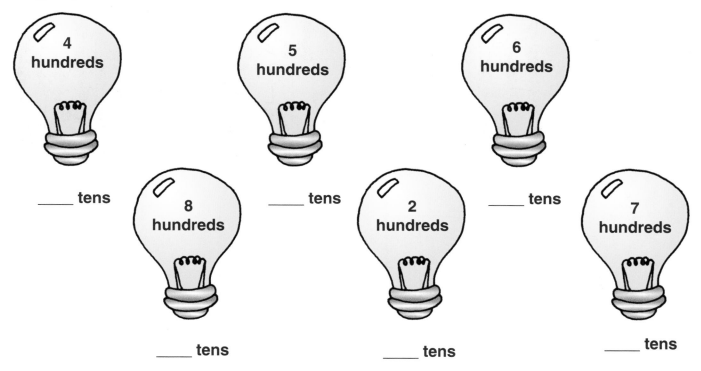

4 hundreds

_____ tens

5 hundreds

_____ tens

6 hundreds

_____ tens

8 hundreds

_____ tens

2 hundreds

_____ tens

7 hundreds

_____ tens

Circle the lightbulb in each box with the greater value yellow.

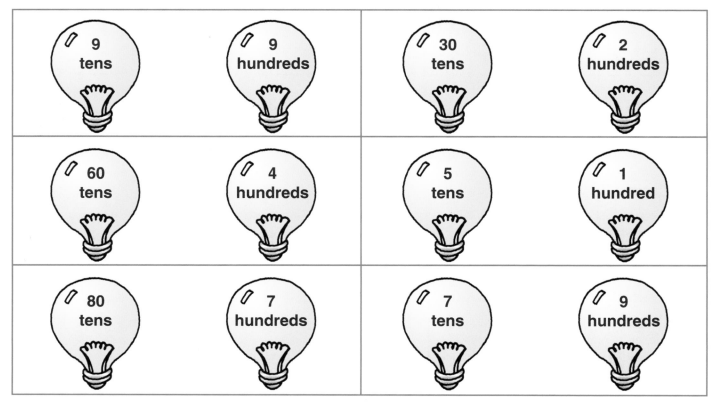

9 tens   9 hundreds   30 tens   2 hundreds

60 tens   4 hundreds   5 tens   1 hundred

80 tens   7 hundreds   7 tens   9 hundreds

A, B, C, . . .

Add.

286 + 668	138 + 289	285 + 269
496 + 188	159 + 190	175 + 189
499 + 446	375 + 469	183 + 289
299 + 158	196 + 378	657 + 285
186 + 287	157 + 267	276 + 566

295 + 675	188 + 185	487 + 385
284 + 439	389 + 188	595 + 289
128 + 379	297 + 179	198 + 199
365 + 378	192 + 579	123 + 589
386 + 189	295 + 379	436 + 538

This letter sounds like a question.

Color each answer with a 4 in the ones place to see!

This letter names a feature on your face.

Color each answer with a 7 in the tens place to see!

Scholastic Professional Books

. . . X, Y, and Z

Add.

P x W N O v O U T v T R Q z Y S

298 + 276	191 + 343	269 + 289
157 + 189	137 + 369	278 + 485
395 + 457	244 + 279	499 + 446
288 + 664	236 + 288	577 + 388
498 + 399	399 + 164	284 + 439

259 + 467	364 + 258	487 + 436
199 + 128	199 + 89	238 + 287
255 + 373	509 + 315	117 + 304
257 + 569	276 + 566	149 + 279
339 + 385	258 + 467	179 + 348

This letter names an icy drink.

Color each answer with a 5 in the hundreds place to see!

This letter names an insect that stings.

Color each answer with a 2 in the tens place to see!

Name _____

Let's Talk

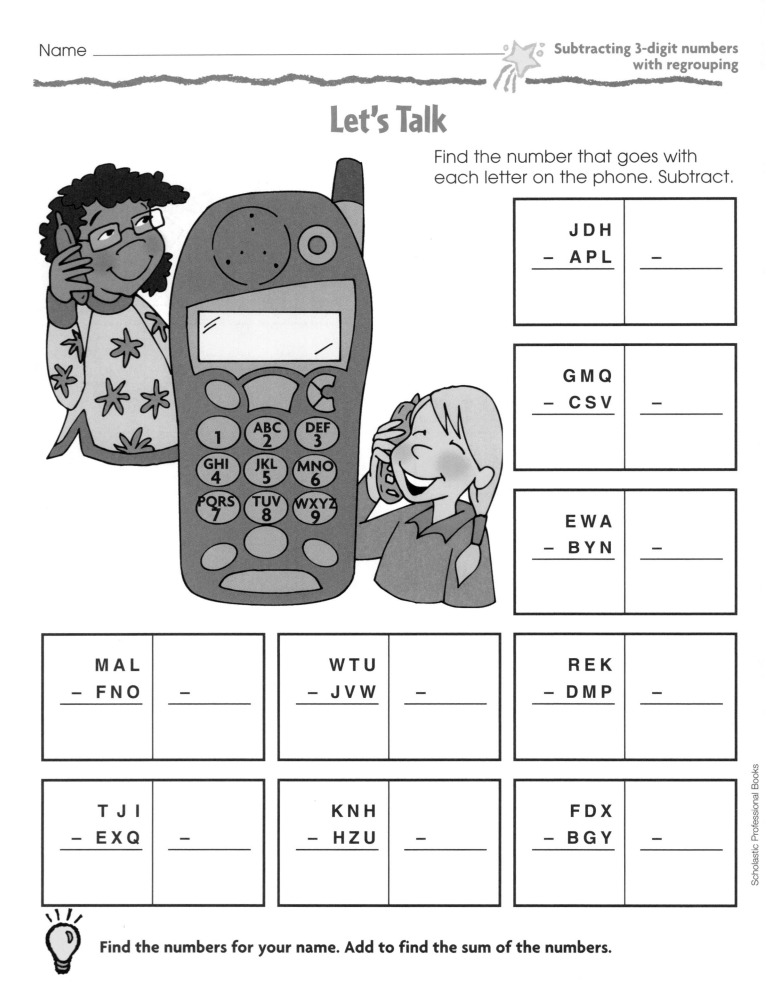

Find the number that goes with each letter on the phone. Subtract.

J D H	
– A P L	– _____

G M Q	
– C S V	– _____

E W A	
– B Y N	– _____

M A L	
– F N O	– _____

W T U	
– J V W	– _____

R E K	
– D M P	– _____

T J I	
– E X Q	– _____

K N H	
– H Z U	– _____

F D X	
– B G Y	– _____

Find the numbers for your name. Add to find the sum of the numbers.

Scholastic Professional Books

Out of This World

Subtract. Use the chart to color the picture.

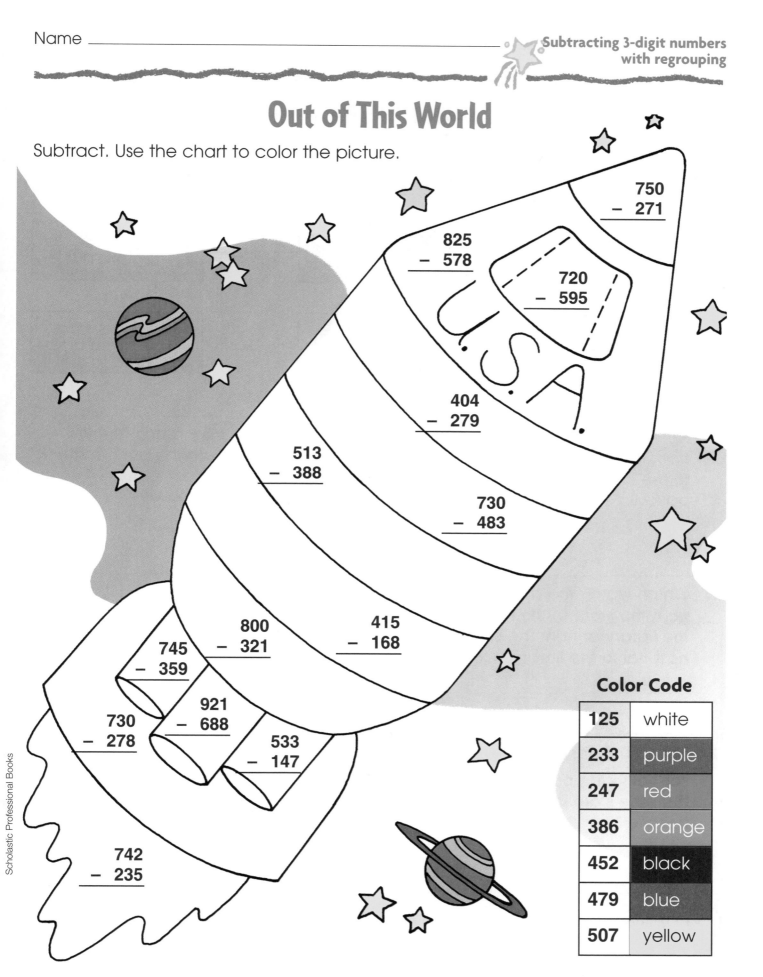

750
− 271

825
− 578

720
− 595

404
− 279

513
− 388

730
− 483

800
− 321

415
− 168

745
− 359

921
− 688

730
− 278

533
− 147

742
− 235

Color Code

125	white
233	purple
247	red
386	orange
452	black
479	blue
507	yellow

Scholastic Professional Books

Your Part of the World

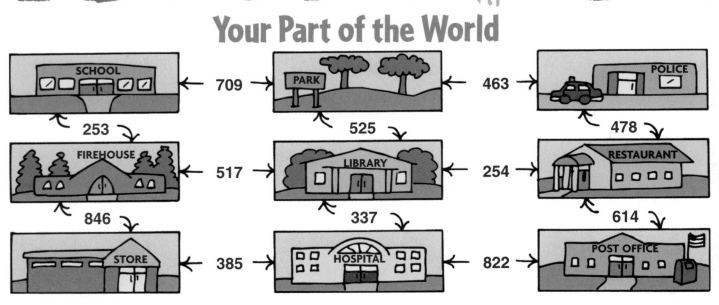

Use the distance between each building to solve each problem.

A. How many feet is it from the firehouse to the library to the park?	**B.** How many feet is it from the post office to the restaurant to the police station?	**C.** How many feet is it from the park to the school to the firehouse?

D. Which way is the shortest route— from the store to the firehouse to the library or from the store to the hospital to the library? Circle.

$$846$$
$$+\ 517$$

$$385$$
$$+\ 337$$

E. How much farther is the

| school to the park than the store to the hospital? | firehouse to the library than the park to the police station? | library to the park than the hospital to the store? |

 On another piece of paper, find which route is the shortest way from the school to the post office. Trace this route on the map above.

Home Sweet Home

Use the coordinates to find each number. Add or subtract.

	1	2	3
A	496	723	379
B	162	215	956
C	547	834	688

	4	5	6
E	668	884	345
F	239	716	188
G	422	578	957

A. (A, 1)
(F, 6) − _____

B. (B, 3)
(E, 4) − _____

C. (C, 1)
(F, 4) + _____

D. (A, 3)
(E, 6) + _____

E. (A, 2)
(B, 1) − _____

F. (G, 4)
(B, 2) − _____

G. (G, 6)
(C, 3) − _____

H. (E, 5)
(C, 2) + _____

I. (B, 3)
(G, 5) − _____

Color the largest number on each house orange. Color the smallest number on each house purple.

Name _____

What a Beautiful World!

Add or subtract.

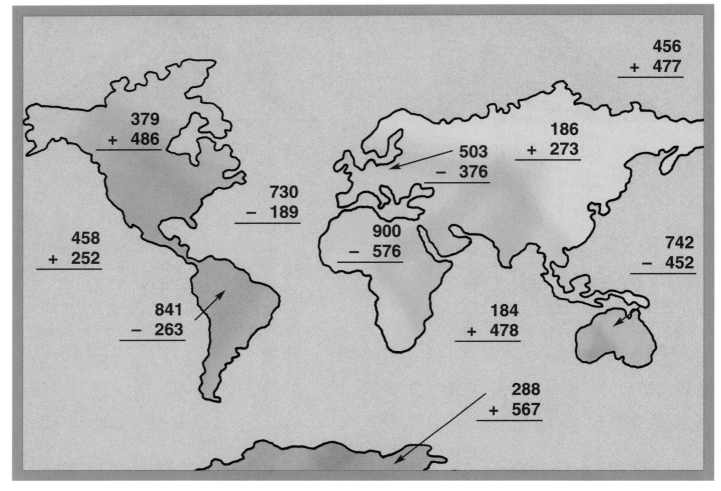

```
                                                              456
                                                            + 477
                                                            ─────

        379                              186
      + 486                   503      + 273
      ─────                 - 376      ─────
                            ─────
                 730
               - 189          900                                  742
  458          ─────        - 576                                - 452
+ 252                       ─────                                ─────

        841                              184
      - 263                            + 478
      ─────                            ─────

                                 288
                               + 567
                               ─────
```

Label the map using the code below.

North America	> 860 and < 927	**Atlantic Ocean**	> 496 and < 560
South America	> 571 and < 658	**Indian Ocean**	> 581 and < 672
Australia	> 189 and < 293	**Pacific Ocean**	> 671 and < 732
Asia	> 423 and < 538	**Arctic Ocean**	> 867 and < 948
Europe	> 85 and < 266		
Antarctica	> 748 and < 864		
Africa	> 297 and < 334		

Add the answers for the oceans together.

Majestic Mountains

Add or subtract. Use the code to name four
different mountain ranges.

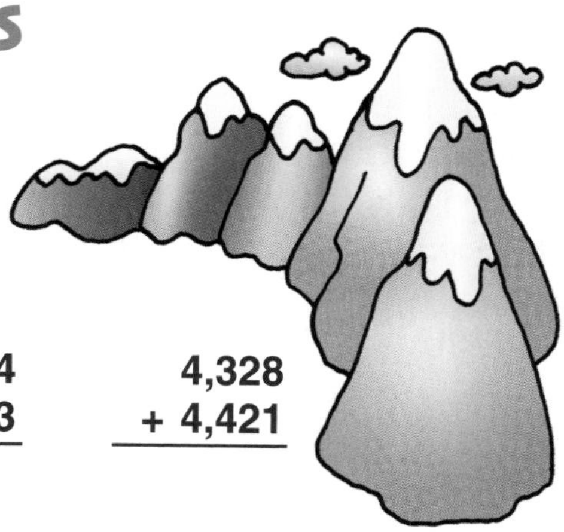

N	6,348
R	8,789
A	5,063
I	7,695
O	2,429
K	5,642
E	7,483
C	3,012
Y	2,351
Z	5,234
L	3,721
U	6,704
P	3,827
S	8,749
D	4,907

2,033
+ 3,030
○

2,411
+ 1,310
○

2,504
+ 1,323
○

4,328
+ 4,421
○

4,258
+ 4,531
○

1,326
+ 1,103
○

1,012
+ 2,000
○

2,321
+ 3,321
○

1,231
+ 1,120
○

1,204
+ 1,225
○

2,113
+ 3,121
○

2,042
+ 3,021
○

3,746
+ 5,043
○

4,131
+ 1,511
○

4,053
+ 1,010
○

2,216
+ 4,132
○

2,506
+ 2,401
○

6,471
+ 1,012
○

7,326
+ 1,423
○

Reach for the Top

Add. Then starting at the bottom row, add the digits in each sum. If the digits total 9, color the box to find your way to the top!

1,021
+ 1,031

3,432   2,130
+ 1,154   + 1,200

1,423   2,423   4,000
+ 1,322   + 1,520   + 4,010

4,024   5,010   3,011   2,240
+ 3,012   + 1,011   + 4,000   + 1,232

1,412   4,201   2,431   4,631   4,302
+ 1,351   + 1,100   + 3,132   + 3,210   + 5,502

3,243   2,031   4,084   1,362   3,025   6,434
+ 4,200   + 1,200   + 2,011   + 1,202   + 1,312   + 3,251

Write an addition problem with four numbers in the answer so the sum of the digits equals 12.

One in a Thousand

Add. Write the letters on the lines below in order from the smallest to the largest sums to find out whose face is on the hundred-dollar bill.

F. $27.41
  + $12.55

N. $59.63
  + $20.33

N. $85.42
  + $14.06

R. $31.75
  + $35.24

K. $64.84
  + $22.15

A. $29.35
  + $50.42

L. $46.96
  + $42.03

I. $73.57
  + $23.43

___ ___ ___ ___ ___ ___ ___ ___ ___

If you have **50** hundred-dollar bills, you have _____ thousand dollars!

If you have **20** hundred-dollar bills, you have _____ thousand dollars!

If you have **80** hundred-dollar bills, you have _____ thousand dollars!

If you have **10** hundred-dollar bills, you have _____ thousand dollars!

If you have **30** hundred-dollar bills, you have _____ thousand dollars!

If you have **70** hundred-dollar bills, you have _____ thousand dollars!

If you have **90** hundred-dollar bills, you have _____ thousand dollars!

If you have **40** hundred-dollar bills, you have _____ thousand dollars!

If you have **60** hundred-dollar bills, you have _____ thousand dollars!

Great Beginnings

Add. Look at each sum. Use the code below to color the picture.

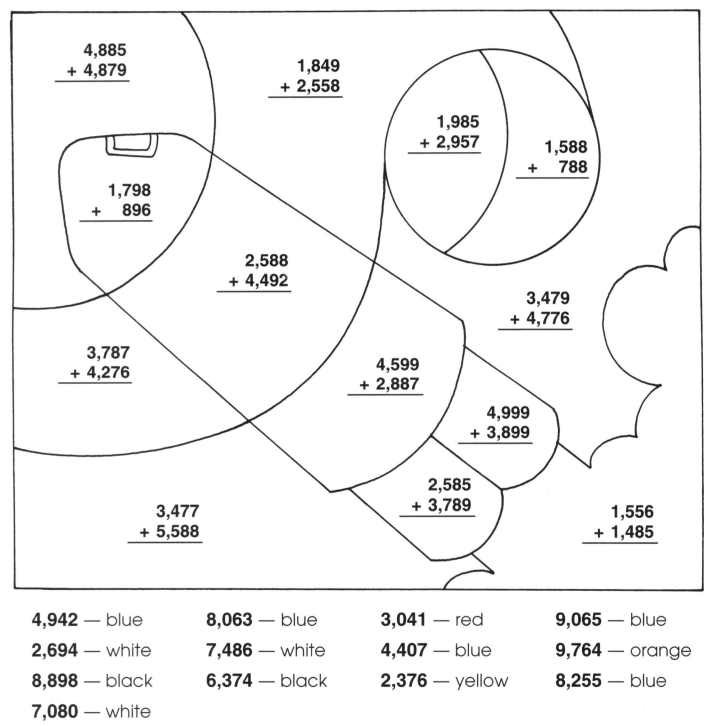

4,885
+ 4,879

1,849
+ 2,558

1,985
+ 2,957

1,588
+   788

1,798
+   896

2,588
+ 4,492

3,479
+ 4,776

3,787
+ 4,276

4,599
+ 2,887

4,999
+ 3,899

3,477
+ 5,588

2,585
+ 3,789

1,556
+ 1,485

4,942 — blue	**8,063** — blue	**3,041** — red	**9,065** — blue
2,694 — white	**7,486** — white	**4,407** — blue	**9,764** — orange
8,898 — black	**6,374** — black	**2,376** — yellow	**8,255** — blue
7,080 — white			

Find the year man first walked on the moon. Add that number to the year it is now.

Scholastic Professional Books

Styles Change

Add. Match the sums to show the hats and shoes that go together.

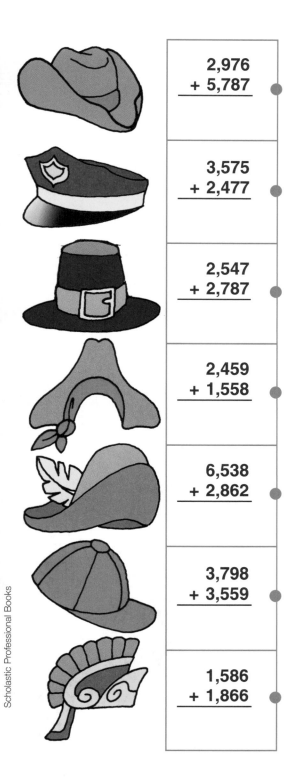

2,976 + 5,787
3,575 + 2,477
2,547 + 2,787
2,459 + 1,558
6,538 + 2,862
3,798 + 3,559
1,586 + 1,866

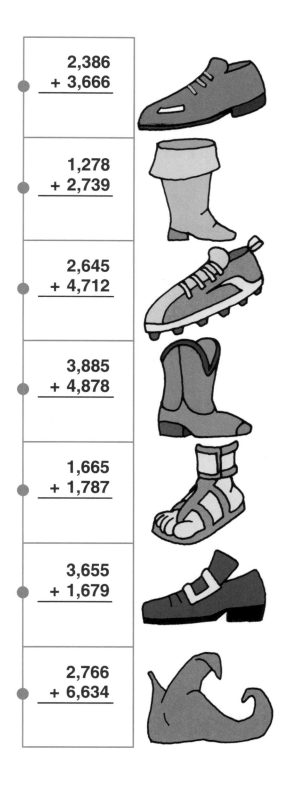

2,386 + 3,666
1,278 + 2,739
2,645 + 4,712
3,885 + 4,878
1,665 + 1,787
3,655 + 1,679
2,766 + 6,634

Scholastic Professional Books

Dynamite Dominoes

Color the connecting squares that equal the same amount the same color.
Remember, 1 thousand equals 10 hundreds.

thousands	20 hundreds	10 hundreds	thousand	thousands
50 hundreds	thousands	90 hundreds	thousands	40 hundreds
30 hundreds	70 hundreds	thousands	10 hundreds	20 hundreds
thousands	thousands	thousands	60 hundreds	thousands

Add. Write the number.

thousands		hundreds		tens		ones		
3	+	1	+	6	+	7	=	
5	+	7	+	0	+	3	=	
6	+	0	+	3	+	9	=	
4	+	5	+	8	+	4	=	
9	+	9	+	4	+	0	=	

Name _____

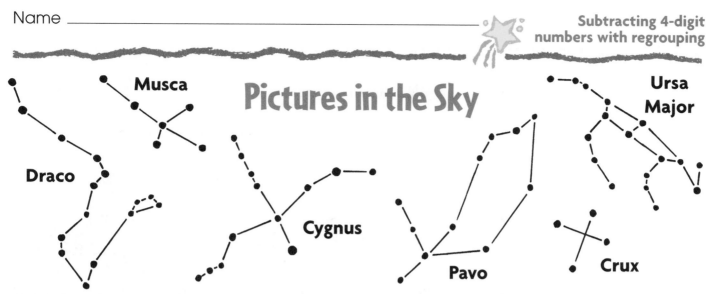

Pictures in the Sky

Subtract. Draw a line between matching sums to connect the Latin and English names for each constellation.

Latin

Draco	7,621 − 5,586
Pavo	7,340 − 3,758
Cygnus	9,317 − 2,858
Ursa Major	8,332 − 3,579
Musca	7,015 − 1,739
Crux	8,150 − 3,166

English

8,533 − 2,074	**Swan**
7,662 − 2,678	**Cross**
8,403 − 6,368	**Dragon**
6,441 − 2,859	**Peacock**
7,031 − 2,278	**Great Bear**
8,133 − 2,857	**Fly**

Name _____

Fun With Numbers

Add or subtract. Then write the problem's letter above its matching answer below.

W.
2,376
+ 2,784

O.
8,500
− 2,763

T.
4,401
− 2,550

A.
2,763
+ 3,857

E.
6,345
− 2,660

H.
8,455
− 1,867

!
4,672
+ 3,885

M.
8,304
− 2,541

M.
2,463
+ 4,908

E.
4,365
− 1,478

A.
1,074
+ 5,988

S.
3,453
+ 2,778

___ ___ ___ ___ **is**
5,763 7,062 1,851 6,588

___ ___ ___ ___ ___ ___ ___ ___
6,620 5,160 2,887 6,231 5,737 7,371 3,685 8,557

Scholastic Success With

MATH

Space Chase Place Value

Use strategies to capture creepy space creatures while learning about place value.

Writing Connection

Describe the strategy you used to play the game and how you think you could improve your score if you played again.

Directions

1. Review place value to the hundred thousands place. You will need this knowledge if you want to do well in the Space Chase game.

2. Partner up with a friend or family member. To make your own spinner, spin a paper clip around a pencil placed at the spinner's center. Players should spin to see who goes first, with the higher spin going first. Players then take turns spinning.

3. On each turn, a player spins and lands on a number. The player then says which creepy space creature he or she will capture on that turn. Players write the number they landed on in the blank that corresponds with the place value of the space creature. (For example: In round 1, Player 1 spins a 5. She decides to capture a Kerpew on this turn. Kerpews represent the ten thousands place. So Player 1 writes a 5 in the ten thousands place of her Round 1 score blanks.) Players record their numbers in the score blanks of the round they are playing.

4. A particular space creature can be captured only once per round. The round ends when both players have captured all six space creatures. Play continues for three rounds. The winner of each round is the player who has written the greater 6-digit number.

Space Chase Place Value

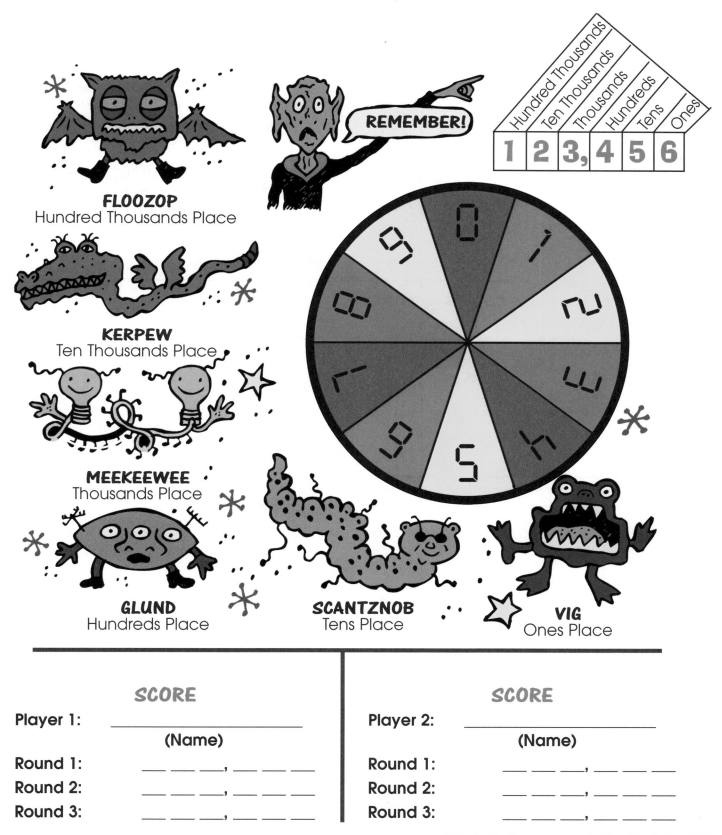

Hundred Thousands	Ten Thousands	Thousands	Hundreds	Tens	Ones
1	2	3,	4	5	6

REMEMBER!

FLOOZOP
Hundred Thousands Place

KERPEW
Ten Thousands Place

MEEKEEWEE
Thousands Place

GLUND
Hundreds Place

SCANTZNOB
Tens Place

VIG
Ones Place

SCORE

Player 1: _____
(Name)

Round 1: __ __ __, __ __ __

Round 2: __ __ __, __ __ __

Round 3: __ __ __, __ __ __

SCORE

Player 2: _____
(Name)

Round 1: __ __ __, __ __ __

Round 2: __ __ __, __ __ __

Round 3: __ __ __, __ __ __

Newspaper Math

What to Do:

Use a newspaper to find the numbers listed below. Cut out your answers from the newspaper and tape them in the box with each question.

EXTRA! EXTRA!
Read All About It!

1. From the weather report, find the temperature in two cities.

2. Pick three items advertised for sale.

3. Find two different times that the same movie is playing.

4. From the TV listings, pick three programs that you would like to watch. Include the channels that those programs will be on.

5. Choose two numbers from an article of your choice.

Scholastic Professional Books

Place-Value Puzzler

What is too much fun for one, enough for two, and means nothing to three?

Find the answer to this riddle by using place value! Take a look at each number below. One digit in each number is underlined. Circle the word in each line that tells the place value of the underlined number. Write the letters next to each correct answer in the blanks below. The first one is done for you.

A.	1<u>5</u>,209	a thousands		i hundreds
B.	4,7<u>2</u>9	n hundreds		s tens
C.	<u>4</u>25	e hundreds		o tens
D.	7,6<u>1</u>8	c tens		g ones
E.	1,<u>1</u>12	p thousands		r hundreds
F.	8,63<u>6</u>	a hundreds		e ones
G.	2<u>2</u>2	t tens		m ones

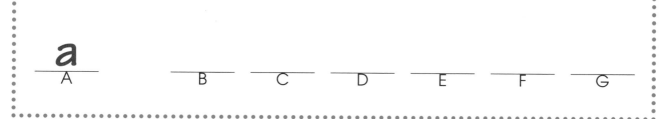

a
A ___ B ___ C ___ D ___ E ___ F ___ G

Bee Riddle

Riddle: What did the farmer get when he tried to reach the beehive?

Round each number. Then use the Decoder to solve the riddle by filling in the spaces at the bottom of the page.

Decoder

400	A
800	W
30	O
10	Y
25	E
500	I
210	J
20	L
40	C
700	U
90	S
100	T
600	G
95	F
50	N
550	V
300	Z
7	H
200	Z

1 Round 7 to the nearest ten _____
2 Round 23 to the nearest ten _____
3 Round 46 to the nearest ten _____
4 Round 92 to the nearest ten _____
5 Round 203 to the nearest hundred _____
6 Round 420 to the nearest hundred _____
7 Round 588 to the nearest hundred _____
8 Round 312 to the nearest hundred _____
9 Round 549 to the nearest hundred _____
10 Round 710 to the nearest hundred _____

A ``B __ __ __ __ `` __ __ __ __ __
    10 5 8 1   4 9 7 3 6 2

Discover Coordinates!

Follow the coordinates to the correct box, then draw in the underlined treasures on this treasure map.

C3   A <u>jeweled crown</u> sparkles.
B1   A <u>ruby necklace</u> can be found.
C5   A <u>golden cup</u> awaits you.
D4   An <u>X</u> marks the spot!
A4   A <u>wooden treasure chest</u> you'll find.
E1   A <u>silvery sword</u> lies here.

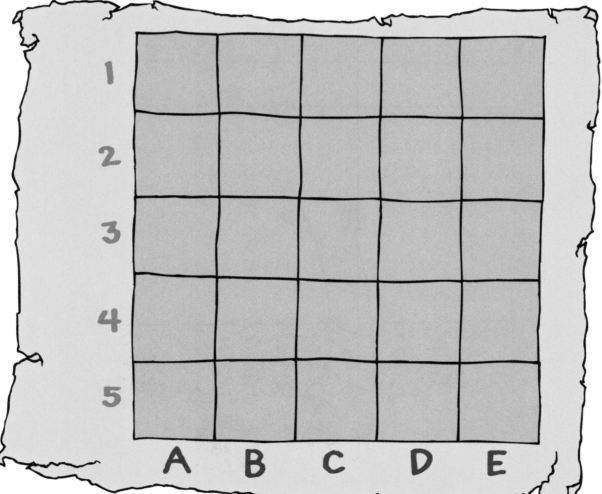

Scholastic Professional Books

Tropical Tree

1. Solve the problems.

2. Find each number pair on the graph. Make a dot for each.

3. Connect the dots in the order that you make them.

4. What picture did you make?

_____

	Across	**Up**
1.	10 – 5 = ____	7 – 0 = ____
2.	19 – 12 = ____	9 – 4 = ____
3.	10 – 4 = ____	18 – 11 = ____
4.	20 – 12 = ____	8 – 2 = ____
5.	9 – 3 = ____	17 – 9 = ____
6.	18 – 10 = ____	15 – 8 = ____

	Across	Up
7.	17 – 11 = ____	19 – 10 = ____
8.	20 – 16 = ____	11 – 2 = ____
9.	19 – 18 = ____	13 – 5 = ____
10.	20 – 17 = ____	15 – 7 = ____
11.	20 – 19 = ____	14 – 8 = ____
12.	18 – 15 = ____	20 – 13 = ____
13.	13 – 12 = ____	16 – 11 = ____
14.	17 – 13 = ____	16 – 9 = ____

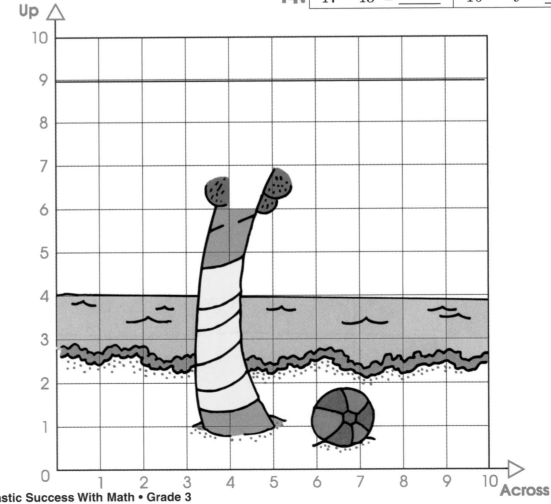

Scholastic Professional Books

Animal Caller

A bar graph shows information. This bar graph shows the speeds of animals in miles per hour. Use the graph to answer the questions.

WHICH ANIMAL IS...

1. THE FASTEST?

_____

2. THE SLOWEST?

_____

3. GOING 40 mph?

_____

4. 20mph FASTER THAN A CAT?

_____

5. HOW MANY 4-FOOTED ANIMALS ARE LISTED?

_____

DO THE BARS SHOW...

6. ANIMAL NAMES AND mph?

_____

7. SPEED OR WEIGHT?

_____

8. INFORMATION ABOUT TIGERS?

_____

What am I doing here?

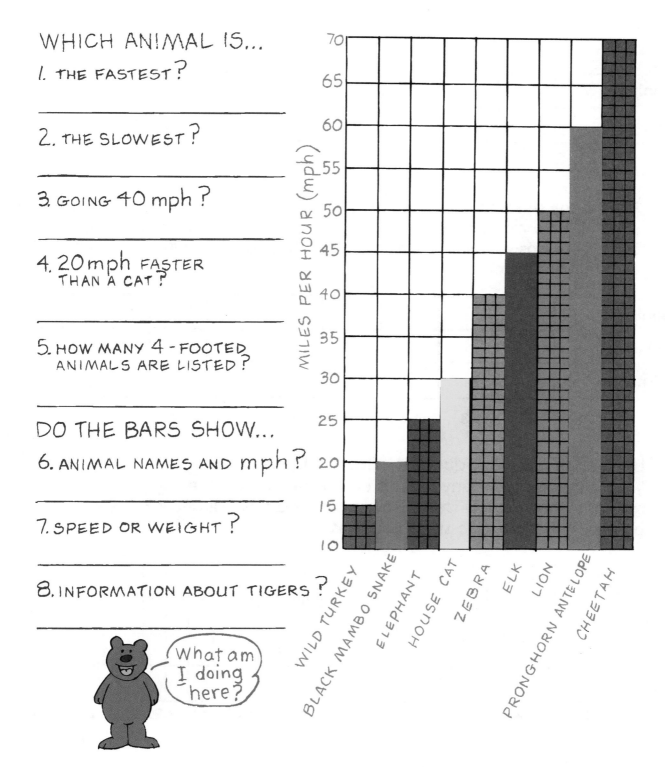

Great Graphing

How many pennies equal 5¢? Color in the boxes on the graph to show your answer. How many nickels equal 5¢? Color in the boxes on the graph to show your answer.

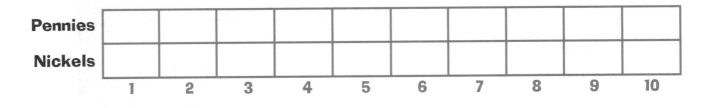

How many pennies equal 10¢? Color in the boxes on the graph to show your answer. How many nickels equal 10¢? Color in the boxes on the graph to show your answer. How many dimes equal 10¢? Color in the boxes on the graph to show your answer.

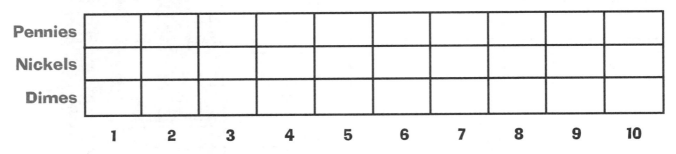

How many pennies equal 25¢? Color in the boxes on the graph to show your answer. How many nickels equal 25¢? Color in the boxes on the graph to show your answer. How many quarters equal 25¢? Color in the boxes on the graph to show your answer.

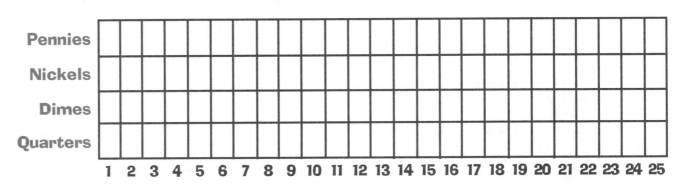

Graph Drafter

A line graph shows how something changes over time. This line graph shows temperature changes during a year in New York City. Use the graph to answer the questions below.

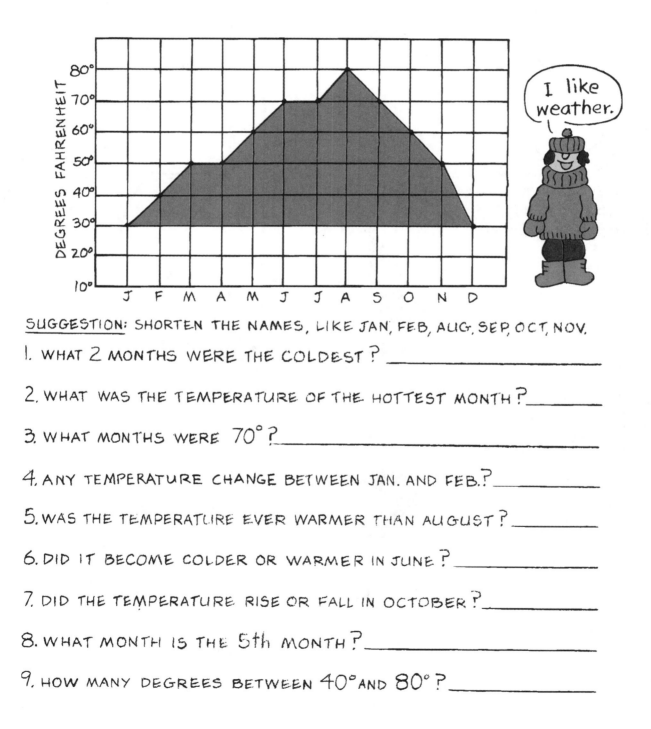

SUGGESTION: SHORTEN THE NAMES, LIKE JAN, FEB, AUG, SEP, OCT, NOV.

1. WHAT 2 MONTHS WERE THE COLDEST? _____

2. WHAT WAS THE TEMPERATURE OF THE HOTTEST MONTH? _____

3. WHAT MONTHS WERE 70°? _____

4. ANY TEMPERATURE CHANGE BETWEEN JAN. AND FEB.? _____

5. WAS THE TEMPERATURE EVER WARMER THAN AUGUST? _____

6. DID IT BECOME COLDER OR WARMER IN JUNE? _____

7. DID THE TEMPERATURE RISE OR FALL IN OCTOBER? _____

8. WHAT MONTH IS THE 5th MONTH? _____

9. HOW MANY DEGREES BETWEEN 40° AND 80°? _____

Code Zero! Code One!

When a number is multiplied by 0, the product is always 0.
When a number is multiplied by 1, the product is always the number being multiplied.

Multiply. Shade all products of 0 yellow. Shade all other products green.

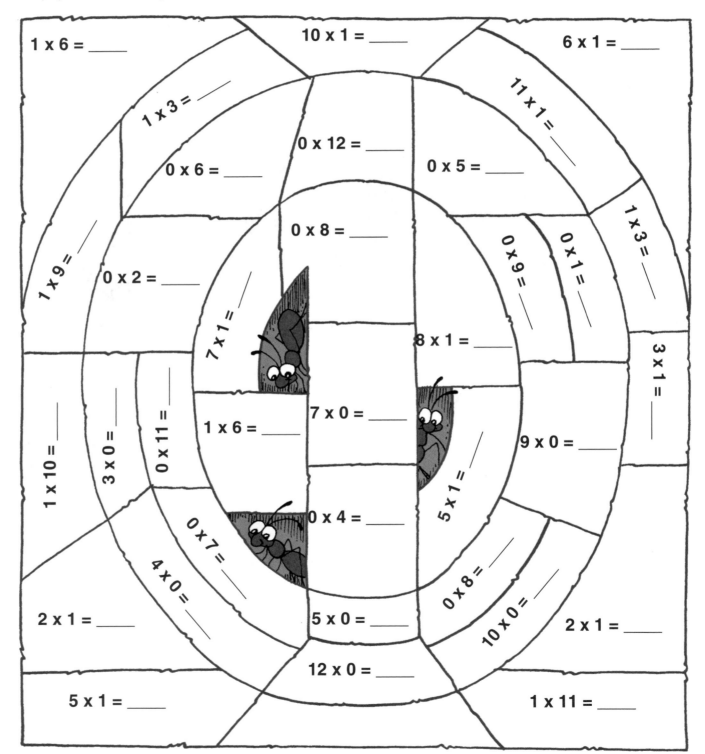

1 x 6 = _____
10 x 1 = _____
6 x 1 = _____
1 x 3 = _____
11 x 1 = _____
0 x 12 = _____
0 x 6 = _____
0 x 5 = _____
0 x 8 = _____
1 x 9 = _____
0 x 2 = _____
0 x 9 = _____
0 x 1 = _____
1 x 3 = _____
7 x 1 = _____
8 x 1 = _____
7 x 0 = _____
1 x 6 = _____
3 x 1 = _____
1 x 10 = _____
3 x 0 = _____
0 x 11 = _____
9 x 0 = _____
5 x 1 = _____
0 x 4 = _____
0 x 7 = _____
4 x 0 = _____
0 x 8 = _____
2 x 1 = _____
5 x 0 = _____
10 x 0 = _____
2 x 1 = _____
12 x 0 = _____
5 x 1 = _____
1 x 11 = _____

Two, Four, Six, Eight, Who Do We Appreciate?

When multiplying by 2, skip count by 2, or think of number line jumping!

Multiply.

A. 2 x 3 = ____   2 x 8 = ____   11 x 2 = ____   2 x 7 = ____

B. 8 x 2 = ____   4 x 2 = ____   2 x 2 = ____   2 x 4 = ____

C. 12 x 2 = ____   5 x 2 = ____   10 x 2 = ____   2 x 12 = ____

D. 9 x 2 = ____   2 x 1 = ____   2 x 10 = ____   7 x 2 = ____

E. 2 x 0 = ____   2 x 6 = ____   3 x 2 = ____   0 x 2 = ____

F. 2 x 5 = ____   2 x 9 = ____

G. 6 x 2 = ____   1 x 2 = ____

H. 2 x 11 = ____   2 x 2 = ____

On another piece of paper, write a rhyme to go with each multiplication fact for 2.
Examples: "2 x 4 = 8, I love math, can you relate?" Or, "2 x 4 = 8, I've got to go, and shut the gate!"

A Positive Answer

What should you say if you are asked, "Do you want to learn the 3s?"

To find out, look at each problem below. If the product is correct, color the space green. If the product is incorrect, color the space yellow.

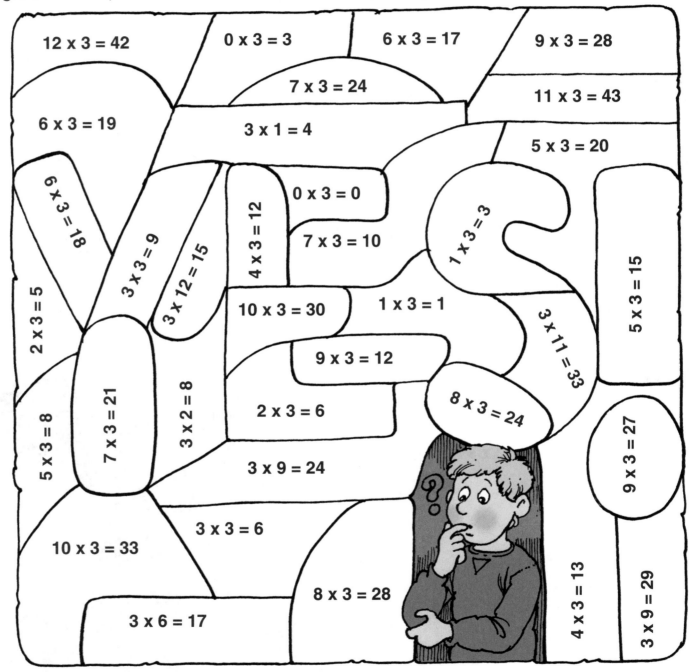

$12 \times 3 = 42$
$0 \times 3 = 3$
$6 \times 3 = 17$
$9 \times 3 = 28$
$7 \times 3 = 24$
$11 \times 3 = 43$
$6 \times 3 = 19$
$3 \times 1 = 4$
$5 \times 3 = 20$
$6 \times 3 = 18$
$0 \times 3 = 0$
$7 \times 3 = 10$
$1 \times 3 = 3$
$2 \times 3 = 5$
$3 \times 3 = 9$
$3 \times 12 = 15$
$4 \times 3 = 12$
$10 \times 3 = 30$
$1 \times 3 = 1$
$3 \times 11 = 33$
$5 \times 3 = 15$
$5 \times 3 = 8$
$7 \times 3 = 21$
$3 \times 2 = 8$
$9 \times 3 = 12$
$2 \times 3 = 6$
$8 \times 3 = 24$
$9 \times 3 = 27$
$3 \times 9 = 24$
$3 \times 3 = 6$
$10 \times 3 = 33$
$8 \times 3 = 28$
$4 \times 3 = 13$
$3 \times 9 = 29$
$3 \times 6 = 17$

How many letters are in the answer to the puzzle? If you wrote this word ten times, how many letters would you write altogether?

Puzzling Facts

Multiply. Write the number word for each product in the puzzle. Don't forget the hyphens!

Across

2. 4 x 9 = _____

4. 4 x 5 = _____

7. 4 x 3 = _____

8. 4 x 7 = _____

9. 4 x 10 = _____

11. 4 x 0 = _____

12. 4 x 11 = _____

Down

1. 4 x 4 = _____

2. 4 x 8 = _____

3. 4 x 12 = _____

5. 4 x 2 = _____

6. 4 x 6 = _____

10. 4 x 1 = _____

 Tracy was missing 4 buttons on 11 different shirts. How many buttons does she need to fix all the shirts?

Scholastic Professional Books

How Many Can You Find?

Complete each multiplication sentence. Then circle each answer in the picture.

A. $2 \times 5 =$ _____

B. $5 \times$ _____ $= 5$

C. _____ $\times 5 = 35$

D. $10 \times 5 =$ _____

E. _____ $\times 5 = 60$

F. $5 \times 6 =$ _____

G. _____ $\times 5 = 55$

H. $5 \times 3 =$ _____

I. $8 \times 5 =$ _____

J. _____ $\times 5 = 45$

K. $2 \times$ _____ $= 10$

L. _____ $\times 5 = 25$

M. $7 \times 5 =$ _____

N. $5 \times 12 =$ _____

O. $5 \times$ _____ $= 20$

Squeaky Squirrel lived in a tree with 4 squirrel friends. If each squirrel collected 12 nuts, how many nuts altogether did the squirrels collect?

Mathematics Fireworks

Multiply. On another piece of paper, find the sum of the products of each star trail. Then use the key to color each star to match its star trail sum.

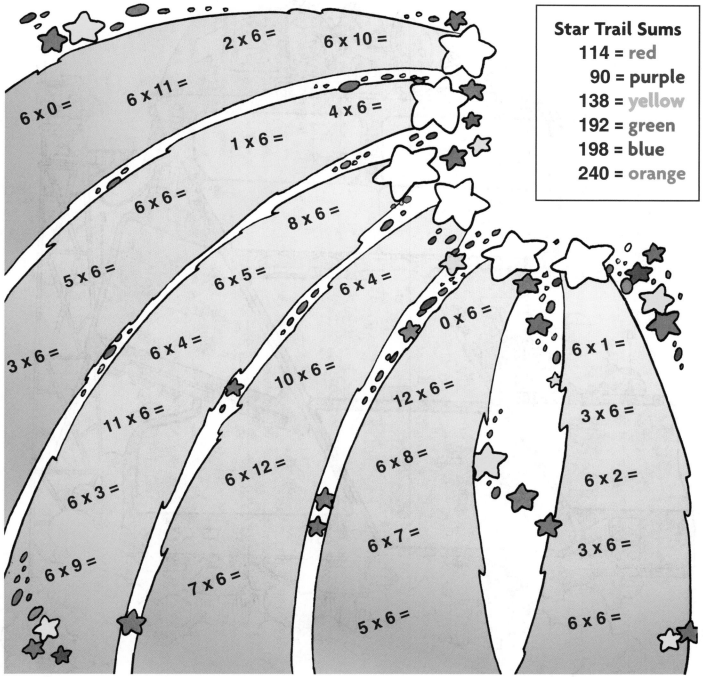

Star Trail Sums
114 = red
90 = purple
138 = yellow
192 = green
198 = blue
240 = orange

2 x 6 =
6 x 10 =
6 x 11 =
4 x 6 =
6 x 0 =
1 x 6 =
6 x 6 =
8 x 6 =
5 x 6 =
6 x 5 =
6 x 4 =
3 x 6 =
6 x 4 =
0 x 6 =
11 x 6 =
10 x 6 =
12 x 6 =
6 x 1 =
6 x 3 =
6 x 12 =
6 x 8 =
3 x 6 =
6 x 2 =
6 x 9 =
7 x 6 =
6 x 7 =
3 x 6 =
5 x 6 =
6 x 6 =

Emma counted the fireworks she watched on the Fourth of July. She counted 6 different fireworks every 15 minutes. The firework show lasted 2 hours. How many fireworks did Emma see?

Name _____

Flying Sevens

Multiply.

7 x 9 = ____
11 x 7 = ____
6 x 7 = ____
7 x 4 = ____

3 x 7 = ____
7 x 7 = ____
7 x 10 = ____
7 x 0 = ____

5 x 7 = ____
7 x 12 = ____
7 x 2 = ____
4 x 7 = ____

7 x 11 = ____
1 x 7 = ____
0 x 7 = ____

7 x 8 = ____
2 x 7 = ____
7 x 1 = ____

7 x 6 = ____
8 x 7 = ____
9 x 7 = ____
10 x 7 = ____

12 x 7 = ____
7 x 3 = ____
7 x 5 = ____

Cassandra's space mission is to orbit Earth seven times, as quickly as she can a total of seven times. How many times altogether will she orbit Earth?

Scholastic Professional Books

Name _____

The Ultimate Eight Track

Use a stopwatch to time how long it takes to multiply around the track.

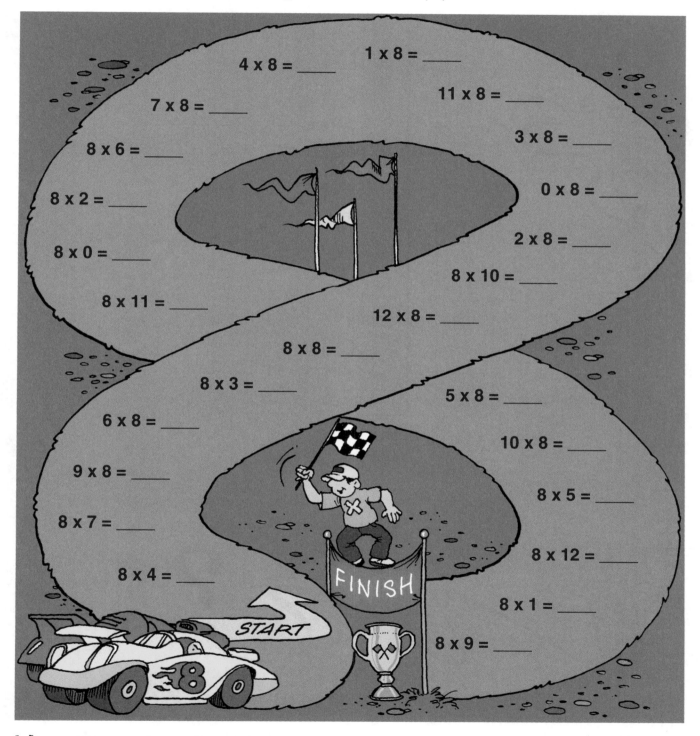

4 x 8 = ____

1 x 8 = ____

7 x 8 = ____

11 x 8 = ____

8 x 6 = ____

3 x 8 = ____

8 x 2 = ____

0 x 8 = ____

8 x 0 = ____

2 x 8 = ____

8 x 11 = ____

8 x 10 = ____

12 x 8 = ____

8 x 8 = ____

8 x 3 = ____

5 x 8 = ____

6 x 8 = ____

10 x 8 = ____

9 x 8 = ____

8 x 5 = ____

8 x 7 = ____

8 x 12 = ____

8 x 4 = ____

8 x 1 = ____

8 x 9 = ____

Racing Ricardo rapidly raced 8 times around the Eight Track. It took him 12 seconds to rapidly race one time around the track. How many seconds did it take him to complete the race?

Cross-Number Puzzle

Multiply. Write the number word for each product in the puzzle. Don't forget the hyphens!

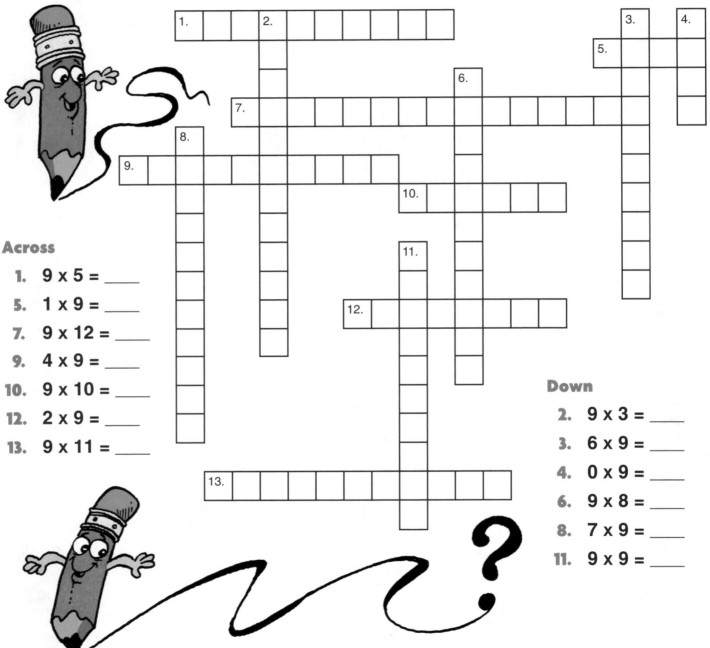

Across

1. 9 x 5 = _____
5. 1 x 9 = _____
7. 9 x 12 = _____
9. 4 x 9 = _____
10. 9 x 10 = _____
12. 2 x 9 = _____
13. 9 x 11 = _____

Down

2. 9 x 3 = _____
3. 6 x 9 = _____
4. 0 x 9 = _____
6. 9 x 8 = _____
8. 7 x 9 = _____
11. 9 x 9 = _____

Justin just finished putting together a puzzle of a castle and wants to know how many pieces are in the puzzle. He knows he put together nine pieces every five minutes. If Justin worked for one hour, how many pieces does the puzzle have?

Scholastic Professional Books

Around Town

Multiply.

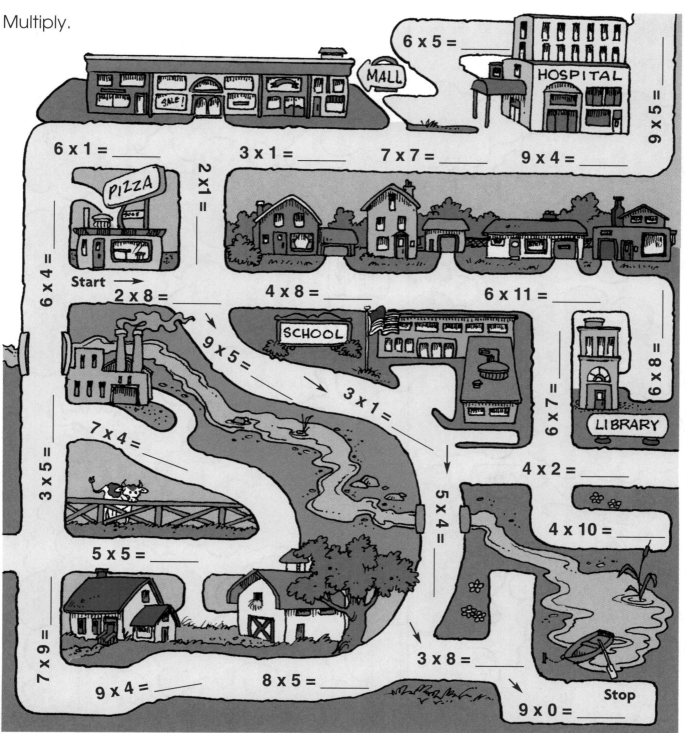

6 x 5 = _____

9 x 5 = _____

6 x 1 = _____   3 x 1 = _____   7 x 7 = _____   9 x 4 = _____

2 x1 = _____

6 x 4 = _____

Start →

2 x 8 = _____   4 x 8 = _____   6 x 11 = _____

9 x 5 = _____

3 x 1 = _____

6 x 7 = _____

6 x 8 = _____

3 x 5 = _____

7 x 4 = _____

4 x 2 = _____

5 x 4 = _____

4 x 10 = _____

5 x 5 = _____

7 x 9 = _____

3 x 8 = _____

9 x 4 = _____   8 x 5 = _____

Stop

9 x 0 = _____

After finishing three slices of pizza at the restaurant, James walked to the pond to meet his dad. James and his dad were going to go canoeing. Add the products on the road James walked along from the pizza restaurant to the pond. Follow the arrows. What multiplication fact has a product equal to this sum?

Cloud Ten

When multiplying by 10, the product always ends in 0.

Multiply.

1 x 10 = _____

10 x 9 = _____

9 x 10 = _____

7 x 10 = _____

10 x 0 = _____

3 x 10 = _____

10 x 5 = _____

10 x 8 = _____

HANG TEN!

10 x 2 = _____

10 x 4 = _____

10 x 3 = _____

10 x 10 = _____

8 x 10 = _____

6 x 10 = _____

WAY COOL!

0 x 10 = _____

4 x 10 = _____

10 x 7 = _____

COOL!

11 x 10 = _____

10 x 1 = _____

10 x 12 = _____

10 x 10 = _____

10 x 11 = _____

2 x 10 = _____

12 x 10 = _____

5 x 10 = _____

10 x 6 = _____

Every morning Miranda chose her favorite ten clouds in the sky. She especially liked clouds which looked like animals. If Miranda did this every morning for a week, how many clouds did she choose altogether?

Scholastic Professional Books

Eleven! Eleven!

When multiplying the factor 11 by a number from 1 to 9, double the number to find the product.

Examples: 11 x 5 = 55   11 x 7 = 77

Look at each multiplication sentence. If the product is correct, circle it. If the product is incorrect, cross it out and write the correct product above it.

8 x 11 = 81

3 x 11 = 33

4 x 11 = 48

5 x 11 = 66

1 x 11 = 12

9 x 11 = 99

11 x 6 = 66

2 x 11 = 22

7 x 11 = 74

6 x 11 = 54

11 x 2 = 21

11 x 3 = 23

11 x 8 = 88

11 x 5 = 55

11 x 7 =

11 x 4 = 44

11 x 9 = 88

11 x 1 = 11

Thinking Thoughts of Twelve

Write a multiplication fact in each box using 12 as a factor for the product on each wastebasket. Use a different sentence for each product.

A.

84   0

B.

96   132   72   144   36

C.

12   60   84   108   48

D.

120   48   96   132   24

Elizabeth wrote 12 different multiplication sentences on each of 6 different pieces of paper. After solving all the problems, she discovered 5 of the problems had the same product. On another piece of paper, show how many multiplication sentences Elizabeth wrote in all. Then write 5 multiplication sentences with the same product.

There Are No Obstacles Too Big for You!

Use a stopwatch to time how long it takes to multiply around the obstacle course.

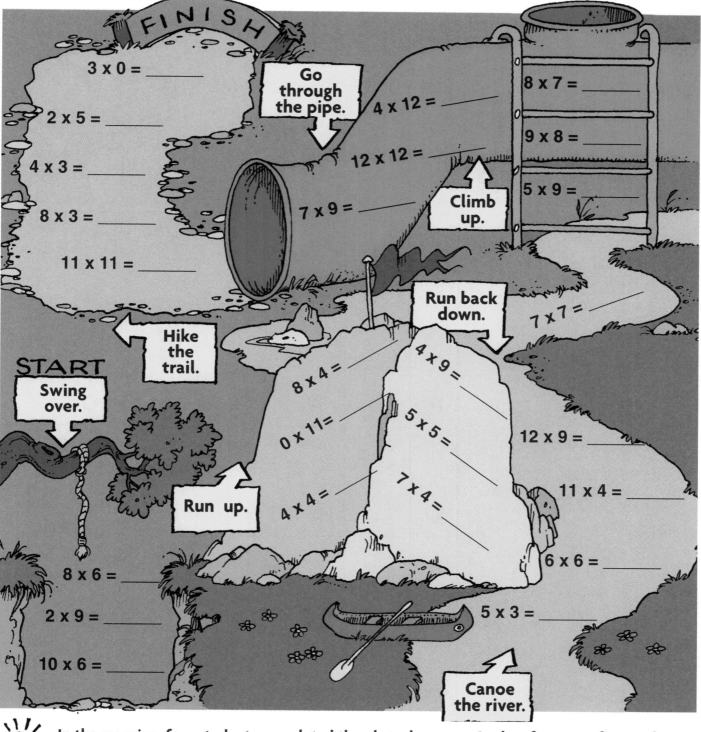

FINISH

3 x 0 = _____

2 x 5 = _____

4 x 3 = _____

8 x 3 = _____

11 x 11 = _____

Go through the pipe.

4 x 12 = _____

12 x 12 = _____

7 x 9 = _____

Climb up.

8 x 7 = _____

9 x 8 = _____

5 x 9 = _____

Hike the trail.

START

Swing over.

8 x 4 = _____

0 x 11 = _____

4 x 4 = _____

Run up.

Run back down.

4 x 9 = _____

5 x 5 = _____

7 x 4 = _____

7 x 7 = _____

12 x 9 = _____

11 x 4 = _____

6 x 6 = _____

8 x 6 = _____

2 x 9 = _____

10 x 6 = _____

5 x 3 = _____

Canoe the river.

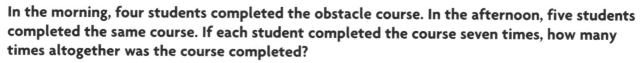

In the morning, four students completed the obstacle course. In the afternoon, five students completed the same course. If each student completed the course seven times, how many times altogether was the course completed?

Friendship

You always have something to give a friend. What is it? _____

To find the answer, do the multiplication problems and then follow the directions below.

Color the squares in row 1 that contain even answers.

Color the squares in row 2 that contain odd numbered answers.

Color the squares in row 3 that contain answers greater than 30 and less than 40.

Color the squares in row 4 that contain answers greater than 50 and less than 60.

Color the squares in row 5 that contain odd-numbered answers.

The letters in the colored squares spell the answer.

6 X 1 Y	6 X 4 O	7 X 7 T	6 X 2 U
7 X 9 R	6 X 3 W	7 X 3 S	7 X 6 O
7 X 4 C	6 X 5 E	6 X 6 M	6 X 9 L
7 X 8 I	7 X 0 F	6 X 7 R	6 X 0 B
7 X 5 L	6 X 8 J	7 X 2 S	7 X 1 E

Scholastic Professional Books

Rainy Day

Solve the problems. Then connect the dot beside each problem to
the dot beside its answer on Line A. One line has been drawn for you.
Some dots on Line A will not be used.

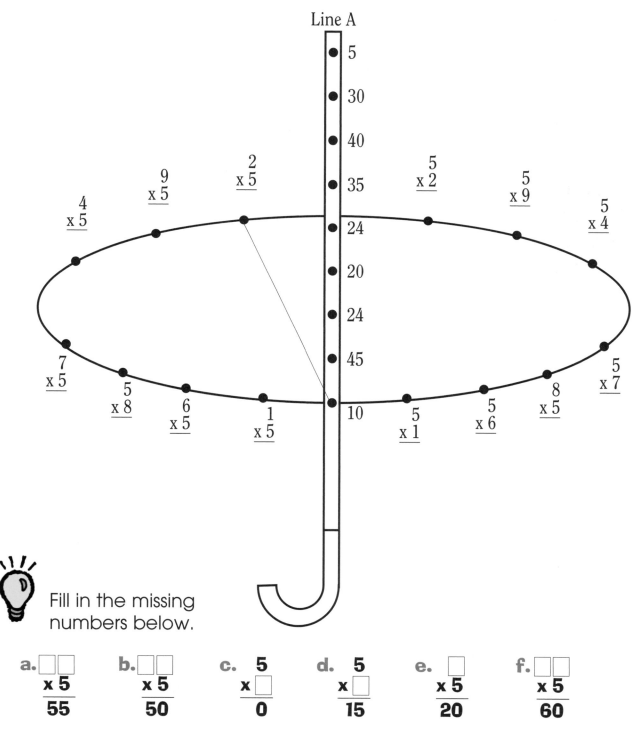

Fill in the missing
numbers below.

a. ☐☐
    x 5
    ─────
     55

b. ☐☐
    x 5
    ─────
     50

c.   5
    x ☐
    ─────
     0

d.   5
    x ☐
    ─────
     15

e.   ☐
    x 5
    ─────
     20

f. ☐☐
    x 5
    ─────
     60

Name _____

Space Traveler

Solve the problems. If the answer is between 0 and 45, color the shape black. If the answer is between 46 and 85, color the shape red. Finish the design by coloring the other shapes with the colors of your choice.

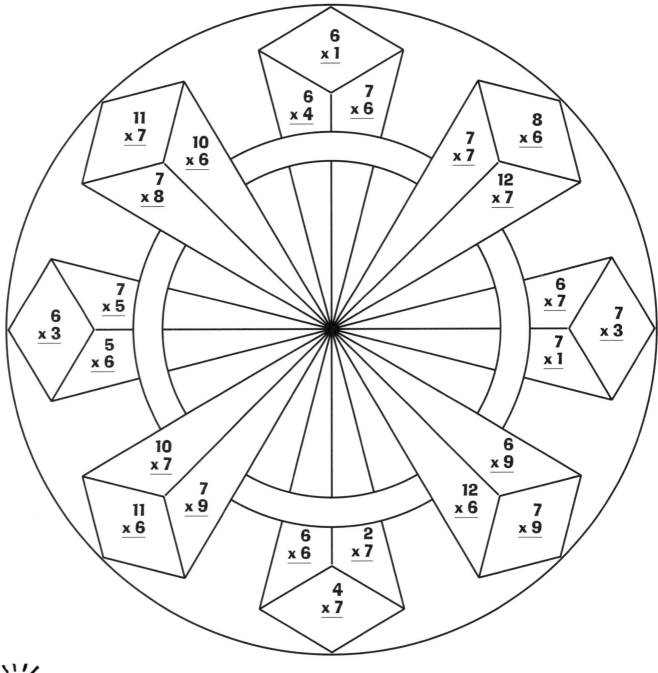

 Look at the four numbers below. Which two numbers, when multiplied together, are greater than 200 but less than 400? 4, 8, 23, 49 _____

Name _____

Eager Seeker

Divide the objects and food equally among the groups of people shown below. How many will each person receive? How much will be left over?

	ITEM	NUMBER OF PEOPLE	EACH	LEFT OVER
1.	28 MARBLES			
2.	15 STICKS OF BUBBLE GUM			
3.	8 ONE DOLLAR BILLS			
4.	15 SLICES OF PIZZA			
5.	4 BALLOONS			
6.	25 MARSHMALLOWS			
7.	6 TOY DINOSAURS			
8.	29 FRENCH FRIES			
9.	12 STRAWBERRIES			
10.	19 COOKIES			

Exploding Star

Solve the problems. If the answer is even, color the shape blue.
If the answer is odd, color the shape orange.

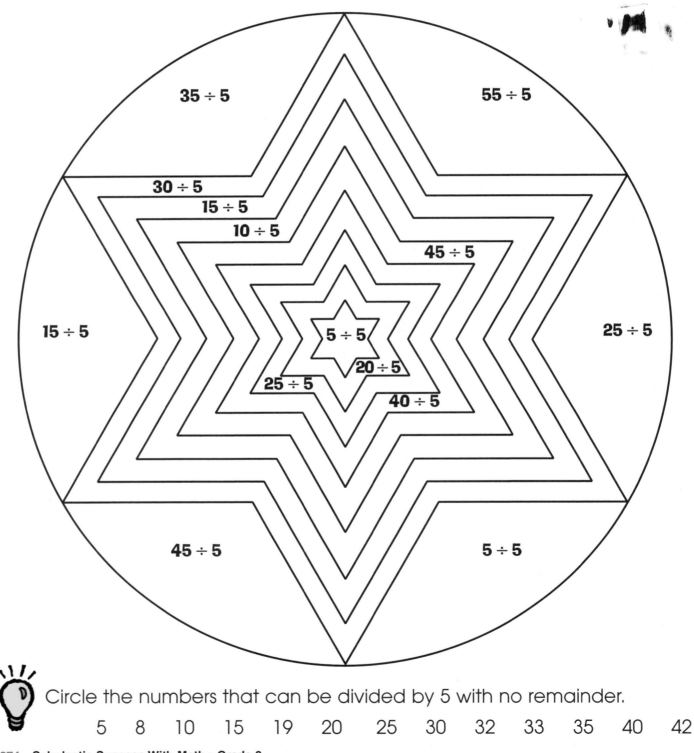

Circle the numbers that can be divided by 5 with no remainder.

5   8   10   15   19   20   25   30   32   33   35   40   42

Flying Carpet

Solve the problems. If the answer is between 100 and 250, color the shape red. If the answer is between 251 and 900, color the shape blue. Finish the design by coloring the other shapes with the colors of your choice.

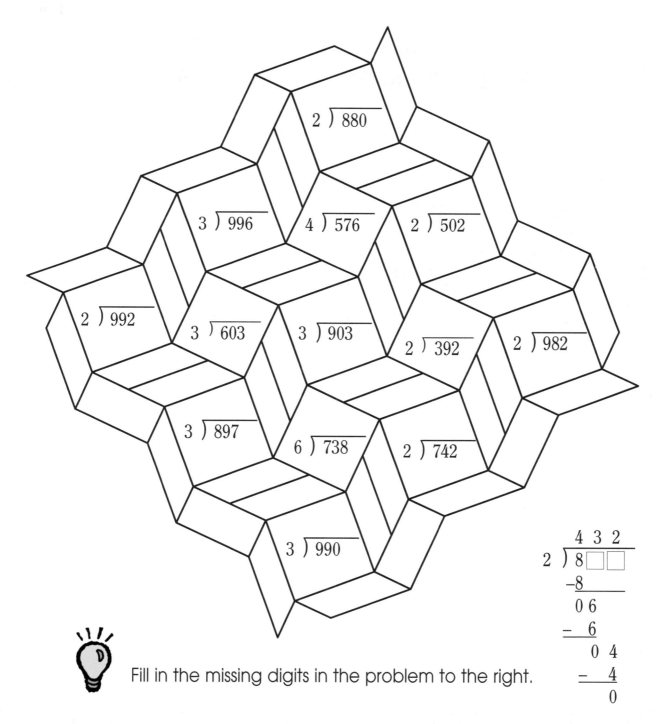

$2 \overline{)\ 880}$

$3 \overline{)\ 996}$ $4 \overline{)\ 576}$ $2 \overline{)\ 502}$

$2 \overline{)\ 992}$

$3 \overline{)\ 603}$ $3 \overline{)\ 903}$ $2 \overline{)\ 392}$ $2 \overline{)\ 982}$

$3 \overline{)\ 897}$

$6 \overline{)\ 738}$ $2 \overline{)\ 742}$

$3 \overline{)\ 990}$

$$
\begin{array}{r}
4\ 3\ 2 \\
2\ \overline{)\ 8\ \square\ \square} \\
-8 \\
\hline
0\ 6 \\
-\ 6 \\
\hline
0\ 4 \\
-\ 4 \\
\hline
0
\end{array}
$$

Fill in the missing digits in the problem to the right.

Who's Got the Button?

Figure it out!

1. If a button is lost every 3 seconds, how many buttons are lost in 60 seconds?

_____

2. Ant Betty finds some buttons. She gives 7 buttons to each of her 8 nieces. How many buttons did she find? _____

3. Molly Mouse organizes 6 groups of mice to look for lost buttons. Each group has 5 mice. How many mice are there in all? _____

4. One group of mice finds many buttons and they put them into 9 bags. Each bag contains 14 buttons. How many buttons did the mice find? _____

5. A second group of mice collects 20 bags containing a total of 160 buttons. Each bag contains the same number of buttons. How many buttons are in each bag? _____

 Suppose 20 mice want to form teams with an equal number of mice on each team. How many different-size teams can they form?

Problems and More

Put on your thinking cap to solve these problems.

1. Magic Square

Using the numbers 1 to 9, fill in the squares so the rows across, down, and diagonally all add up to 15.

2. Pocket Change

I have 19 coins in my pocket. I have twice as many dimes as nickels, three more pennies than nickels, and one more dime than the number of pennies. My coins add up to $1.07. How many of each coin do I have?

_____ dimes

_____ nickels

_____ pennies

3. Connect the Dots

Can you connect all of the dots with four straight lines? Here's the catch: You can't lift your pencil!

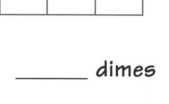

4. A Sneaky Puzzle

Something is hiding under your bed! To find out what it is, do this problem on a calculator:
5,000 + 45,842 + 2,203.
Turn the calculator upside down to reveal the answer.

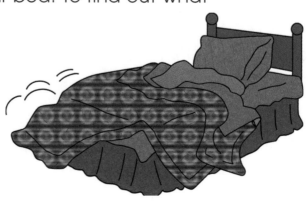

More Problems and More

1. Tricky Triangles

How many triangles can you find
in this shape? Share ideas with
your classmates. Who found the
most triangles?

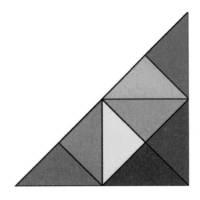

2. Time After Time

How are the clocks the same?
How are they different?

3. Half Again

Draw the missing half
of each shape.

4. A Code for You!

ABC	DEF	GHI	JKL	MNO	PQR	STU	VWX	YZ
1	2	3	4	5	6	7	8	9

Use the code. Write your name. Then add to find the value of all the
letters in your name.

Name _____ Value _____

Find the value of some other words you know.

Scholastic Professional Books

Brain Power!

Put on your thinking cap to solve these problems!

1. How Many Students?

Estimate the number of students in your school. How did you do it?

_____

_____

_____

2. Upside Down

What two-digit number reads the same upside down as it does right side up?

_____

3. Cats In Line

One cat walked in front of two cats. One cat walked behind two cats. One cat walked between two cats. How many cats were there? (Hint: Draw a picture!)

_____

4. Number Pattern

Here are the first five figures in a pattern. Draw the next figure.

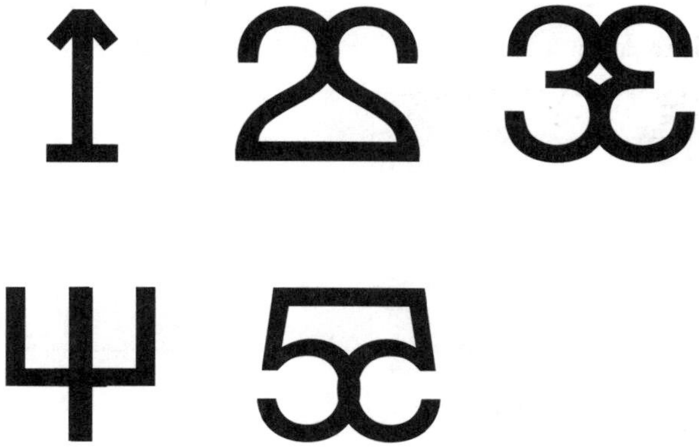

5. Cutting The Cake!

What is the fewest number of cuts you could make in order to cut a cake into six slices? (Hint: Draw a picture!)

_____

Flag Wagger

Write a fraction for the section of the flag next to the arrow.

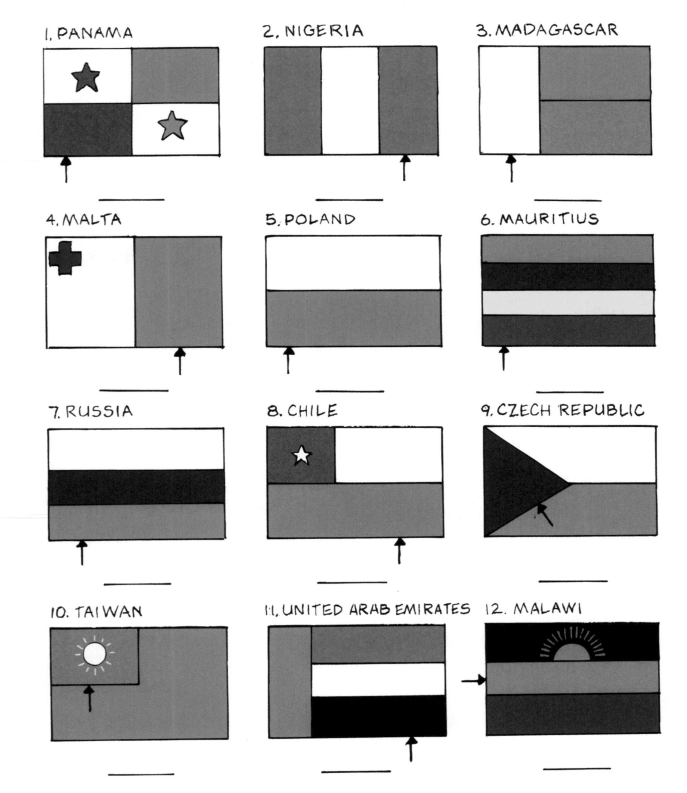

1. PANAMA

2. NIGERIA

3. MADAGASCAR

4. MALTA

5. POLAND

6. MAURITIUS

7. RUSSIA

8. CHILE

9. CZECH REPUBLIC

10. TAIWAN

11. UNITED ARAB EMIRATES

12. MALAWI

Scholastic Professional Books

Goody for Fractions!

Wash your hands, then gather the recipe ingredients and equipment listed below. To prepare the peanut butter–oatmeal drops, simply mix the ingredients together, roll the dough into balls, and place the balls on the wax paper. Chill the finished drops for about an hour, then enjoy your tasty "fractions" with family or friends!

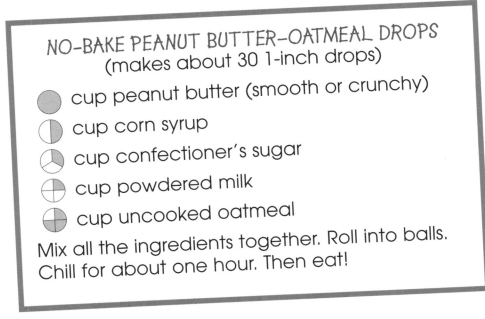

NO-BAKE PEANUT BUTTER–OATMEAL DROPS
(makes about 30 1-inch drops)

cup peanut butter (smooth or crunchy)

cup corn syrup

cup confectioner's sugar

cup powdered milk

cup uncooked oatmeal

Mix all the ingredients together. Roll into balls. Chill for about one hour. Then eat!

Now try these fraction pictures. Can you write the fraction each picture shows?

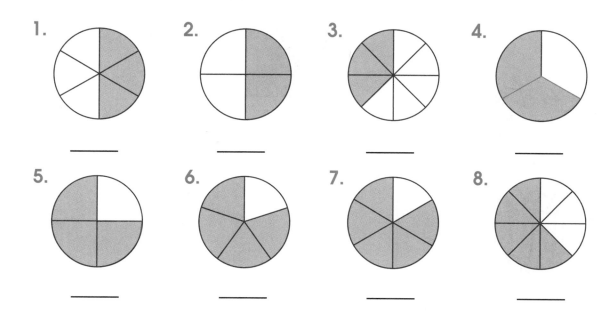

1. _____   2. _____   3. _____   4. _____

5. _____   6. _____   7. _____   8. _____

Flower Shop Fractions

Choose 2 colors for each bunch of flowers. Color some
of the flowers one color. Color the rest of the flowers
the other color. Write a fraction to tell how many
flowers there are of each color.

1.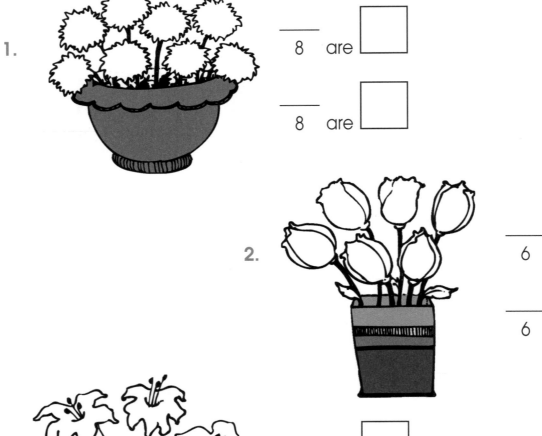

$\dfrac{}{8}$ are ☐

$\dfrac{}{8}$ are ☐

2.

$\dfrac{}{6}$ are ☐

$\dfrac{}{6}$ are ☐

3.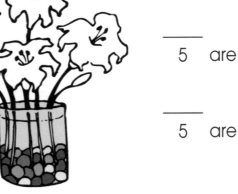

$\dfrac{}{5}$ are ☐

$\dfrac{}{5}$ are ☐

Cooking With Fractions

The recipe below explains how to make peanut-butter balls.

Read the recipe. Then answer the questions.

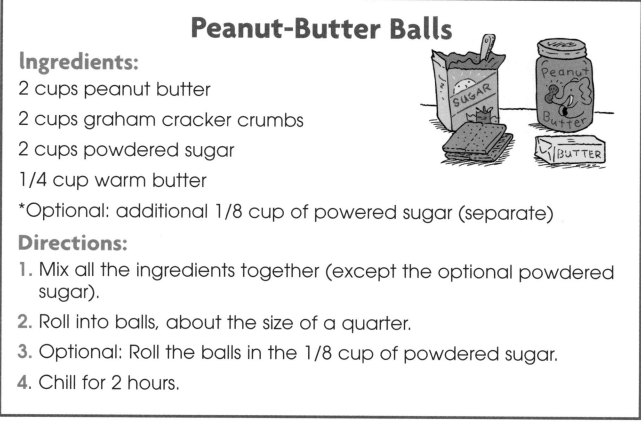

Peanut-Butter Balls

Ingredients:

2 cups peanut butter

2 cups graham cracker crumbs

2 cups powdered sugar

1/4 cup warm butter

*Optional: additional 1/8 cup of powered sugar (separate)

Directions:

1. Mix all the ingredients together (except the optional powdered sugar).

2. Roll into balls, about the size of a quarter.

3. Optional: Roll the balls in the 1/8 cup of powdered sugar.

4. Chill for 2 hours.

Several classmates want to help make the peanut-butter balls.

1. How many students would be needed if each measured 1/2 cup of the peanut butter?

_____

2. How many students would be needed if each measured 1/4 cup of the graham cracker crumbs?

_____

3. How many students would be needed if each measured 1/3 cup of the powdered sugar?

_____

Into Infinity

Solve the problems. Then rename the answers in lowest terms.

If the answer is $\frac{1}{4}$, $\frac{1}{8}$, or $\frac{1}{16}$, color the shape purple.

If the answer is $\frac{1}{2}$, $\frac{1}{3}$, or $\frac{1}{7}$, color the shape blue.

If the answers $\frac{2}{3}$, $\frac{3}{4}$, or $\frac{7}{8}$, color the shape green.

If the answer is $\frac{3}{5}$, $\frac{4}{5}$, or $\frac{5}{7}$, color the shape yellow.

If the answer is $\frac{9}{10}$ or $\frac{11}{12}$, color the shape red.

Finish the design by coloring the other shapes with colors of your choice.

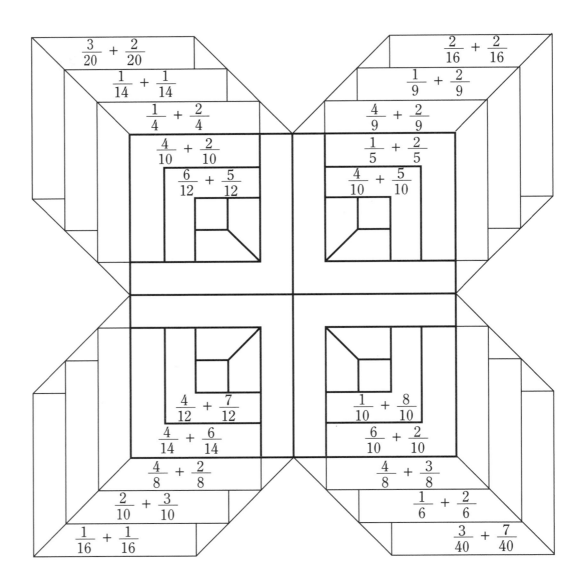

Scholastic Professional Books

Put the Brakes on Math Mistakes!

Take a look at the signs on Bob's store. Circle any mistakes you see. Then fix the mistakes so that the signs are correct.

BOB'S BIKE BARN

Bike Helmets $14.999

OPEN 9:30 AM - 8:75 PM

OPEN 8 DAYS A WEEK

* SALE *
$10 off selected Mountain Bikes
Were $139.99
Now $129.00

Handlebar Tape
$3.99 a roll
Buy two for $7.99
SAVE $1.00

Bicycle Baskets
$12.99 each
Two for $25.00
SAVE $.98

* FREE *
Bicycle Stickers
$.10 each

Bicycle Chain
$.50 an inch
That's only $5.00 a foot

½ off all Bicycle Seats
Were $17.00
Now $9.50

Autumn Harvest

Circle the coins that you need to pay for each thing in the picture on page 387.

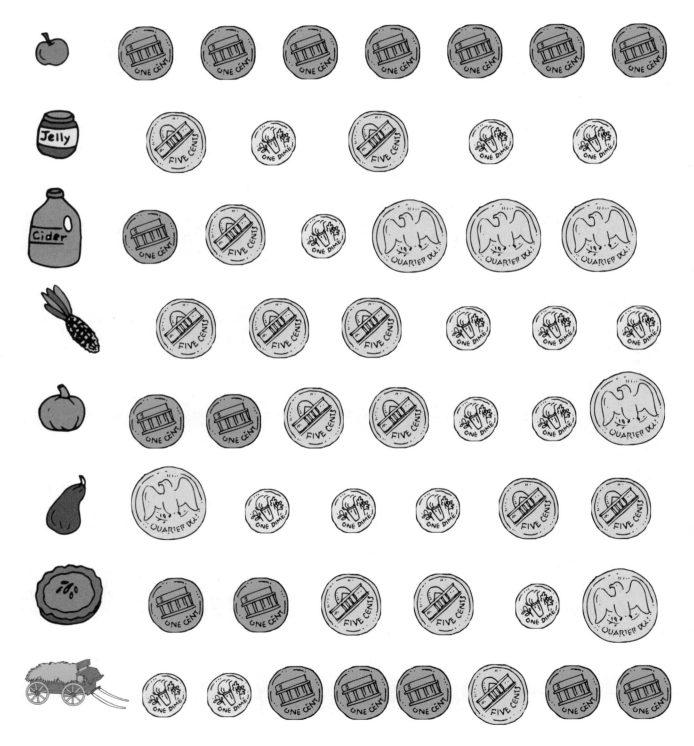

Dollar Scholar

How many ways can you make a dollar? Write the number of coins you will need.

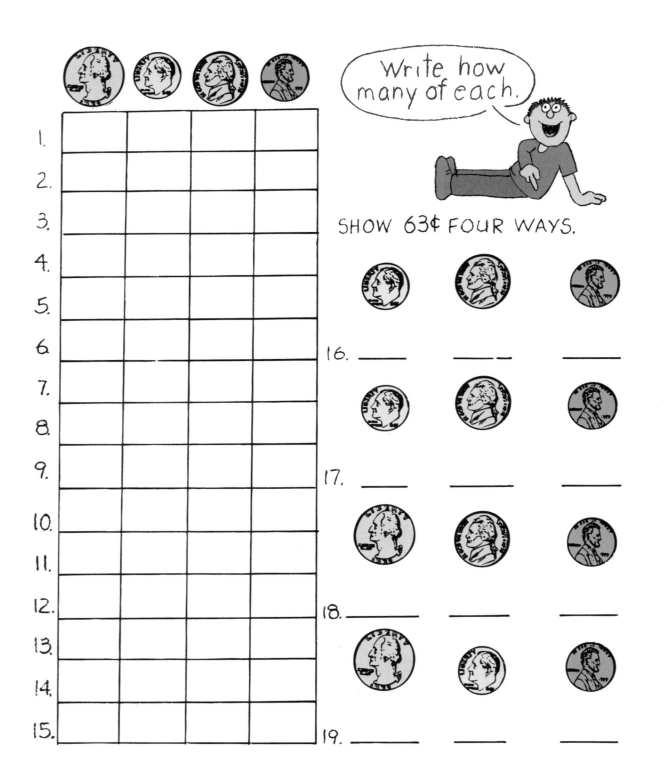

Write how many of each.

SHOW 63¢ FOUR WAYS.

16. ____ ____ ____

17. ____ ____ ____

18. ____ ____ ____

19. ____ ____ ____

Time for a Riddle!

Read the riddle. To find the answer, find the clockface that matches the time written under each blank line. Then write the letter under that clockface on the blank line.

Riddle: **What did the little hand on the clock say to the big hand?**

Answer.   "____ ____ ____ ____ ____ ____ ____
              10:00   3:30   3:30   6:05   2:25   3:45   6:15

____ ____ ____ ____ ____ ____ !"
4:45   6:05   2:55   3:45   3:45   2:55

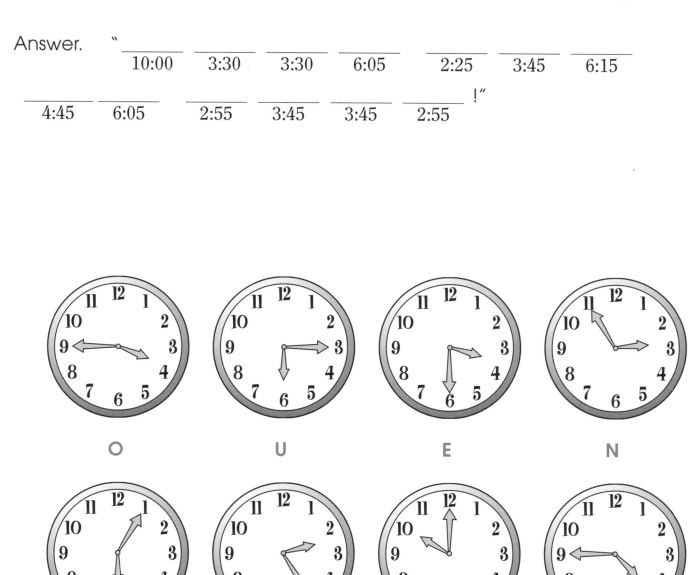

O   U   E   N

T   Y   M   A

Curves Ahead!

How long is each curved line? Guess. Then check by measuring.

1. My guess _____

   Actual length _____

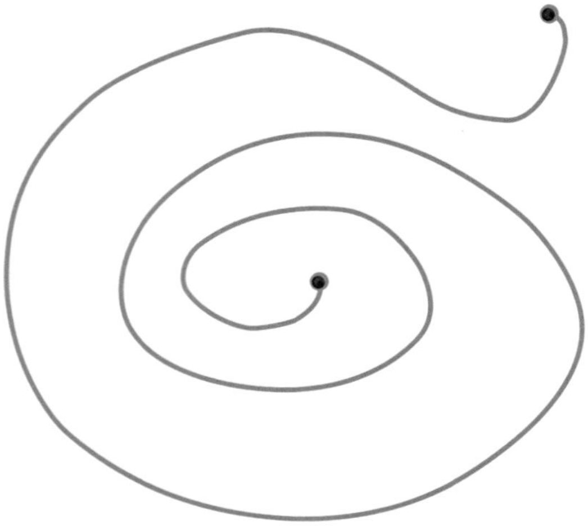

2. My guess _____

   Actual length _____

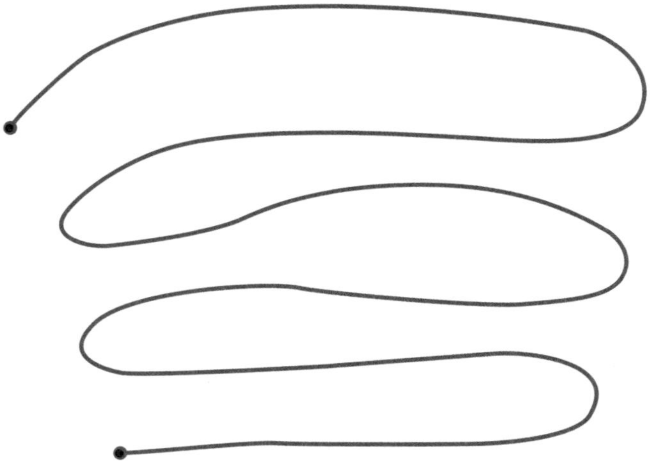

3. My guess _____

   Actual length _____

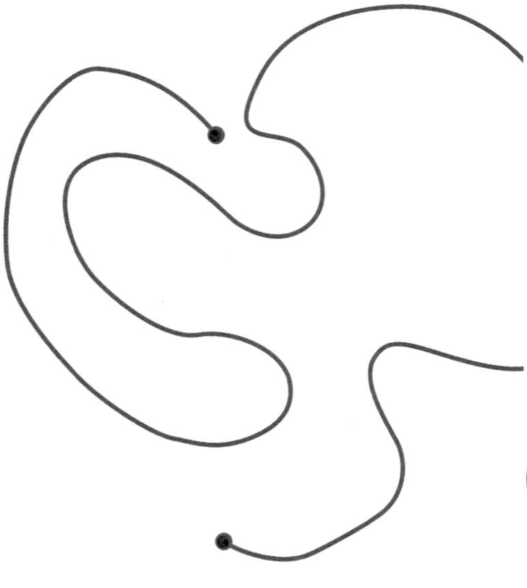

4. My guess _____

   Actual length _____

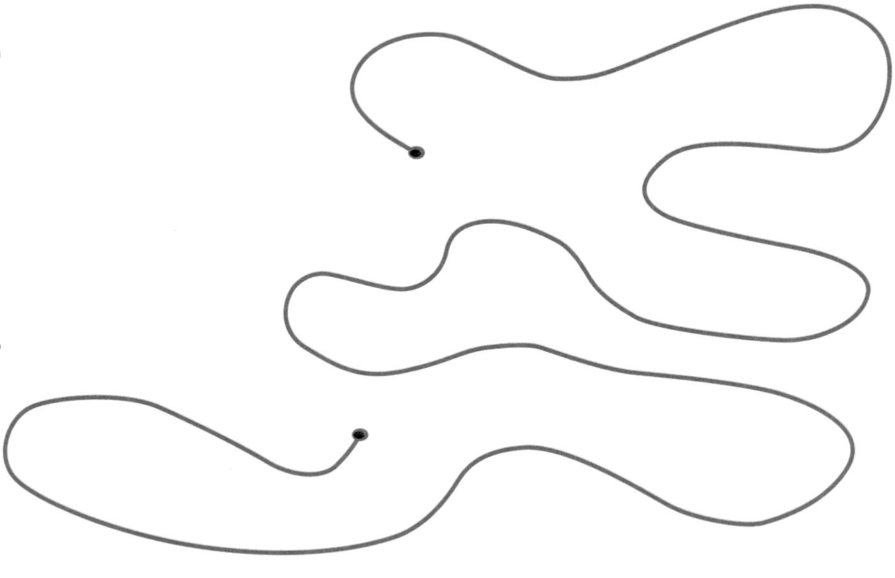

Measure With Me

Cut a piece of string or yarn that is equal to your height. Measure each object below and check the correct box.

Object	Longer than my string	Shorter than my string	The same as my string

⊚ Measure something else. Draw a picture of it on another piece of paper. Write a sentence to show what you found out.

_____

_____

⊚ Have someone measure you. Who measured you? _____

How tall are you? _____

Weight Watcher

Weight can be measured in ounces (oz.) and pounds (lb.). 16 oz. = 1 lb. Which unit of measure would you use to weigh the items below? Underline the more sensible measure.

1. An apple

    ounces   pounds

2. A pair of sneakers

    ounces   pounds

3. A bar of soap

    ounces   pounds

4. A bicycle

    ounces   pounds

5. A watermelon

    ounces   pounds

6. A baseball player

    ounces   pounds

7. A balloon

    ounces   pounds

8. A jam sandwich

    ounces   pounds

9. A baseball bat

    ounces   pounds

10. A pair of socks

    ounces   pounds

11. A slice of pizza

    ounces   pounds

12. A full backpack

    ounces   pounds

13. A large dog

    ounces   pounds

14. A loaf of bread

    ounces   pounds

15. A paintbrush

    ounces   pounds

Put me down!

Scholastic Professional Books

Degree Overseer

Temperature is measured in degrees. Fahrenheit (°F) is a common measure. Celsius (°C) is a metric measure. Circle the more sensible temperature in which to do the activities below.

1. FRY AN EGG

90°F
50°F

2. ICE SKATE

0°C
30°C

3. GO TO THE BEACH

60°C
30°C

4. RAKE LEAVES

55°F
75°F

5. BUILD A SNOWMAN

30°F
50°F

6. DRINK HOT COCOA

75°F
40°F

7. STUDY IN SCHOOL

68°F
40°F

8. FLY A KITE

40°C
20°C

9. DRINK COLD JUICE

75°F
25°F

10. EAT ICE CREAM

30°F
80°F

°C   °F

50—
45—   —120
40—   —110
35—   —100
30—   —90
25—   —80
20—   —70
15—   —60
10—   —50
5—   —40
0—   —30
-5—   —20
-10—   —10
          —0

Fact Finder

Numbers can be used to count and to measure. Complete the measures below by writing how many are in each.

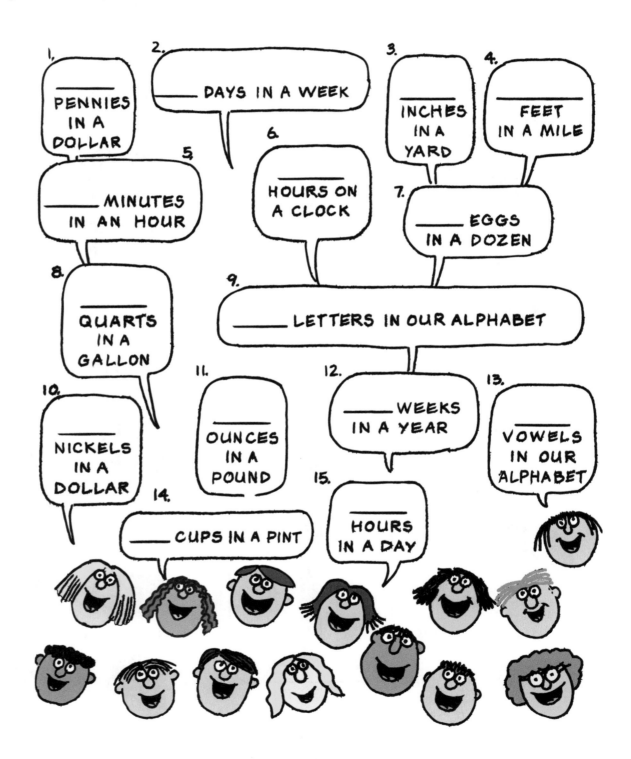

1. _____ PENNIES IN A DOLLAR

2. _____ DAYS IN A WEEK

3. _____ INCHES IN A YARD

4. _____ FEET IN A MILE

5. _____ MINUTES IN AN HOUR

6. _____ HOURS ON A CLOCK

7. _____ EGGS IN A DOZEN

8. _____ QUARTS IN A GALLON

9. _____ LETTERS IN OUR ALPHABET

10. _____ NICKELS IN A DOLLAR

11. _____ OUNCES IN A POUND

12. _____ WEEKS IN A YEAR

13. _____ VOWELS IN OUR ALPHABET

14. _____ CUPS IN A PINT

15. _____ HOURS IN A DAY

Amount Counter

How many triangles and squares can you count in these geometric figures?

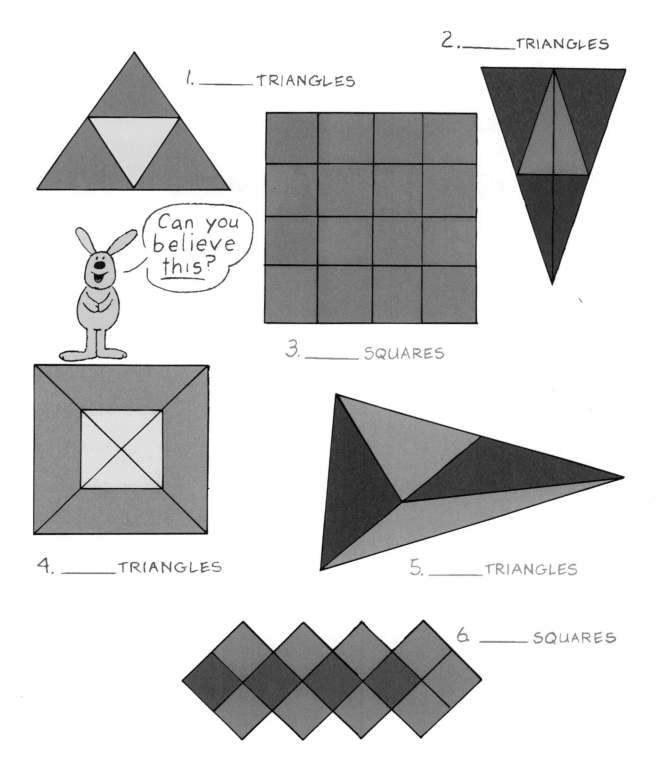

1. _____ TRIANGLES

2. _____ TRIANGLES

Can you believe this?

3. _____ SQUARES

4. _____ TRIANGLES

5. _____ TRIANGLES

6. _____ SQUARES

Shape Gaper

FLAT SHAPES HAVE LENGTH AND WIDTH.

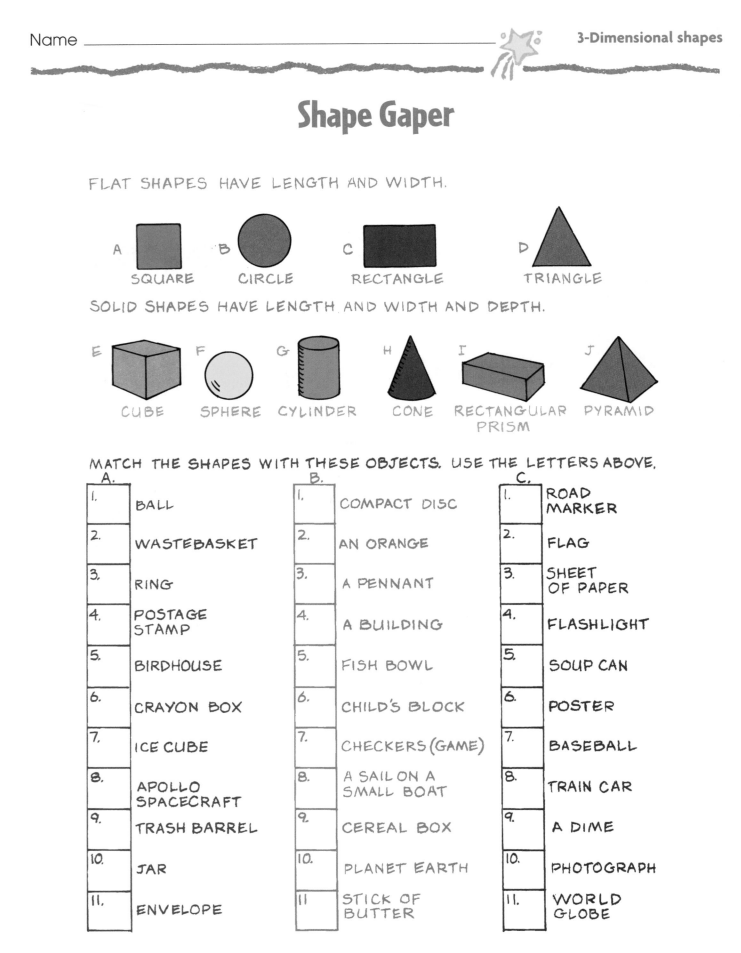

A SQUARE   B CIRCLE   C RECTANGLE   D TRIANGLE

SOLID SHAPES HAVE LENGTH AND WIDTH AND DEPTH.

E CUBE   F SPHERE   G CYLINDER   H CONE   I RECTANGULAR PRISM   J PYRAMID

MATCH THE SHAPES WITH THESE OBJECTS. USE THE LETTERS ABOVE.

A.
1. BALL
2. WASTEBASKET
3. RING
4. POSTAGE STAMP
5. BIRDHOUSE
6. CRAYON BOX
7. ICE CUBE
8. APOLLO SPACECRAFT
9. TRASH BARREL
10. JAR
11. ENVELOPE

B.
1. COMPACT DISC
2. AN ORANGE
3. A PENNANT
4. A BUILDING
5. FISH BOWL
6. CHILD'S BLOCK
7. CHECKERS (GAME)
8. A SAIL ON A SMALL BOAT
9. CEREAL BOX
10. PLANET EARTH
11. STICK OF BUTTER

C.
1. ROAD MARKER
2. FLAG
3. SHEET OF PAPER
4. FLASHLIGHT
5. SOUP CAN
6. POSTER
7. BASEBALL
8. TRAIN CAR
9. A DIME
10. PHOTOGRAPH
11. WORLD GLOBE

Riddle Teller

Read the riddle. Then draw the shape it describes.

I have 3 sides and 3 corners. One of my corners is at the top.

> 1

I have no corners. One half of me is like the other half.

> 2

I have 4 corners and 4 sides. You can draw me by joining 2 triangles.

> 3

I have 5 sides and 5 corners. Draw a square and a triangle together.

> 4

I am not a square, but I have 4 sides and 4 corners.

> 5

I have 4 sides and 4 corners. My 2 opposite sides are slanted.

> 6

Terrific Tessellations

What do math and art have in common?
Everything—if you're making tessellations!

A **tessellation** (tess-uh-LAY-shun) is a design made of shapes that fit together like puzzle pieces. People use tessellations to decorate walls and floors, and even works of art.

This sidewalk is formed from rectangles.

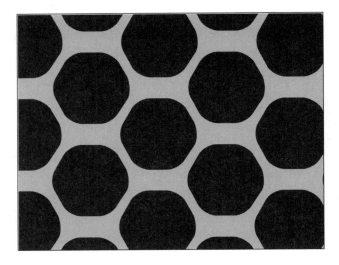

Hexagons form this beehive.

Here is a tessellation made from more than one shape.

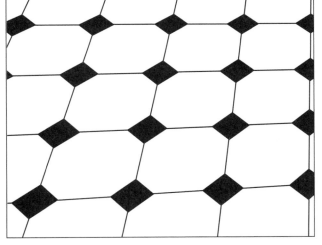

Squares and octagons form a tile floor.

Terrific Tessellations

You Need:
heavy paper • scissor
tape • crayons

What to Do:
Here's how you can make
your own tessellation.

1. Start with a simple shape
   like a square. (Cut your
   shape from the heavy
   paper). Cut a piece out of
   side A . . .

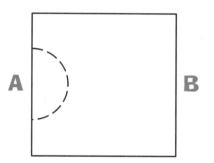

2. . . . and slide it over to side B. Make
   sure it lines up evenly with the cut
   out side, or your tessellation won't
   work. Tape it in place on side B.

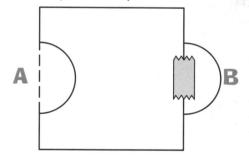

3. If you like, do the same
   thing with sides C and D.
   Now you have a new
   shape.

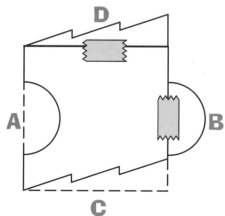

4. Trace your new shape on paper. Then
   slide the shape so it fits together with the
   one you just traced. Trace it again. Keep
   on sliding and tracing until your page is
   filled. Decorate your tessellation.

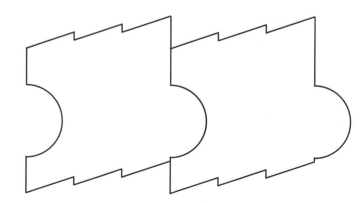

Pattern Block Design

How many total pieces are in this pattern block design?

2 + 2 + 2 + 4 = _____

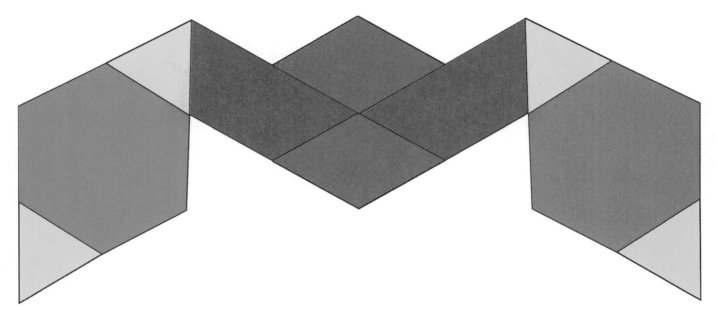

Now make your own design. Use 10 pattern blocks different from those used above. Cut out the shapes and trace or glue them in the space below. You may need to use a shape more than once.

Write an equation to show how many of each shape you used.

Equation: _____

Answer Key

READING COMPREHENSION

Page 13
1. Alexander Graham Bell;
2. teacher of the deaf; 3. "Mr. Watson, come here! I want you!";
4. Mr. Bell's assistant; 5. Bell demonstrated it to many people.

Page 14
Main Idea: The Milky Way is our galaxy.; Details: 1. stars; 2. outer; 3. spiral; 4. white; 5. sun; 6. 200

Page 15
Life on a wagon train was hard and dangerous.;1. oiling; 2. gathering; 3. cooking; 4. hauling; 5. hunting; 6. watching; 7. waiting; 8. crossing; 9. getting

Page 16
Main Idea: Elephants have very useful noses.; Sentences that do not belong: Some people like to ride on elephants.; Giraffes are the tallest animals in the world.; (The rest of the sentences are details.)

Page 17
The answer is 20.

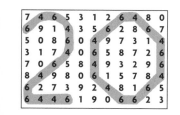

1. Mr. Jefferson, Riley, Rhonda; 2. C; 3. B; 4. Riley

Page 19
1. B; 2. E, A, D; 3. G; 4. F; 5. C, F

Page 20
1. land by the sea; 2. weather; 3. happens regularly; 4. outer covering of trees; 5. illness; 6. wood cut into boards; 7. no longer existing

Page 21

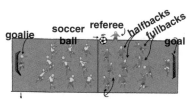

soccer field   forwards

Page 22
A. 2, 1, 3; B. 1, 3, 2; C. 3, 2, 1; D. 2, 1, 3; E. 3, 1, 2; F. 3, 1, 2; G. 1, 3, 2; H. 2, 1, 3; I. 2, 1, 4, 3; J. 2, 4, 1, 3

Page 23
4, 6, 1, 3, 5, 2

Page 24
7, 4, 8, 1, 5, 3, 6, 2

Page 25
Check students' pages.

Page 26
1. venomous; 2. sneaky; 3. camouflage; 4. jungle; 5. rattlesnakes; 6. sand; 7. coral snake; Watch out for sneaky snakes!

Page 27
1. The palindromes are wow, dad, mom, noon, deed. (The other words are not.); 2. screech, pow, slurp, boom, click, sizzle, crunch; 3. knot–not; break–brake; flu–flew; sore–soar; right–write; rode–road; 4. pear, shoe, soccer, like, oven, hen, neither

Pages 28–29
1. Holly was being so quiet.
2. Holly's voice sounded so far away.
3. She thought Holly might be hiding.
4. She had fallen headfirst into the toy box and couldn't get out. 5. The piano was at the bottom of the toy box.
6. Mom and Holly will play on the swings in the park.

Page 30
1. Potato chips were invented by accident. 2. George Crum was a Native American chef. 3. The complaining diner actually caused something good to happen. 4. Mr. Crum was angry when the diner sent the potatoes back, but he was probably glad later on because his chips became famous. 5. Saratoga Chips were named after the town where they were invented. 6. The reason we have potato chips today is because of what happened at Moon Lake Lodge in 1853.

Page 31
Check students' drawings.

Page 33
1. way back yonder—many years ago; 2. buckboard—wagon; 3. Lend me your ears.—Listen to me.; 4. Put a spring in your step.—makes you feel peppy; 5. heavenly elixir—wonderful tonic; 6. special blend of secret ingredients—I won't tell what's in it.; 7. bustin' broncs—making wild horses gentle; 8. war whoop—loud yell; 9. It's a steal!—You are getting it for a low price.; 10. mosey—walk slowly; 11. kept my eye on him—watched him closely; 12. hornswoggled—cheated; tricked; 13. hightailed it—ran quickly; 14. no-good varmint—evil creature; 15. behind bars—in jail

Page 34
1. an illness; 2. shoreline of a river or creek; 3. a measurement; 4. a small, furry animal; 5. hot bread; 6. applause; 7. am able to; 8. area that is fenced in

Page 35
1. in a cave; 2. at a movie; 3. on a roller coaster; 4. on an airplane; 5. at a wedding; 6. at the vet; 7. at a candy store; 8. in a garden

Page 36
Toolbox: saw, screwdriver, wrench, pliers, hammer; Baseball: bat, pitcher, bases, catcher, glove; Horse: pony, donkey, horse, mule, zebra; Water: lake, river, ocean, sea, creek

Page 37
Medicine Chest: aspirin, cough syrup, bandages, eyedrops; Linen Closet: blankets, sheets; pillowcases, quilts; Silverware Drawer: forks, knives, teaspoons, serving spoons; Pantry: cereal, canned soup, crackers, cake mix; Garage Shelves: motor oil, toolbox, fishing tackle, car wax; Bookshelf: dictionary, novels, atlas, encyclopedias

Page 38
Wording of answers may vary: 1. Kinds of Languages; 2. Things That Are Hot; 3. Computer Equipment; 4. Musical Instruments; 5. Kinds of Trees; 6. Holidays; 7. Air Transportation; 8. Careers (or Occupations); 9. Kinds of Flowers

Page 39
1. views; 2. views; 3. news; 4. views; 5. news; 6. news; 7. views; 8. news; 9. views

Page 40
Burgers: O, F; Sports Car: O, F; In-line Skates: O, F; Video Game: F, O; Movie: O, O, F, F, F

Page 41
Facts: 1, 2, 3, 4, 6, 9, 10, 13
Opinions: 5, 7, 8, 11, 12

Page 43
1. Color the picture of Homer in his cage. 2. Homer had many exciting adventures after crawling out of his cage. 3. Answers will vary.

Page 45
1. Underline: The man found the other Mary, his girlfriend, and gave her the ring.; Mary's mom turned the 9 over to make a 6 again and nailed it tight so their apartment number would be correct.; Mark an X on: The man sent Mary a bill because she ate the chocolates.; Nine-year-old Mary sent the man a dozen roses.; 2. "Love Me Always"; 3. a dozen red roses; 4. Answers will vary.; 5. Friday; 6. Mary's apartment

Page 46
1. chicken nuggets; 2. green beans; 3. applesauce; 4. roll; 5. carrots; 6. corn; 7. salad

Page 47

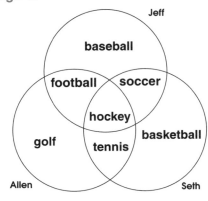

1. hockey; 2. football; 3. soccer; 4. tennis; 5. baseball; 6. golf; 7. basketball

Page 49
1. whale shark; 2. pygmy shark; 3. great white shark; 4. mako shark; 5. all; 6. all; 7. goblin shark; 8. hammerhead shark; 9. all; 10. cookie cutter shark; 11. sawshark; 12. tiger shark

Page 50
1, 3, 4, 6, 8, 9

Page 51
Gravity pulls the swimmer from the **top** of the slide to the **bottom**.
Rushing **water** causes the **slide** to be **slippery**.

Page 53

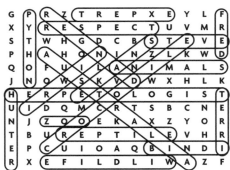

Facts will vary.

Page 54
Answers will vary.

TESTS: READING

TEST 1   Pages 57–60
Sample: 1.C   2.B

Passage A
1.D   2.A   3.C   4.A

Passage B
1.B   2.D   3.B   4.A

Passage C
1.C   2.D   3.C

Passage D
1.C   2.C

Passage E
1.A   2.C   3.B   4.D

Vocabulary Synonyms
Sample: B
1.C   2.B   3.B   4.A   5.D   6.B   7.C

Antonyms
Sample: D
1.A   2.C   3.B   4.C   5.A   6.D   7.A

TEST 2   Pages 61–64
Sample: 1.B   2.C

Passage A
1.B   2.D   3.A   4.D

Passage B
1.A   2.B   3.D   4.A

Passage C
1.C   2.A   3.C   4.A

Passage D
1.B   2.A   3.B

Passage E
1.D   2.A   3.B   4.C

Vocabulary Synonyms
Sample: B
1.D   2.C   3.D   4.C   5.A   6.B   7.C

Antonyms
Sample: C
1.B   2.A   3.C   4.C   5.A   6.D   7.B

TEST 3   Pages 65–68
Sample: 1.C   2.A

Passage A
1.B   2.D   3.C   4.B

Passage B
1.C   2.A   3.A   4.C

Passage C
1.B   2.A   3.D   4.C

Passage D
1.B   2.C   3.A   4.D

Passage E
1.A   2.C   3.B   4.B

Vocabulary
Synonyms
Sample: A
1.C   2.A   3.D   4.B   5.D   6.B
 7.D   8.C

Antonyms
Sample: A
1.C   2.D   3.A   4.D
5.B   6.B   7.C   8.A

TEST 4   Pages 69–72
Sample: 1.C   2.B

Passage A
1.A   2.D   3.B

Passage B
1.A   2.B   3.B   4.B

Passage C
1.D   2.B   3.D   4.C

Passage D
1.C   2.B   3.A   4.B

Passage E
1.D   2.B   3.C

Vocabulary
Synonyms
Sample: B
1.A   2.C   3.C   4.D   5.C   6.A   7.C

Antonyms
Sample: D
1.A   2.D   3.C   4.B   5.C   6.B   7.D

TEST 5   Pages 73–76
Sample: 1.B   2.C

Passage A
1.D   2.C   3.A   4.B

Passage B
1.B   2.D   3.A   4.B

Passage C
1.C   2.C   3.B

Passage D
1.A   2.B   3.C   4.D

Passage E
1.C   2.A   3.A   4.B

Vocabulary
Synonyms
Sample: C
1.D   2.C   3.C   4.A
5.B   6.B   7.C   8.A

Antonyms
Sample: D
1.B   2.C   3.B   4.A
5.C   6.A   7.B   8.A

TEST 6   Pages 77–80
Sample: 1.C   2.A

Passage A
1.B   2.D   3.A   4.C

Passage B
1.C   2.A   3.B

Passage C
1.C   2.C   3.A

Passage D
1.D   2.A   3.B

Passage E
1.A   2.B   3.D

Vocabulary
Sample: C; A
1.A   2.D   3.C   4.B   5.C   6.B   7.A

TEST 7   Pages 81–84
Sample: 1.C   2.A

Passage A
1.D   2.B   3.C

Passage B
1.C   2.B

Passage C
1.D   2.C   3.B

Passage D
1.C   2.B

Passage E
1.B   2.A   3.B

Passage F
1.C   2.A   3.C   4.D

Vocabulary
Synonyms
Sample: D
1.B   2.C   3.A   4.D
5.A   6.A   7.D

Multiple Meanings
Sample: A
1.C   2.D   3.A   4.B

TEST 8   Pages 85–88
Sample: 1.B   2.C

Passage A
1.C   2.B   3.D   4.A   5.B

Passage B
1.B   2.C   3.A   4.C

Passage C
1.D   2.B   3.A

Passage D
1.A   2.D   3.B   4.D

Passage E
1.B   2.D   3.C

Vocabulary
Synonyms
Sample: D
1.B   2.C   3.D   4.B
5.A   6.A   7.D   8.C

Multiple Meanings
Sample: C
1.B   2.D   3.B   4.D   5.C

TEST 9   Pages 89–92
Sample: 1.B   2.C

Passage A
1.D   2.A   3.B   4.B

Passage B
1.D 2.C 3.A 4.B
Passage C
1.B 2.A 3.D 4.C
Passage D
1.B 2.C 3.A 4.C
Passage E
1.D 2.B 3.C

Vocabulary
Synonyms
Sample: A
1.D 2.B 3.A 4.C 5.B 6.B 7.B
Multiple Meanings
Sample: B
1.D 2.C 3.A 4.B 5.A

TEST 10   Pages 93–96
Sample: 1.A 2.C
Passage A
1.B 2.C 3.B 4.D 5.A
Passage B
1.D 2.D 3.A 4.B
Passage C
1.A 2.B 3.A 4.A
Passage D
1.A 2.A 3.C 4.B
Passage E
1.A 2.C 3.A 4.C

Vocabulary
Synonyms
Sample: B
1.A 2.D 3.B 4.A 5.B
6.D 7.A 8.C
Multiple Meanings
Sample: B
1.D 2.C 3.B 4.A 5.C

TEST 11   Pages 97–100
Sample: 1.C 2.A
Passage A
1.C 2.B 3.A 4.C
Passage B
1.A 2.C 3.B 4.B

Passage C
1.C 2.B 3.A 4.C 5.D
Passage D
1.B 2.A 3.C
Passage E
1.A 2.B 3.C 4.B

Vocabulary
Synonyms
Sample: B
1.D 2.D 3.B 4.C 5.B 6.A 7.B
Antonyms
Sample: D
1.C 2.A 3.B 4.D 5.A 6.D 7.C

TEST 12   Pages 101–104
Sample: 1.B 2.C
Passage A
1.B 2.C 3.C
Passage B
1.A 2.B 3.B
Passage C
1.B 2.D
Passage D
1.A 2.D
Passage E
1.D 2.C 3.B
Passage F
1.B 2.D 3.D 4.A
Study Skills
Reading a Table of Contents
1.C 2.B 3.D 4.A
Reading a Pictograph
1.D 2.C 3.B 4.A

TEST 13   Pages 105–108
Sample: 1.C 2.A
Passage A
1.B 2.C 3.B 4.A
Passage B
1.B 2.B 3.D 4.C
Passage C
1.B 2.C 3.D 4.B

Passage D
1.B 2.D 3.A 4.C
Passage E
1.C 2.B 3.B 4.C

Vocabulary
Which Word Is Missing?
Sample: C; B
1.A 2.D 3.B 4.C 5.D 6.C 7.B

TEST 14   Pages 109–112
Sample: 1.A 2.C
Passage A
1.C 2.A 3.B 4.C
Passage B
1.B 2.A 3.D 4.C
Passage C
1.D 2.B 3.C 4.B
Passage D
1.B 2.C 3.A
Passage E
1.B 2.C 3.C

Vocabulary
Which Word Is Missing?
Sample: C; B
1.C 2.A 3.D 4.A 5.B 6.C 7.D

TEST 15   Pages 113–116
Sample: 1.B 2.C
Passage A
1.A 2.C 3.D 4.C
Passage B
1.B 2.C 3.A 4.C
Passage C
1.A 2.C 3.B 4.A
Passage D
1.D 2.A 3.C 4.B
Passage E
1.B 2.C 3.C 4.C

Vocabulary
Which Word Is Missing?
Sample: D;B
1.B 2.C 3.C 4.B 5.A 6.B 7.B

GRAMMAR

Page 164
A. 1. Q 2. S 3. S 4. Q 5. Q 6. S
7. S 8. Q

B. 1. How did the ant carry the crumb? 2. She carried it herself.

Page 165
A. 1. Can we take a taxi downtown?
2. Where does the bus go? 3. The people on the bus waved to us.
4. We got on the elevator. 5. Should I push the elevator button?

B. 1. Answers will vary.
2. Answers will vary.

Page 166
1. correct as is 2. help. 3. would not help 4. the Ants 5. cousins. 6. The man 7. correct as is 8. from the ant.
9. strongest. 10. Do you

Page 167
A. 1. E 2. C 3. C 4. E 5. E 6. C
7. E 8. C

B. Answers will vary.

Page168
A. 1. There's a Gila monster at the airport! 2. Look at the buffaloes.
3. Pack your toys and games.

B. 1. sentence 2. sentence
3. not a sentence; I want to be a subway driver. 4. sentence
5. not a sentence; I hope there are kids on our street. 6. sentence

Page 169
1. correct as is 2. excited! 3. pack.
4. adorable! 5. correct as is 6. Help me find a game. 7. correct as is 8. It will be great! 9. to write to me.
10. team won the game!

Page 170
A. 1. S 2. S 3. P 4. S 5. P

B. 1. sisters 2. pockets 3. fingers
4. parents 5. girls

C. Singular: train, cow
Plural: fences, gates

Page 171
A. ch, sh, ss, x: Possible answers: beach, fox, box, dress, boss, dish, fish y: Possible answers: baby,

bunny, city, berry, family, diary f: Possible answers: calf, hoof, shelf, half, wolf

B. 1. cherries 2. bushes
3. peaches 4. boxes 5. shelves
6. classes

C. Answers will vary

Page 172
1. boxes 2. teeth 3. correct as is
4. glasses 5. faxes 6. brushes
7. groceries 8. correct as is
9. mice 10. stories

Page 173
A. 1. common 2. common
3. proper

B. 1. (April), brother, sister
2. (Julius), May 3. (Taiwan), parents 4. (April), Saturday, school 5. (Mandarin), language
6. (May), (Middle Ages), book

C. Common Nouns: camp, children, picnic Proper Nouns: August, David, Fourth of July

Page 174
A. 1. Common: doctor; Proper: Pat
2. Common: park; Proper: Atlanta
3. Common: football; Proper: Tangram

B. Answers will vary.

Page 175
1. Fourth of July 2. correct as is 3. Tom's apple pie 4. teacher, Dr. Ruffin 5. correct as is 6. Kansas City, Missouri 7. New Year's Day
8. school on Monday 9. pets in North America 10. the movies on Saturday

Page 176
A. 1. S 2. S 3. P 4. P 5. S

B. 1. Singular: It 2. Singular: She
3. Plural: We 4. Plural: They

C. 1. he or she 2. it 3. they
4. she

Page 177
A. 1. us, P 2. him, S 3. her, S
4. it, S 5. me, S 6. them, P

B. 1. us 2. me 3. her 4. them

5. him

C. Sample answer: It is inside the house. I will get it.

Page 178
1. us 2. me 3. correct as is 4. It
5. them 6. He 7. correct as is
8. correct as is 9. It 10. I

Page 179
A. 1. cheered 2. added 3. give
4. serves 5. emptied

B. 1. paraded 2. whispered
3. gobbled 4. skipped
5. bounced

C. 1. laughed 2. sighed
3. whispered

Page 180
A.1. snatched 2. cracked
3. nibbled 4. scrambled

B. 1. honked 2. grabbed
3. shouted 4. ran 5. bounced

C. Answers will vary

Page 181
A. 1. arrived 2. hugged
3. roasted 4. ate 5. cheered

B. 1. chased 2. dashed
3. peeked 4. leaped 5. grabbed

Page 182
A. 1. past 2. past 3. present
4. past 5. past 6. past
7. present 8. present
9. present 10. past

B. 1. The man crossed the river.

2. He rows his boat.

Page 183
A. 1. fills 2. watches 3. takes
4. leave 5. go

B.1. looked 2. stared 3. walked
4. helped

C.1. Answers will vary.

Page 184
1. correct as is 2. washes and peels 3. correct as is 4. enjoy 5. entered 6. traveled 7. arrived 8. awarded 9. correct as is 10. enjoyed

Page 185
A.1. was 2. is 3. are 4. am 5. were

B. 1. past 2. present 3. present 4. past 5. present

C. 1. am 2. are 3. is

Page 186
A. 1. is, being 2. carried, action 3. were, being 4. are, being

B. 1. am 2. are 3. was 4. is 5. were

C. Answers will vary.

Page 187
1. are 2. correct as is 3. correct as is 4. were 5. am 6. was 7. were 8. were 9. correct as is 10. am

Page 188
A.1. M 2. H 3. H 4. M 5. H 6. M 7. H 8. M

B. 1. will watch 2. is going 3. are reading 4. have lifted 5. had climbed

Page 189
A. 1. (had) built 2. (has) painted 3. (is) building 4. (will) fly 5. (will) bring 6. (am) buying

B. 1. is 2. had 3. going 4. using 5. will 6. have

C. Answers will vary.

Page 190
A. 1. reading 2. playing 3. walked 4. come 5. share

B. 1. has 2. is 3. will 4. will 5. have

Page 191
A. 1. is 2. am 3. was 4. were 5. are 6. will be

B. 1. am, present 2. was, past 3. are, present 4. were, past

5. is, present

C. 1. am 2. was 3. are

Page 192
A. 1. S 2. S 3. P 4. P 5. S

B. 1. was 2. were 3. am 4. is 5. are

C. Answers will vary.

Page 193
A. 1. is 2. am 3. are 4. were 5. was

B. 1. is 2. was 3. are 4. were 5. will be

Page 194
A. 1. All of the families | traveled to California. 2. Baby Betsy, Billy, Joe, and Ted | stayed in the cabin. 3. My father | told us stories. 4. I | baked a pie.

B. 1. Betsy 2. miners 3. baby 4. feet 5. man

C. 1. made 2. rolled 3. added 4. bakes 5. loves

Page 195
A. 1. class | took Simple subject: class; Simple predicate: took
2. paintings | hung Simple subject: paintings; Simple predicate: hung
3. Maria | saw Simple subject: Maria; Simple predicate: saw
4. children | looked Simple subject: children; Simple predicate: looked
5. Paul | pointed Simple subject: Paul; Simple predicate: pointed
6. friend | liked Simple subject: friend; Simple predicate: liked
7. Everyone | laughed Simple subject: Everyone; Simple predicate: laughed
8. people | visited Simple subject: people; Simple predicate: visited
9. bus | took Simple subject: bus; Simple predicate: took

B. Answers will vary.

Page 196
A. 1. complete subject 2. complete predicate 3. complete subject 4. complete predicate 5. complete

subject

B. 1. simple predicate 2. simple subject 3. simple subject 4. simple subject 5. simple predicate

Page 197
A. 1. big, sweet 2. many, hot 3. red, four 4. ripe, juicy 5. large, round 6. delicious, colorful

B. Answers will vary.

C. Answers will vary.

Page 198
A.1. sparkling 2. clear 3. Large 4. Busy 5. fresh

B. Answers may include:

1. red 2. green 3. sweet 4. loud 5. sour

Page 199
A.1. Several 2. six 3. many 4. blue 5. colorful

B.1. delicious 2. many 3. some 4. five 5. wonderful

Page 200
A.1. The, the 2. an 3. A, a, a 4. an 5. The, the, the 6. The, a 7. The, an, on 8. an, the

B. 1. a 2. the 3. the 4. an 5. an 6. the 7. a 8. a

Page 201
A. 1. an 2. a 3. an 4. an 5. an 6. a

B. Answers will vary.

C. Answers will vary.

Page 202
A.1. the 2. the 3. an 4. the 5. The

B.1. elephant 2. airport 3. umbrella 4. crab 5. lobster

Page 203
A. 1. King's 2. palace's 3. flower's 4. trees' 5. gardner's 6. birds' 7. singers' 8. sun's 9. diamond's 10. Visitors'

B.1. king's 2. palace's 3. gardener's 4. sun's 5. diamond's

C. 1. flowers' 2. trees' 3. birds' 4. singers' 5. Visitors'

Scholastic Professional Books

Page 204

A. 1. Anna's, S 2. birds', P 3. Brad's, S 4. butterfly's, S 5. turtle's, S 6. chipmunks', P 7. animals', P

B. 1. Carol's 2. Jim's 3. sister's 4. brother's 5. dad's 6. sneaker's 7. dog's

Page 205

A. 1. Kramer's 2. mother's 3. brother's 4. librarian's 5. Joan's

B. 1. astronomers' 2. engines' 3. spectators' 4. scientists' 5. astronauts'

Page 206

A. 1. We 2. It 3. I 4. She 5. He 6. They 7. You

B. 1. He 2. She 3. They 4. He 5. It 6. They 7. We

Page 207

A. 1. us 2. it 3. him 4. you 5. me 6. her 7. them

B. 1. them 2. her 3. it 4. him 5. us

C. Answers will vary.

Page 208

1. us 2. It 3. She 4. her 5. them 6. They 7. He 8. We 9. him 10. us

Page 209

A. 1. I, my 2. you, your 3. He, his 4. She, her 5. It, its 6. We, our 7. They, their

B. 1. their 2. Her 3. his 4. His 5. My 6. Your 7. Its 8. Our

Page 210

A. 1. our 2. her 3. my 4. his 5. its 6. your 7. their

B. 1. his 2. our 3. her 4. its 5. His 6. Their

C. Answers will vary.

Page 211

A. 1. her 2. Its 3. our 4. my 5. his

B. 1. Her 2. his 3. Its 4. Their 5. our

Page 212

A. 1. Laura (and) Ramona 2. Pa, Ma, (and) Laura 3. dog (and) horses 4. Ma (and) Pa 5. Grass (and) trees

B. 1. swayed (and) creaked 2. hummed (and) sang 3. twisted (and) turned 4. neighed (and) snorted 5. stopped (and) stared

C. Answers will vary.

Page 213

A. 1. Mike and Jody, CS 2. call and e-mail, CP 3. jogs and swims, CP 4. Phil and Jan, CS 5. Juan and Yoshi, CS 6. speak and read, CP 7. Lori, Sam, and Beth, CS 8. practiced and presented, CP 9. clapped and smiled, CP 10. The parents and the principal, CS

B. 1. barked and jumped 2. My dad and sister

Page 214

A. 1. compound subject 2. compound predicate 3. compound subject 4. compound predicate 5. compound subject

B. 1. Paul, Luz, and Annie 2. teacher and students 3. wrote and proofread 4. stamped and mailed 5. ran, skipped, and jumped

Page 215

A. 1. It's 2. We're 3. They've 4. I'm 5. she'll 6. They're

B. 1. I've I have 2. What's What is 3. It's It is 4. they're they are 5. I'm I am

C. 1. he'll 2. they're 3. who's 4. I'm 5. we'll 6. there's

Page 216

1. What's 2. it's 3. I'm 4. Aren't 5. can't 6. doesn't 7. They're 8. didn't 9. I've 10. don't 11. there's

Page 217

A. 1. We are 2. You will 3. We have 4. I am 5. It is

B. 1. Who's 2. There's 3. she'll 4. doesn't 5. Don't

Page 218

A. 1. "I have a strange case," 2. "What's strange about it?" 3. "Seventeen years ago Mr. Hunt found an elephant," 4. "Where did he find it?" 5. The elephant just appeared in his window," 6. "He must have fainted!" 7. "No, Mr. Hunt brought him,"

B. 1. Huntsville, Alabama 2. Street, Huntsville, Alabama 3. January 8, 2001 4. January 22, 2001 5. Peachtree Lane, Farley, Alabama 6. Redstone Park, Alabama 7. September 29, 2000 8. Draper Road, Newportville, Pennsylvania

Page 219

A. 1. Mrs. Wu's bank is located at 92 Maple Avenue, Inwood, Texas 2. September 8, 2001 3. Lakewood, Texas 4. weekdays, Saturdays, and 5. Saturdays, Sundays, and 6. Ms. Ames, Mr. Pacheco, and Mrs. Jefferson 7. checks, bills, and deposits 8. May 2, 1974

B. 1. "My favorite author is Jerry Spinelli," said Rick. 2. Spinelli was born on Feburary 1, 1941. 3. His home town is Norristown, Pennsylvania. 4. "What are your favorite books by him?" asked Teresa. 5. "I like Maniac Magee, Dump Days, and Fourth Grade Rats," replied Rick.

Page 220

A. 1. underlining 2. commas 3. quotation mark 4. comma

B. 1. "I have a new baby sister!" 2. April 3, 2002 3. correct as is 4. tiny fingers, tiny toes, and a big scream

Page 221

A. 1. told 2. was 3. came 4. saw 5. knew 6. fell 7. lit 8. threw

B. 1. knew 2. saw 3. threw 4. fell

C. Answers will vary.

Page 222

A. 1. bought 2. ate 3. grew 4. began 5. gave 6. sat

B. 1. came 2. won 3. went 4. was 5. fell 6. said

C. Answers will vary.

WRITING

Page 224
1. S; 2. F; 3. S; 4. S; 5. F; 6. F;
7. S; 8. F; 9. F; 10. F; 11. S; 12. S

Page 225
1. Some of these things are wood, plants, and nectar. 2. Flower nectar makes good food for bees. 3. Wasps build nests to store their food. 4. Termites are wood eaters. 5. A butterfly caterpillar eats leaves. 6. Mosquitoes bite animals and people.

Page 226
1. One type is called igneous.
2. They are formed by layers of rocks, plants, and animals.
3. Rocks are found everywhere in our world.

Page 227
1. There are three types of rocks on our planet. 2. The melted rock inside the earth is more than 2000°F. 3. Most igneous rocks are formed inside the earth. 4. Marble is a metamorphic rock. 5. Fossils are found in sedimentary rock.

Page 228
1. Why is that car in a tree?
2. Should that monkey be driving a bus? 3. Did you see feathers on that crocodile? 4. Can elephants really lay eggs? 5. Is that my mother covered in spots?

Page 229
Questions will vary.

Page 230
1. period; 2. question mark; 3. period; 4. exclamation point; 5. question mark; 6. period; 7. question mark; 8. period; 9. question mark; 10. exclamation point; 11. period; 12. exclamation point; When reading an exclamation, a voice shows strong feeling.

Page 231
1. The Sahara Desert is in Africa.
2. Do people live in the Sahara Desert? 3. The Sahara Desert is about the same size as the United States. 4. How high is the temperature in the Sahara Desert? 5. Once the temperature reached 138°F!

Page 232
Every sentence begins with a capital letter.; A statement ends with a period.; A question ends with a question mark.; An exclamation ends with an exclamation point.; Sentences will vary.; Did it snow ten inches last night?, It snowed ten inches last night!

Page 233
The kids at Elm School had been waiting for a snowstorm. They knew school would be canceled if the storm brought a lot of snow. Last week their wish came true. It snowed 12 inches! School was canceled, and the kids spent the day sledding, building snowmen, and drinking hot chocolate. It was a great snow day!; Students may correct any two of the sentences containing two mistakes.

Page 234
D, B, F, E, A, C

Page 235
Sentences will vary.

Page 236
Sentences will vary.

Page 237
Sentences will vary.

Page 238
1. I ordered a hamburger and a milkshake. 2. I like salt and ketchup on my French fries. 3. My mom makes great pork chops and applesauce. 4. My dad eats two huge helpings of meat loaf and potatoes! 5. My brother helps set the table and clean the dishes. 6. We have cookies and ice cream for dessert.

Page 239
1. We are eating out tonight because Mom worked late. 2. We are going to Joe's Fish Shack although I don't like fish. 3. Dad said I can play outside until it's time to leave. 4. We can play video games while we are waiting for our food. 5. We may stop by Ida's Ice Cream Shop after we leave the restaurant.

Page 240
Lists of words will vary.

Page 241
Possible answers: 1. The melting snow cone sat in the bright sun. 2. Many excited children ran toward the crashing ocean waves. 3. My new friends built a large sandcastle. 4. My younger brother grabbed his favorite beach toys. 5. Our playful dog tried to catch flying beach balls.

Page 242
Words will vary.

Page 243
Words will vary.

Page 244
Dialogue sentences will vary.

Page 245
1. I think it's fun to splash in the puddles. 2. Rain, rain, don't go away! 3. Wow! I should have worn my bathing suit! 4. It's a perfect day to go sailing.

Page 246
Examples: "Somebody turned out the lights!" shouted the cowboy.; "What makes you think I've been eating cookies?" asked the guilty boy.; "My parents finally let me get my ears pierced," said the proud girl.

Page 247
Drew woke up early on Saturday. "No school today," he said. He found his mom working in the garden. "What are you doing?" he asked.

"I am planting these flowers," she answerered.

Drew looked down.

He couldn't believe it. "A four-leaf clover!" he shouted. "This should help us win our big game today," he said.

Scholastic Professional Books

Drew's entire day was perfect.His sister shared her toys, the ice-cream truck brought his favorite flavor, and his team won the big game. "What a day!" he whispered to himself as he fell asleep that night.

Page 248
Sentences will vary.

Page 249
Paragraphs will vary.

Page 250
Lists of ideas will vary.

Page 251
Sentences that do not belong: My favorite kind of dog is a boxer.; Not much is known about the history of Chinese flags.; Hurricanes have strong, powerful winds.

Page 252
Topic sentences will vary. Examples: Guinea pigs make good pets.; It is easy to make a peanut butter and banana sandwich.; Frogs are different from toads.

Page 253
Topic sentences will vary.

Page 254
The following sentences should be crossed out: My three-year-old brothers both have blonde hair.; Her favorite sport is gymnastics.;
I wish I had a fish tank in my room.; The rewritten paragraph should omit the above sentences.

Page 255
Supporting sentences will vary.

Page 256
2, 1, 4, 3; Paragraph sentences will vary but should follow the same order as the numbered sentences.

Page 257
Supporting sentences will vary.

Page 258
1. Of all the seasons, autumn is the best. 2. Though dangerous, the job of an astronaut is exciting. 3. There are many subjects in school, but math is the most difficult.4. Some

gardeners in Florida and Texas can enjoy their flowers all year long. 5. Life would never be the same without computers.

Page 259
Closing sentences will vary.

Page 260
Paragraphs will vary.

Page 261
Paragraph plans and paragraphs will vary.

Page 262
Sentences will vary, and paragraph plans will vary.

Page 263
Drawings and paragraph plans will vary.

Page 264
Paragraph plans and paragraphs will vary.

Page 265
Paragraph plans and paragraphs will vary.

Page 266
Letters will vary.

MAPS

Pages 268–269
1. Mill Town   2. hospital   3. grass
4. Sable River   5. bridge   6. Doe Avenue   7. fire house, school, library
8. Grand Street

Page 270
1. North Pole   2. South Pole   3. west   4. E

Page 271
1. south   2. north   3. east   4. no
5. clothing shop

Pages 272
1. no   2.North America, South America, Asia, Africa, Australia, Antarctica, Europe 3. Indian, Arctic, Pacific, Atlantic   4. Western and Southern

Page 273
1. Eastern   2. Arctic   3. right   4. top

5. Hemisphere
Code word: Earth

Page 274
1. southeast   2. northeast
3. southeast   4. northwest
5. SW

Page 275
1. north   2. southeast
3. southwest   4. north
5. northwest

Page 276
1. library   2. D4   3. A2, B2, C2, D2
4. D4, D5   5. yes

Page 277
1. fire department   2. A5   3. A5, B5, C5, D5   4. store   5. go to the movies   My tour: apartment building; library; store; park; movie theater

Page 278
1. boat house   2. stable
3. office   4. arts and crafts
5. tennis court

Page 279
1. 25 miles   2. 45 miles   3. Luna City   4. Clark City to Dover to Luna City to Terra View; 81 miles
5. Far HIlls

Page 280
1. 40 feet   2. 10 feet   3. 10 feet
4. 30 feet

Page 281
1. 125 feet   2. 100 feet
3. 75 feet   4. about 150 feet
5. 200 feet

Pages 282–283
1. 150   2. 200   3. 300   4. shorter
5. Amarillo   6. less   7. kilometers
8. 500   9. 800   10. kilometers

Pages 284–285
1. Minnesota 2. 150 miles
3. Map 2 4. 1,000 miles
5. about 2,500 6. 1,500 miles
7. North America 8. more land is shown on Map 3 9. Map 1

Pages 286–287
1. Mississippi 2. Kansas and Nebraska 3. Lake Erie
4. Mississippi River 5. Alaska and Hawaii 6. Juneau 7. west
8. North Carolina, Tennessee, Arkansas, Oklahoma, New Mexico, Arizona, California

Page 288
1. south 2. Belize, Guatemala 3. Canada 4. Alaska
5. Atlantic; Pacific 6. Arctic
7. Ottawa 8. Rio Grande

Page 290
1. c 2. b 3. c 4. b 5. c 6. a 7. a 8. c

Page 292
1. mountain, hill, plateau
2. canyon, valley 3.Both are low land. A valley doesn't have as high, steep walls as a canyon, and it isn't as narrow as a canyon.

Page 293
1. It is more sheltered; the water might be calmer. 2. Both are partially enclosed by land. 3. peninsula 4. An island is completely surrounded by water while a peninsula is surrounded except for one side. 5. An island is surrounded by water. A lake is surrounded by land.

Page 294
1. valley 2. red 3. plateau
4. Mississippi River 5. east and south

Page 295
1. north 2. Kodiak 3. Alaska Peninsula 4. mountains
5. Yukon

page 296
1. People use them to make things.
2. roads, sandboxes, concrete

3. because natural gas burns

Page 297
1. true 2. true 3. false 4. false
5. true 6. true

Pages 298–299
1. 38 to 40 inches of rain a year
2. north and west 3. 40 to 44
4. Houlton 5. Lewiston
6. greater 7. less than 38

Pages 300–301
1. northwest 2. Missouri River
3. Fort Laramie 4. Rocky Mountains 5. Snake River 6. The trail followed rivers and valleys. 7. The weather was better during spring and summer.

Word scramble: Oregon, Idaho, Nebraska, Kansas

Pages 302–303
1. picnic area 2. southwest
3. Take Kinney Road to Bajada Loop heading northeast. Go right onto Golden Gate Road. Then turn left on Picture Rocks Road. 4. Saguaro cacti 5. waterhole; to drink
6. Sandario Road

Pages 304–305
1. Hudson River; East River
2. east to west 3. north to south
4. southern 5. 59th Street; Fifth Avenue and Central Park West
6. Fifth Avenue and 42nd Street
7. east 8. west 9. It is easier to find places.

Pages 306-307
1. Fremont-Daly City Route
2. blue 3. Concord-Daly City
4. yes 5. Concord, Daly City, Richmond, Fremont 6. It's a transfer stop where people can change trains. 7. Richmond-Fremont
8. northeast 9. San Francisco Bay
10. over bridges, by boat, by plane

Page 308
1. 5 to 10 inches of rain
2. coasts 3. 10 to 20 inches
4. less than 5 inches a year

5. Canberra 6. Indian, Pacific
7. southeast 8. All are true.

Page 309
1. Map 1 2. 200 3. 10
4. Sacramento 5. 500 6. Pacific Ocean 7. Nevada, Arizona
8. national border

Page 310

ADDITION & SUBTRACTION

Page 314
7, 4, 13, 10, 15, 5, 9, 16, 8, 12, 3, 6, 18, 11, 14; Charity, Constance, Edward, Humility, Jasper, Oceanus, Peregrine, Priscilla, Prudence, Remember, Resolve, Samuel, Solomon, Susan, Thomas

Page 315

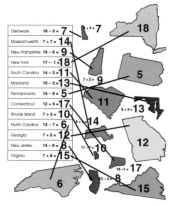

Scholastic Professional Books

Page 316

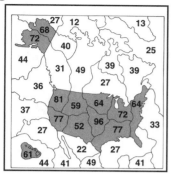

Page 317

Check that each student has circled the correct number of stars. 3 tens, 4 ones, 34; 4 tens,
5 ones, 45; 2 tens, 7 ones, 27; 7 tens, 0 ones, 70; 5 tens, 3 ones, 54;
6 tens, 5 ones 65; 3 tens, 6 ones, 36; 8 tens, 0 ones, 80; 13, 13 + 50 = 63, 6 tens, 3 ones

Page 318

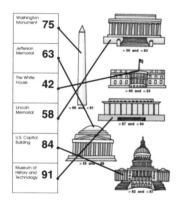

Page 319

52, 53, 82, 61, 96, 52, 82, LINCOLN; 37, 83, 42, 42, 83, 78, 66, 96, 82, JEFFERSON; 98, 72, 64, 65, 53, 82, 45, 47, 96, 82, WASHINGTON

Page 320

37: 3 tens 7 ones, 2 tens 17 ones;
52: 5 tens 2 ones, 4 tens 12 ones;
85: 8 tens 5 ones, 7 tens 15 ones;
43: 4 tens 3 ones, 3 tens 13 ones;
68: 6 tens 8 ones, 5 tens 18 ones;
26: 2 tens 6 ones, 1 ten 16 ones

Page 321

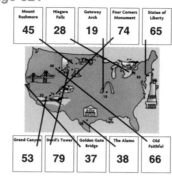

Page 322

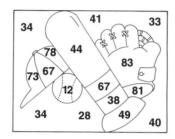

Check child's coloring.
32, 34, 36, 38, 40, 42, 44, 46, 48, 50

Page 323

16 + 87 = 103, 57 + 11 = 68, 91 + 45 = 136, 39 + 49 = 133, 68 + 29 = 97, 25 + 73 = 98, 83 + 32 = 115, 44 + 58 = 102, 72 + 66 = 138; 87 − 16 = 71, 57 − 11 = 46, 91 − 45 = 46, 94 − 39 = 55, 68 − 29 = 39, 73 − 25 = 48, 83 − 32 = 51, 58 − 44 = 14, 72 − 66 = 6;
A. 41; B. 90; C. 34; D. 58

Page 324

24, 91, 47, 53,
16, 92, 65, 38

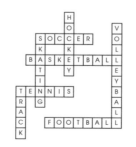

Page 325

56 + 38 = 94, 18 + 24 + 35 = 77, 38 + 34 + 18 = 90, 47 + 24 = 71; 90 −

77 = 13, 94 − 77 = 17, 90 − 71 = 19, 94 − 71 = 23; 47 − 38 = 9; 56 − 18 = 38; 252

Page 326

S. 75; I. 24; A. 65; R. 38;
R. 84; W. 57; H. 58; I. 64;
U. 33; O. 72; L. 51; M. 34;
B. 71; L. 80; G. 69; U. 48; WILLIAM BURROUGHS

Page 327

324 + 632 = 956, 241 + 551 792;
155 + 331 = 486, 213 + 313 = 526;
415 + 322 = 737, 143 + 146 = 289,
202 + 216 = 418, 431 + 422 = 853;
142 + 233 = 375, 541 + 134 = 675,
335 + 333 = 668, 712 + 232 = 944;
220 + 314 = 534, 514 + 334 = 848,
224 + 143 = 367, 416 + 132 = 548;
Joe brought $5.40, and Ellie brought $4.35.

Page 328

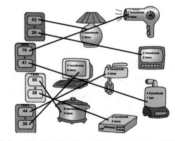

200, 40, 7, 247; 400, 70, 6, 476; 300, 90, 2, 392; 100, 90, 3, 193; 500, 60, 1, 561

Page 329

40, 50, 60; 80, 20, 70; 9 hundreds, 30 tens; 60 tens, 1 hundred; 80 tens, 9 hundreds

Page 330

954	427	554		970	373	872
684	349	364		723	577	884
945	844	472		507	476	397
457	574	942		743	771	712
473	424	842		575	674	974

Page 331

574	534	558
346	506	763
852	523	945
952	524	965
897	563	723

726	622	923
327	288	525
628	824	421
826	842	428
724	725	527

Page 332

534 – 275 = 259; 467 – 278 = 189;
392 – 296 = 96; 625 – 366 = 259,
988 – 589 = 399, 735 – 367 = 368;
854 – 397 = 457, 564 – 498 = 66,
339 – 249 = 90

Page 333

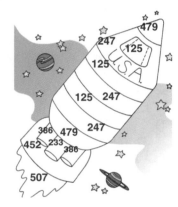

Check child's coloring.

Page 334

A. 517 + 525 = 1,042;
B. 614 + 478 = 1,092;
C. 709 + 253 = 962;
D. 1,363, 722 E. 709 – 385 = 324,
517 – 463 = 54, 525 – 385 = 140;
253 + 517 + 254 + 614 = 1,638

Page 335

A. 496 – 188 = 308; B. 956 – 668 =
288; C. 547 + 239 = 786; D. 379 +
345 = 724;
E. 723 – 162 = 561; F. 422 – 215 =
207; G. 957 – 688 = 269; H. 884 +
834 = 1,718; I. 956 – 578 = 378

Page 336

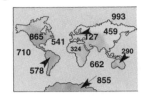

Check labeling.

Page 337

5,063; 3,721; 3,827; 8,749; ALPS;
8,789; 2,429; 3,012; 5,642; 2,351;
ROCKY; 2,429; 5,234; 5,063; 8,789;
5,642; OZARK; 5,063; 6,348; 4,907;
7,483; 8,749; ANDES; 2.846

Page 338

Page 339

F. $39.96; N. $79.96;
N. $99.48; R. $66.99;
K. $86.99; A. $79.77;
L. $88.99; I. $97.00; FRANKLIN; 5,
2, 8, 1, 3, 7, 9, 4, 6

Page 340

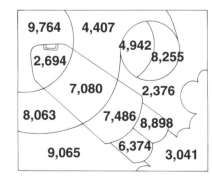

Check child's coloring.

Page 341

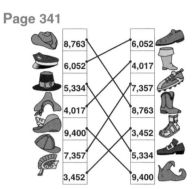

Page 342

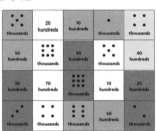

3,167; 5,703; 6,039; 4,584; 9,940

Page 343

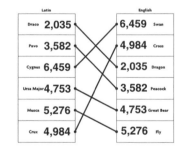

Page 344

MATH is AWESOME!

MATH

Page 346–347
Scores will vary.

Page 348
Answers will vary.

Page 349
A. thousands; B. tens; C. hundreds;
D. tens E. hundreds; F. ones;
G. tens
The answer to the secret riddle is "a secret."

Page 350
1. 10; 2. 20; 3. 50; 4. 90; 5. 200
6. 400; 7. 600; 8. 300; 9. 500;
10. 700

What did the farmer get when he tried to reach the beehive?

A "buzzy" signal

Page351
C3: jeweled crown; B1: ruby necklace; C5: golden cup D4: X; A4: wooden treasure chest; E1: silvery sword

Page 352

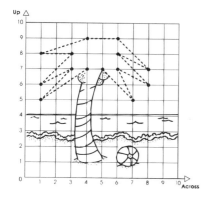

Page 353
1. cheetah; 2. wild turkey; 3. zebra
4. lion; 5. 7; 6. yes; 7. speed; 8. no

Page 354
5 pennies equal 5 cents, one nickel equals 5 cents

10 pennies equal 10 cents, 2 nickels equal 10 cents, one dime equals 10 cents

25 pennies equal 25 cents, 5 nickels equal 25 cents, one quarter equals 25 cents

Page 355
1. January and December; 2. 80º
3. June, July, and September; 4. Yes;
10º 5. No 6. Warmer 7. Fall 8. May
9. 40 degrees

Page 356

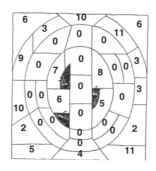

Page 357
A. 6, 16, 22, 14; B. 16, 8, 4, 8; C. 24, 10, 20, 24; D. 18, 2, 20, 14; E. 0, 12, 6, 0; F. 10, 18; G. 12, 2; H. 22, 4; Rhymes will vary.

Page 358

3, 30 letters

Page 359

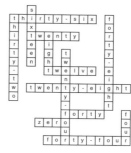

44 buttons

Page 360
A. 10; B. 1; C. 7; D. 50; E. 12; F. 30; G. 11; H. 15; I. 40; J. 9; K. 5; L. 5; M. 35; N. 60; O. 4; 60 nuts

Page 361
yellow: 0 + 66 + 12 + 60 = 138; red: 18 + 30 + 36 + 6 + 24 = 114; orange: 54 + 18 + 66 + 24 + 30 + 48 = 240; blue: 42 + 72 + 60 + 24 = 198; green: 30 + 42 + 48 + 72 + 0 = 192; purple: 36 + 18 + 12 + 18 + 6 = 90; 48 fireworks

Page 362

49 times

Page 363
32, 56, 72, 48, 24, 64, 96, 80, 16, 0, 24, 88, 8, 32, 56, 48, 16, 0, 88, 40, 80, 40, 96, 8, 72; 96 seconds

Page 364

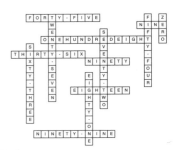

108 pieces

Page 365

Page 366

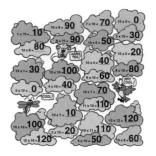

70 clouds

Page 367

Page 368

A. 12 x 7 = 84, 12 x 0 = 0; B. 12 x 8 = 96, 12 x 11 = 132, 12 x 6 = 72, 12 x 12 = 144, 12 x 3 = 36; C. 12 x 1 = 12, 12 x 5 = 60, 7 x 12 = 84, 12 x 9 = 108, 12 x 4 = 48; D. 12 x 10 = 120, 4 x 12 = 48, 8 x 12 = 96, 11 x 12 = 132, 2 x 12 = 24 72 sentences; Answers will vary.

Page 369

9 x 7 = 63

Page 370

YOUR SMILE

6 x 1 = 6; 6 x 4 = 24; 7 x 7 = 49; 6 x 2 = 12; 7 x 9 = 63; 6 x 3 = 18; 7 x 3 = 21; 7 x 6 = 42; 7 x 4 = 28; 6 x 5 = 30; 6 x 6 = 36; 6 x 9 = 54; 7 x 8 = 56; 7 x 0 = 0; 6 x 7 = 42; 6 x 0 = 0 7 x 5 = 35; 6 x 8 = 48; 7 x 2 = 14; 7 x 1 = 7

Page 371

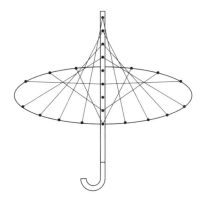

a. 11 b. 10 c. 0 d. 3 e. 4 f. 12

Page 372

6 x 1 = 6; 6 x 4 = 24; 7 x 6 = 42; 11 x 7 = 77; 7 x 8 = 56; 10 x 6 = 60; 8 x 6 = 48; 7 x 7 = 49; 12 x 7 = 84; 6 x 3 = 18; 7 x 5 = 35; 5 x 6 = 30; 6 x 7 = 42; 7 x 1 = 7; 7 x 3 = 21; 10 x 7 = 70 11 x 6 = 66; 7 x 9 = 63; 6 x 9 = 54; 12 x 6 = 72; 7 x 9 = 63; 6 x 6 = 36; 2 x 7 = 14; 4 x 7 = 28

Taking It Further: 8 x 49 = 392

Page 373

1. 9R1; 2. 3R3 3. 4R0; 4. 5R0
5. 2R0; 6. 6R1 7. 3R0; 8. 9R2
9. 6R0; 10. 4R3

Page 374

35 ÷ 5 = 7; 55 ÷ 5 = 11; 30 ÷ 5 = 6
15 ÷ 5 = 3; 10 ÷ 5 = 2; 45 ÷ 5 = 9
15 ÷ 5 = 3; 5 ÷ 5 = 1; 25 ÷ 5 = 5
20 ÷ 5 = 4; 25 ÷ 5 = 5; 40 ÷ 5 = 8
45 ÷ 5 = 9; 5 ÷ 5 = 1

Taking It Further: 5, 10, 15, 20, 25, 30, 35, 40

Page 375

880 ÷ 2 = 440; 996 ÷ 3 = 332; 576 ÷ 4 = 144; 502 ÷ 2 = 251; 992 ÷2 = 496; 603 ÷3 = 201; 903 ÷ 3 = 301; 392 ÷ 2 = 196; 982 ÷ 2 = 491; 897 ÷ 3 = 299; 738 ÷ 6 = 123; 742 ÷ 2 = 371; 990 ÷ 3 = 330

Taking It Further:

$$
\begin{array}{r}
4\ 3\ 2 \\
2\ )\overline{\ 8\ 6\ 4} \\
-\ 8 \\
\overline{\ 0\ 6} \\
-\ 6 \\
\overline{\ 0\ 4} \\
-\ 4 \\
\overline{\ 0}
\end{array}
$$

Page 376

1. 20 buttons; 2. 56 buttons; 3. 30 mice 4. 126 buttons; 5. 8 buttons

Super Challenge: 6 teams

Page 377

1. Here is one way to complete the square. (Child may invert the rows and columns.)

6	1	8
7	5	3
2	9	4

2. 8 dimes, 4 nickels, and 7 pennies
3. Here is one way to "connect the dots":

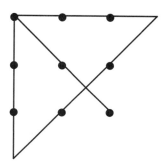

4. SHOES (53045)

Page 378

1. 17 triangles 2. They show the same time in different ways.
3. Child should complete the shapes.
4. Answers will vary.

Page 379

1. Answers will vary. Child may take an average class size of 30 students and multiply 30 by the number of classes in the school.

2. Answers include 11, 88, 69, and 96.

3. 3 cats

4.

𝟞𝟞

5. three cuts

Page 380

1. 1/4; 2. 1/3; 3. 1/3; 4. 1/2; 5. 1/2
6. 1/4; 7. 1/3; 8. 1/2; 9. 1/4; 10. 1/4
11. 1/4; 12. 1/3

Page 381

1. 3/6; 2. 2/4; 3. 3/8; 4. 2/3
5. 3/4; 6. 4/5; 7. 5/6; 8. 5/8

Page 382

Answers will vary.

Page 383

1. 4 students; 2. 8 students;
3. 6 students

Page 384

3/20 + 2/20 = 1/4;
2/16 + 2/16 = 1/4;
1/14 + 1/14 = 1/7
1/9 + 2/9 = 1/3;
1/4 + 2/4 = 3/4;
4/ 9 + 2/9 = 2/3
4/10 + 2/10 = 3/5;
1/5 + 2/5 = 3/5;
6/12 + 5/12 = 11/12
4/10 + 5/10 = 9/10;
4/12 + 7/12 = 11/12;
1/10 + 8/10 = 9/10
4/14 + 6/14 = 5/7;
6/10 + 2/10 = 4/5;
4/8 + 2/8 = 3/4
4/8 + 3/8 = 7/8;
2/10 + 3/10 = 1/2;
1/6 + 2/6 = 1/2
1/16 + 1/16 = 1/8;
 3/40 + 7/40 = 1/4

Page 385

Check that children have found all of the mistakes and that they have fixed the mistakes with reasonable corrections. Mistakes: 8 days a week should be 7; 8:75 pm is not possible; $10.99 off mountain bikes; bicycle chain is $6.00 a foot; bike helmets are $14.99; you save only $.01, not $1.00, on 2 rolls of tape; free stickers can't be 10 cents each; half-price bicycle seats should be $8.50.

The additional mistake—a clock with three hands.

Pages 386–387

apple: 5 pennies

jelly: 2 dimes or 1 dime + 2 nickels

cider: 1 quarter + 1 nickel

corn: 3 dimes + 1 nickel or 2 dimes + 3 nickels

pumpkin: 4 dimes + 1 nickel or 1 quarter + 2 dimes or 1 quarter + 1 dime + 2 nickels

squash: 1 quarter + 2 dimes + 1 nickel

pie: 1 quarter + 1 dime + 1 nickel

hay ride: 2 dimes + 1 nickel or 2 dimes + 5 pennies

Page 388

Page 389
Answer: "Meet you at noon!"

Page 390
The actual measurements will vary somewhat,but they should be close to the following:

1. 14 1/2 inches
2. 19 inches
3. 13 1/2 inches
4. 21 inches

Page 391
Answers will vary.

Page 392
1. ounces; 2. pounds; 3. ounces; 4. pounds 5. pounds; 6. pounds; 7. ounces; 8. ounces 9. pounds; 10. ounces; 11. ounces; 12. pounds 13. pounds; 14. ounces; 15. ounces

Page 393
1. 90°F; 2. 0°C; 3. 30°C; 4. 55°F; 5. 30°F 6. 40°F; 7. 68°F; 8. 20°C; 9. 75°F; 10. 80°F

Page 394
1. 100; 2. 7; 3. 36; 4. 5280; 5. 60 6. 12; 7. 12; 8. 4; 9. 26; 10. 20 11. 16; 12. 52; 13. 5; 14. 2; 15. 24

Page 395
1. 5; 2. 11; 3. 30; 4. 12; 5. 8; 6. 17

Page 396
A. 1F, 2G, 3B, 4C or A, 5E, 6I, 7E, 8H, 9G, 10G, 11C

B. 1B, 2F, 3D, 4,I 5F, 6E, 7A, 8D, 9I, 10F, 11I

C. 1I, 2C, 3C, 4G, 5G, 6C, 7F, 8I, 9B, 10C or A, 11F

Page 397

I HAVE 3 SIDES AND 3 CORNERS. ONE OF MY CORNERS IS AT THE TOP.

I HAVE NO CORNERS. ONE HALF OF ME IS LIKE THE OTHER HALF.

I HAVE 4 CORNERS AND 4 SIDES. YOU CAN DRAW ME BY JOINING 2 TRIANGLES.

I HAVE 5 SIDES AND 5 CORNERS. DRAW A SQUARE AND A TRIANGLE TOGETHER.

I AM NOT A SQUARE BUT I HAVE 4 SIDES AND 4 CORNERS.

I HAVE 4 SIDES AND 4 CORNERS. MY 2 OPPOSITE SIDES ARE SLANTED.

Pages 398–399
Children's Tessellate patterns will vary.

Page 400
10; Answers will vary.